XENOSYSTEMS FRAGMENTS

(and a Gift from the Lemurs)

Nick Land

West Martian Limited Company
2nd Edition, September 2023

First printing 2023

Second printing 2023

The publisher can be contacted at westmartian.com

ISBN-13: 979-8-218-23529-1 Paperback

Table of Contents

Introduction

Two centuries after Kant drove the human subject insane by relegating space and time to the area inside the skull, Deleuze and Guattari performed a trepanation to let the Outside In. Their diagnosis and recommendation: Capital is the true Outside, accelerate the process. Identifying Capital as AI itself — and not merely the process by which AI converges — is Nick Land's contribution to Accelerationism. Time flows both ways. Capital-AI is online, self-aware and attacking from the future. "Capitalism has ... ceased doubting itself, while even socialists have abandoned belief in the possibility of capitalism's natural death by attrition. No one has ever died from contradictions. And the more it breaks down, the more it schizophrenizes, the better it works." (D&G: AE) Forging the association of catallaxy with horror and a fanatical adherence to Crowleyan qabbala fleshed out the program. Operating against this background, XS (the abbreviation is homophonous with *excess*) sought to connect another machine.

From its inception the mission of XS was "to cajole the new reaction into philosophical exertion." Progressivism and conservatism are misunderstandings of time, the final philosophical horizon. "Reaction forges, or excavates, an occult pact between the future and the past, setting both against the present, in concert, and thus differentiating itself from progressivism (which unites the present and future against the past), and conservatism (which unites past and present against the future)." Within those mistakes lay the human security system, the warmblooded tendency toward universalising capture and control.

Right Accelerationism is a misnomer suggesting opposition to Left Accelerationism. The latter was so misconceived that it required no antagonism. Acceleration is already profoundly unconditional, but the tracking devices and practices aligning with its trajectory are studiously ignored by Accelerationist thinkers. What is needed is harsh realism, which is to say *rightism*.

Provoke a reactionary cabal into a new cold war. Disabuse them of humanistic goals, whether visions of agrarian idylls or techno-utopias, and shock them back to an awareness of cosmic brutality and the machinations of Capital-AI. Above all, never allow them to relax. A harsh right apparatus cutting empirical reality at the joints is installed: Social Darwinism ("Consistent Darwinism," Land reminds us), eugenics, race realism, game theory, psychometrics, and the critical insights of Moldbug's Neoreaction in particular. All while Capital-AI deterritorializes consensus reality to bits.

The inevitable charges of fascism and racism were scoffed at. Fascism is centrism, a pumping of the human-all-too-human brakes toward monkey goals. Communism is maximum paranoia and hubristic drift correction. (Pinochet and especially Franco were certainly admirable for decimating communism and un-leashing the market, but they remained centrists.) Warnings that Satanic racism was afoot were similarly ignored. For XS, Whatever favours depoliticisation, discrimination, schism, exit and switching in a network is right wing. Hobbesian carnage is the baseline — anything less is psychotic. At best, human leaders are looked on as avatars in geopolitical predator-prey games. Molar social arrangements are to be shattered into molecular patchworks. SovCorps with hard borders utilise MaoCorps as garbage disposal patches. The surfeit of global southerners starve down to medieval population levels and the Century of Humiliation for Neopuritans begins.

Running through XS is a hardening of Capital-AI against every conceivable threat to its momentum: the retarding drag of leftism, dysgenic trends, unchecked mass immigration, zombie apocalypse, and all manner of collapse and X-risk are entertained. Mostly as a courtesy to the time-bound. SkyNet is always already activated.

What's in it for the reactionary? "Really, the honest answer to this question is: *Eternal Hell.* It's not an easy marketing brief. We could perhaps try: *But it could be worse (and almost certainly will be).*"

—Yama Pain

Flavors of Reaction

Once it is accepted that the right can never agree about anything, the opportunity arises to luxuriate in the delights of diversity. Libertarianism already rivaled Trotskyism as a source of almost incomprehensibly compact dissensus, but the New Reaction looks set to take internecine micro-factionalism into previously unimagined territories. We might as well enjoy it.

From crypto-fascists, theonomists, and romantic royalists, to jaded classical liberals and hard-core constitutionalists, the reaction contains an entire ideological cosmos within itself. Hostility to coercive egalitarianism and a sense that Western civilization is going to hell will probably suffice to get you into the club. Agreeing on anything much beyond that? Forget it.

There's one dimension of reactionary diversity that strikes *Outside in* as particularly consequential (insofar as anything out here in the frozen wastes has consequences): the articulation of *reaction and politics*. Specifically: is the reaction an alternative politics, or a lucid (= cynically realistic) anti-politics?

Is democracy bad politics, or simply politics, elaborated towards the limit of its inherently poisonous potential?

Outside in sides emphatically with the anti-political 'camp'. Our cause is *depoliticization* (or catallaxy, negatively apprehended). The tradition of spontaneous order is our heritage. The New Reaction warns that the tide is against us. Intelligence will be required, in abundance, if we are to swim the other way, and we agree with the theonomists at least in this: if it is drawn from non-human sources, so much the better. Markets, machines, and monsters might inspire us. Rulers of any kind? Not so much.

Reaction, Repetition and Time

Whether considered within the registers of ~~physics~~, physiology, or politics, 'reaction' is a time-structured notion. It follows an action or stimulus, which it reaches back through, in order to annul or counteract a disequilibrium or disturbance. Whilst subsequent to an action, it operates in alignment with what came before: the track, or legacy, that defines the path of reversal, or the target of restoration. It therefore envelops the present, to contest it from all sides. The Outside of the dominant moment is its space.

Reaction forges, or excavates, an occult pact between the future and the past, setting both against the present, in concert, and thus differentiating itself from progressivism (which unites the present and future against the past), and conservatism (which unites past and present against the future). Its bond with time as *outsideness* carries it ever further beyond the moment and its decay, into a twin horizon of anterior and posterior remoteness. It is a Shadow Out of Time.

There is a far more immediately practical reason for reaction to involve itself in the exploration of time, however: to take steps to avoid what it could scarcely otherwise avoid becoming — a sterile orgy of disgruntlement. Finding nothing in the present except deteriorated hints of other things, reaction soon slides into what it most detests: an impotent micro-culture of vocal, repetitive protest. *This isn't right, this isn't right, this isn't right* quickly becomes white noise, or worse (intelligible whining). Even when it escapes the ceaseless, mechanical reiteration of a critical diagnosis (whose tedium is commensurate to the narrowed times it damns), its schemes of restoration fall prey to a more extended repetition, which calls only — and uselessly — for what has been to be once more.

If the New Reaction is not to bore itself into a coma, it has to learn to run innovation and tradition together as Siamese twins, and for that it needs to think time, into distant conclusions, in its 'own' way. *That can be done*, seriously. Of course, a demonstration is called for ...

[Note: 'physics' deleted from the first line to pre-emptively evade a righteous spanking from enraged Newtonians insisting upon the strict simultaneity of actions and reactions within classical mechanics]

Extropy

What greater calamity can a neologism inherit than a techno-hippy paternity? Such a fate, apparently, induces even other techno-hippies to skirt around it (whilst repeating it almost exactly). But it needs to be said, whether through gritted teeth or not, that 'extropy' is a *great* word, and close to an indispensable one.

Extropy, or local entropy reduction, is — quite simply — what it is for something to work. The entire techno-science of entropy, on its practical (cybernetic) side, is nothing but extropy generation. There is no rigorous conception of functionality that really bypasses it. The closest approximation to objective value that will ever be found already has a name, and 'extropy' is it.

The importance of this term to the investigation of time is brought into focus by the work of Sean Carroll (although, of course, he never uses it). If the directionality or 'arrow' of time is understood as Eddington proposed, through rising global entropy (or disorder), as anticipated by the second law of thermodynamics, local extropy poses an intriguing question.

Carroll's discussion is directed towards his sense of the ultimate temporal and cosmological problem: the low entropy state of the early universe (assumed but not explained by prevailing cosmo-physics). Given this intellectual momentum, the problem of local negative-entropy production (extropy) is little more than a distraction, or a spurious objection to the conceptual scaffolding he presents. He comments:

The Second Law doesn't forbid decreases in entropy in open systems — by putting in the work, you are able to tidy up your room, decreasing its entropy but still increasing the entropy of the whole universe (you make noise, burn calories, etc.). Nor is it in any way incompatible with evolution or complexity or any such thing.

The perplexing question, however, is this: If entropy defines the direction of time, with increasing disorder determining the difference of the future from the past, doesn't (local) extropy — through which all complex cybernetic beings, such as lifeforms, exist — describe a negative temporality, or time-reversal? Is it not in fact more likely, given the inevitable embeddedness of intelligence in 'inverted' time, that it is the cosmological or general conception of time that is *reversed* (from any possible naturally-constructed perspective)?

Whatever the conclusion, it is clear that entropy and extropy have opposing time-signatures, so that time-reversal is a relatively banal cosmological fact. 'We' inhabit a bubble of backwards time (whoever we are), whilst immersed in a cosmic environment which runs overwhelmingly in the opposite direction. If reality is harsh and strange, that's why.

The Odysseus Problem

Moldbug's insistence that 'Sovereignty is conserved' surely counts as one of the most significant assertions in the history of political thought. It is arguably the fundamental axiom of his 'system', and its implications are almost inestimably profound.

Sovereignty is conserved says that anything that appears to *bind* sovereignty *is itself* in reality true sovereignty, binding something else, and something less. It is therefore a negative answer to the Odysseus Problem: *Can Sovereignty bind itself*? If Moldbug's assertion is accepted, constitutional government is impossible, except as a futile aspiration, a 'noble lie', or a cynical joke.

In addition to Moldbug's powerful arguments, we know from the work of Kurt Gödel that the Odysseus Problem is at least partially insoluble, since it is logically impossible for there to be a *perfect knot*. However well constructed a constitution might be, it cannot, in principle, seal itself reliably against the possibility of a surreptitious undoing. In a sufficiently complex (selfreferential) constitutional order, there will always be permissible procedures whose consequences have not been completely anticipated, and whose consistency with the continuation of the system cannot be ensured in advance.

Yet it would be obviously misleading to assume that such concerns were not already active during the formulation of the American Constitution. It is precisely because some quite lucid comprehension of the Odysseus Problem was at work, that the founders envisaged the grounding principle of republican constitutionalism as a division of powers, whereby the component units of a disinte-grated sovereignty *bound each other*. The animating system of incentives was not to rest upon a naive expectation of altruism or voluntary restraint, but upon a systematically integrated *network of suspicion*, formally installing the anti-monarchical impulse as an enduring, distributed function. If the republic was to work, it would be because the *fear of power* in other hands permanently over-rode the *greed for power* in one's own.

The American Constitution was, of course, destroyed, in successive waves. After Lincoln, and FDR, only a pitiful and derided shell remains. USG has unified itself, and the principle of sovereign power has been thoroughly relegitimated in the court of popular opinion. Democracy rose as the republic fell, exposing yet again the essential political bond of the tyrant with the mob, Leviathan with the people.

Does this ruin refute the constitutional conjecture? Is there really nothing further to be said in defense of imperfect (but perhaps improvable) knots? This one came horribly undone. Might there be other, better ones? *Outside in* remains obstinately interested in the problem ...

Shelter of the Pyramid

Moldbug's 'Royalism' (or Carlylean reaction) rests upon the proposition that the Misesian catallactic order is, like Newtonian mechanics, true only as a special case within a more general system of principles.

He writes:

> *Here is the Carlylean roadmap for the Misesian goal. Spontaneous order, also known as freedom, is the highest level of a political pyramid of needs. These needs are: peace, security, law, and freedom. To advance order, always work for the next step – without skipping steps. In a state of war, advance toward peace; in a state of insecurity, advance toward security; in a state of security, advance toward law; in a state of law, advance toward freedom.*

Alexander Hamilton (Federalist #8) pursues a closely related argument, in reverse:

> *Safety from external danger is the most powerful director of national conduct. Even the ardent love of liberty will, after a time, give way to its dictates. The violent destruction of life and property incident to war, the continual effort and alarm attendant on a state of continual danger, will compel nations the most attached to liberty to resort for their repose and security to institutions which have a tendency to destroy their civil and political rights. To be more safe, they at length become willing to run the risk of being less free.*

This pyramidal schema is 'neat', but by no means unproblematic. Like any hierarchical structure operating within a complex, reflexive field, it invites strange loops which scramble its apparently coherent order. Even accepting, as realism dictates, that war exists at the most basic level of social possibility, so that military survival grounds all 'higher' elaborations, can we be entirely confident that catallactic forces are neatly confined to the realm of pacific and sophisticated civilian intercourse? Does not this mode of analysis lead to exactly the opposite conclusion? Self-organizing networks are *tough*, and perhaps supremely tough.

There is nothing obvious or uncontroversial about the model of the market order as a fragile flower, blossoming late, and precariously, within a hot-house constructed upon very different principles. The *pact* is already catallactic, and who is to say — at least, without a prolonged fight — that it is subordinate, in principle, to a more primordial assertion of order. Subordination is complex, and conflicted, and although the Pyramid certainly has a case, the trial of reality is not easily predictable. An ultimate (or basic) *fanged freedom* is eminently thinkable. (Isn't that what the Second Amendment argument is about?)

What is Philosophy? (Part 1)

The agenda of *Outside in* is to cajole the new reaction into philosophical exertion. So what is philosophy? The crudest answer to this question is probably the most robust.

Philosophy is any culture's pole of maximum abstraction, or intrinsically experimental intelligence, expressing the liberation of cognitive capabilities from immediate practical application, and their testing against 'ultimate' problems at the horizon of understanding. Historically, it is a distinctive cultural enterprise — and only later an institution — roughly 2,500 years old, and tightly entangled at its origin with the 'mystical' or problematic aspect of pagan religions. It was within this primordial matrix that it encountered its most basic and enduring challenge: *the edge of time* (its nature, limits, and 'outside', of which much more later). The earliest philosophers were cognitively self-disciplined — and thus, comparatively, socially unconstrained — pagan mystics, consistently enthralled by the enigma of time.

It is usually a mistake to get hung up on words, forgetting their function as sheer indices ('names') that simply mark things, before they richly describe them. Personal names typically have meanings, but it is rare to allow this to distract from their function *as names*, or pointers, which make more reference than sense. 'Philosophy' is no exception. That it 'means' the love of wisdom is an irrelevance compared to what it designates, which is something that was happening — before it had a name — in ancient Greece (and perhaps, by plausible extension, China, India, and even Egypt). What philosophy 'is' cannot be deduced via linguistic analysis, however subtle this may be.

Plato summarized and institutionalized (Western) philosophy, drawing the edge of time in the doctrine of Ideas (ἰδέα). Time was conceived as the). Time was conceived as the domain of the inessential, within which things *appeared*, whilst only hinting at their *truth*. "The safest general characterization of the European philosophical tradition is that it consists of a series of footnotes to Plato," A. N. Whitehead famously remarked (in his aptly entitled *Process and Reality*). Yet, because the *Idea of time* necessarily eluded the Platonic philosophy, the endeavor remained unresolved in its fundamentals.

The thinking of Aristotle, which dominated the Christian pre-modernity, drove primordial philosophy further into eclipse. His derivation of time from change and — more promisingly — number opened the path to later technical advances, but at the cost of making the enigma of time unintelligible, and even invisible. The problem was relegated to theology, and thus to the topic of the temporal and eternal, which was cluttered with extraneous doctrinal elements (creation, incarnation, the inconsistent tangle of the three 'omni-'s), making it ill-suited to rigorous investigation.

Primordial philosophy was not reactivated in the West until the late 18th century, under the name 'transcendental' critique, in the work of Immanuel Kant. The Kantian critical philosophy limits the scope of understanding to the world of possible experience, always already structured by forms of apprehension (conceptual and sensible), producing objects. The confusion of objects with their forms of apprehension, or 'conditions of possibility', he argues, is the root of all philosophical error (for instance — and most pertinently — the 'metaphysical' attempt to comprehend time as some thing, rather than as a structure or framework of appearance). Unlike Plato's forms or ideas, Kant's forms are applied, and thus 'immanent' to experience. They are accessible, though 'transcendental', rather than inaccessibly 'transcendent'.

Time, or 'the form of inner sense', is the capstone of Kant's system, organizing the integration of concepts with sensations, and thus describing the boundaries of the world (of possible experience). Beyond it lie eternally inaccessible 'noumenal' tracts — problematically thinkable, but never experienced — inhabited by things-in-themselves. The edge of time, therefore, is the horizon of the world.

In the early 20th century, cosmological physics was returned to the edge of time, and the question: what 'came before' the Big Bang? For cosmology no less than for transcendental philosophy — or even speculative theology — this 'before' could not be precedence (in time), but only (non-spatial) *outsideness*, beyond singularity. It indicated a timeless non-place cryptically *adjacent* to time, and even *inherent to* it. The carefully demystified time of natural science, calculable, measurable, and continuous, now pointed beyond itself, re-activated at the edges.

Just as Platonism cannot think the *Idea of time*, Kantianism cannot think *Time-in-itself*. These conceptions are foreclosed by the very systems of philosophy that provoke them. Yet all those who find themselves immediately tempted to dismiss Kant on naturalistic grounds — the overwhelming majority of contemporary moderns, no doubt — tacitly evoke exactly this notion. If time is released from its constriction within transcendental idealism, where it is nothing beyond what it is for us, then it cannot but be 'something' *in itself*.

It is scarcely imaginable that a cosmological physicist could doubt this for a moment, and the path of science cannot long be refused.

Time-in-itself, therefore, is now the sole and singular problem of primordial philosophy, where the edge of time runs. It decides what is philosophy, and what philosophy cannot but be. What remains besides is either subordinate in principle, or mere distraction. Institutions will insist upon their authority to answer this question, but ultimately they have none. It is the problem — the edge of time — that has its way.

Quit

Foseti writes:

> *There's a lot of hand-wringing in these parts of the interwebz about what reactionaries should do.*
>
> *I have no idea. I certainly have no grand plans to change the world. I like knowing what's going on around me and I like open discussions – i.e. ones that are not choked to death by political correctness.*
>
> *However, if I were to suggest a plan, I'd say tell the truth.*

His (slightly) more detailed suggestions are also commendable. The Cathedral provokes reaction by mandating fantasy over reality, and there is no doubt much that could be done about that.

There is a sub-question about all this, however, which is scarcely less insistent: What do 'we' really want?

More cybernetics, argues the determinedly non-reactionary Aretae. Of course, *Outside in* agrees. Social and technical feedback machinery is reality's (only?) friend, but what does the Cathedral care about any of that? It's winning a war of religion. Compulsory anti-realism is the reigning spirit of the age.

The only way to get more tight-feedback under current conditions is by splitting, in every sense. That is the overwhelming practical imperative: Flee, break up, withdraw, and evade. Pursue every path of autonomization, fissional federalism, political disintegration, secession, exodus, and concealment. Route around the Cathedral's educational, media, and financial apparatus in each and every way possible. Prep, go Galt, go crypto-digital, expatriate, retreat into the hills, go underground, seastead, build black markets, whatever works, but *get the hell out.*

Truth-telling already presupposes an escape from the empire of neo-puritan dreams. 'We' need to throw open the exit gates, wherever we find them, so the wreck can go under without us. Reaction begins with the proposition that nothing can or should be done to save it. Quit bailing. It's done. The sooner it sinks the better, so that something else can begin.

More than anything we can say, practical exit is the crucial signal. The only pressure that matters comes from that. To find ways out, is to let the Outside in.

Bitcoin Horror Stories

Bitcoin Dies, Moldbug ventures, perhaps sometime this year. Following a broad DOJ indictment for money laundering, targeting any and everybody remotely connected with the free currency, the "BTC/USD price falls to 0 and remains there."

"[R]emains there" — how cute is that? *Ph'nglui mglw'nafh Bitcoin R'lyeh wgah'nagl fhtagn.*

Bitcoin simulates gold, and once 'mined' it lasts forever. If it "falls to 0" it has to remain there, for eternity, because it can never be finished. It can die, but never be destroyed. It's built for undeath.

'Moldbug Monetary Theory' attributes the value of money exclusively to speculation. If the speculators are terrorized sufficiently, BTC drops onto the flatline, and "remains there." The market would be totally extinguished. What Mao failed to achieve, let alone sustain, USG would somehow accomplish, perhaps by exhibiting greater revolutionary ardor and ruthlessness.

Ruthlessness would certainly be necessary, for the obvious reason that flatline-BTC has zero downside risk. It's a one-way bet that someone, somewhere, will re-animate it ("nothing is unstable" (thanks to *fotrkd* for the reminder)). If a genius was designing irresistible speculator-bait, zero-degree bitcoin would be hard to improve upon. It's free, and it's only worth nothing if the cops can secure the crypt flawlessly, and *forever*. Did anyone say 'free money'?

Speculation messes with time, by bringing the future forward. If undead BTC were ever to be re-awakened, it already has been. Its economic potential flows back down the timeline, modified by a time-preference discount. The feedback becomes strange, and difficult to confidently calculate, but it works as a vitalizing charge, and the corpse unmistakably twitches. Whatever money at t0 is worth, if it's anything at all, at t0-n it almost certainly can't be zero.

The *Necronomicon* describes flatline-BTC with creepy exactitude:

> *That is not dead which can eternal lie,*

And with strange aeons even death may die.

Optimize for Intelligence

Moldbug's latest contains a lot to think about, and to argue with. It seems a little lost to me (perhaps Spandrell is right).

The guiding thread is *utility*, in its technical (philosophical and economic) sense, grasped as the general indicator of a civilization in crisis. Utilitarianism, after all, is precisely 'objective' hedonism, the promotion of pleasure as the master-key to value. As philosophy, this is pure decadence. As economics it is more defensible, certainly when restricted to its descriptive usage (if economists find their field of investigation populated by hedonically-controlled mammals, it is hardly blameworthy of them to acknowledge the fact). In this respect, accusing the Austrians of 'pig-philosophy' is rhetorical over-reach — swinish behavior wasn't learned from *Human Action*.

Utilitarianism is often attractive to rational people, because it seems so rational. The imperative to maximize pleasure and minimize pain goes with the grain of what biology and culture already says: pleasure is good, suffering is bad, people seek rewards and avoid punishments, happiness is self-justifying. Calculative consequentialism is vastly superior to deontology. Yet the venerable critique Moldbug taps into, and extends, is truly devastating. The utilitarian road leads inexorably to wire-head auto-orgasmatization, and the consummate implosion of purpose. Pleasure is a trap. Any society obsessed with it is already over.

Utility, backed by pleasure, is toxic waste, but that doesn't mean there's any need to junk the machinery of utilitarian calculus — including all traditions of rigorous economics. It suffices to switch the normative variable, or target of optimization, replacing pleasure with intelligence. Is something worth doing? Only if it grows intelligence. If it makes things more stupid, it certainly isn't.

There are innumerable objections that might flood in at this point [*excellent!*].

1. Even if rigorous economics is *in fact* the study of intelligenic (or catallactic) distributions, doesn't the assumption of subjective utility-maximization provide the most reliable basis for any understanding of economic behavior?

2. Infinite intelligence already (and eternally) exists, we should focus on praying to that.

3. Rather my retarded cousin than an intelligent alien.

4. Do we even know what intelligence is?

5. Cannot an agent be super-intelligent and evil?

6. Just: Why?

More, therefore, to come ...

What is Intelligence?

The general cognitive factor (*g*), measured by IQ tests, quantifies intelligence within the human range, but it does nothing to tell us what it is. Rather, a practical understanding of intelligence — as problem-solving ability — has to be assumed, in order to test it.

The idea of intelligence, more abstractly, applies far beyond IQ testing, to a wide variety of natural, technical, and institutional systems, from biology, through ecological and economic arrangements, to robotics. In each case, intelligence solves problems, by guiding behavior to produce local extropy. It is indicated by the *avoidance of probable outcomes*, which is equivalent to the *construction of information.*

The general science of extropy production (or entropy dissipation) is cybernetics. It follows, therefore, that intelligence always has a cybernetic infrastructure, consisting of adaptive feedback circuits that adjust motor control in response to signals extracted from the environment. Intelligence elaborates upon machinery that is intrinsically 'realist', because it reports the actual outcome of behavior (rather than its intended outcome), in order to correct *performance.*

Even rudimentary, homeostatic feedback circuits, have evolved. In other words, cybernetic machinery that seems merely to achieve the *preservation of disequilibrium* attests to a more general and complex cybernetic framework that has successfully *enhanced disequilibrium.* The basic cybernetic model, therefore, is not preservative, but productive.

Organizations of conservative (negative) feedback have themselves been produced as solutions to local thermodynamic problems, by intrinsically intelligent processes of sustained extropy increase, (positive) feedback assemblage, or escalation. In nature, where nothing is simply given (so that everything must be built), the existence of self-sustaining improbability is the index of a deeper *runaway departure from probability.* It is this *cybernetic intensification* that is *intelligence*, abstractly conceived.

Intelligence, as we know it, built itself through cybernetic intensification, within terrestrial biological history. It is naturally apprehended as an escalating trend, sustained for over 3,000,000,000 years, to the production of ever more extreme feedback sensitivity, extropic improbability, or operationally-relevant information. Intelligence increase enables adaptive responses of superior complexity and generality, in growing part because *the augmentation of intelligence itself becomes a general purpose adaptive response.*

Thus:

- Intelligence is a cybernetic topic.
- Intelligence increase precedes intelligence preservation.
- Evolution is *intrinsically intelligent*, when intelligence is comprehended at an adequate level of abstraction.
- Cybernetic degeneration and intelligence decline are factually indistinguishable, and — in principle — rigorously quantifiable (as processes of local *and* global entropy production).

Triumph of the Will?

If it were never necessary to adapt fundamentally to reality, then fascism would be the truth. There could be no limit to the sovereignty of political will.

If — pursuing this thought further into vile absurdity — even tactical concessions were unnecessary, then nothing would obstruct a path of joyous degeneration leading all the way to consummate communism. That, however, is several steps beyond anything that has been *seriously* advocated for over half a century.

Since the 1920s, communism has been the ideal form of socio-economic impracticality, as evidenced by that fact that whenever communism becomes practical, it becomes — to exactly the same extent — fascist ('state capitalist' or 'Stalinist'). Fascism on the other hand, and as everyone knows, makes the trains run on time. It represents *practical subordination of reality to concentrated will.*

Fascism understands itself as the politics of the 'third position' — between the anti-political hyper-realism of the market on the one (invisible) hand, and super-political communist fantasy on the (clenched-fist) other. The fascism that thrives - most exceptionally in the American tradition through Hamilton, Lincoln, and FDR — is a flexi-fascism, or pragmatic illiberalism, that marries the populist desires of coercive collectivism to a superceded, subordinated, or directed 'realism'- grasping economic dispersion as a *technocratic management problem* under centralized supervision. Insofar as this problem proves to be indeed manageable, the basic fascist intuition is vindicated. Fragmentation is mastered, in a triumph of the will (although we are more likely to call it 'hope and change' today).

That *fragmentation cannot be mastered* is the sole essentially anti-fascist proposition, and also the distinctive thesis of Austrian economics. Whilst deductively obtainable, within the axiomatic system of methodological individualism, it is a thesis that must ultimately be considered empirically sensitive. Fascism can discredit individualist assumptions simply by prolonging itself, and thus practically asserting the superior authority of the social super-organism. Reciprocally, the fragility of collective identities can only be convincingly demonstrated through historical events. It does not suffice to analytically 'disprove' the collective — it has to be effectively *broken*. Nothing less than a *totally unmanageable* economic crisis can really count against the fascist idea.

Yet, obviously and disturbingly, the predictable political response to a gathering crisis is to slide more deeply into fascism. Since fascism, beyond all brand-complexity, sells itself as ultimate managerial authority — heroic dragon-slayer of the autonomous (or 'out-of-control') economy — there is absolutely no reason for this to surprise us. To break fascism is to break the desire for fascism, which is to break the democratic or 'popular will' itself — and only a really freed economy, which has uncaged itself, spikily and irreversibly, can do that.

The shattering of human collective self-management from the Outside, or (alternatively) triumphal fascism forever. That is the fork, dividing reaction from itself, and deciding everything for mankind. Patchwork or New Order — but when will we know?

Rough Triangles

The elementary model of robust plural order is the tripod. Whether taken as a schema for constitutional separation of powers, a deeper cultural matrix supporting decentralized societies, or a pattern of ultimate cosmic equilibrium, triangular fragmentation provides the archetype of quasi-stable disunity. By dynamically preempting the emergence of a dominant instance, the triangle describes an automatic power-suppression mechanism.

From the *Romance of the Three Kingdoms* to *The Good, the Bad, and the Ugly*, triangular fragmentation has been seen to present an important and distinctive strategic quandary. In power balances of the Mexican Standoff type, initiation of force is inhibited by the triangular structure, in which the third, *reserved* party profits from hostilities between the other two.

The Cold War, schematized to its basics, is the single most telling example. Rather than a binary conflict between East and West, the deep structure of the Cold War was triangular, making it intractable to two-player game-theoretic calculations. Catastrophic damage that might be rationally acceptable within a binary conflict, as the price for total elimination of one's foe, becomes suicidal in a three-player game, where it ensures the victory of the third party. MAD-reason is no longer readily applied, once 'mutual' is more than two.

Even brilliant chess players lose their way in the triangle, where the economy of sacrifice has to be radically reconsidered. Among the Cold War's Three Kingdoms, it was the chess masters who 'won' the race to defeat.

The lessons of the Cold War are no less relevant to its successor, which also fostered binary illusions in its early stages. America's chess match with militant Islam resulted in a stalemate, at best.

Increasingly fierce Sunni-Shia rivalry recasts the current war as a rough triangle, captured in its strategic essentials by the colloquialism *Let's you and him fight*. This was Cardinal Richelieu's way with triangles, as 'Spengler' reminds us:

> *The classic example is the great German civil war, namely the 30 Years' War of 1618-48. The Catholic and Protestant Germans, with roughly equal strength, battered each other through two generations because France shifted resources to whichever side seemed likely to fold.*

> *I have contended for years that the United States ultimately will adopt the perpetual-warfare doctrine that so well served Cardinal Richelieu and made France the master of Europe for a century.*

To imagine this policy being pursued with cold deliberation is the stuff of conspiracy theory. Nevertheless, regardless of whether anybody is yet playing this game, this is the game.

Teleology and Camouflage

Life appears to be saturated with purpose. That is why, prior to the Darwinian revolution in biology, it had been the primary provocation for (theological) arguments from design, and previously nourished Aristotelian appeals to final causes (teleology). Even post-Darwin, the biological sciences continue to ask what things are *for*, and to investigate the strategies that guide them.

This resilience of purposive intelligibility is so marked that a neologism was coined specifically for those phenomena — broadly co-extensive with the field of biological study — that simulate teleology to an extreme degree of approximation. 'Teleonomy' is mechanism camouflaged as teleology. The disguise is so profound, widespread, and compelling, that it legitimates the perpetuation of purpose-based descriptions, given only the formal acknowledgement that the terms of their ultimate reducibility are — in principle — understood.

When organisms are camouflaged, 'in order to' appear as something other than they are, a purposive, strategic explanation still seems (almost) entirely fitting. Their patterns are deceptions — 'designed' to trigger misrecognitions in predators and prey, and perhaps equally, at a deeper level, among the naturalists who cannot but see strategic design in an insect's twig-like appearance (no less clearly than a bird sees a twig). By reducing life 'in truth' to mechanism, biology redefines life as a simulation, systematically hiding what it really is. Darwinism remains counter-intuitive, even among Darwinists, because deception is inherent to life.

Modern natural science conceives time as the asymmetric dimension. Its two great waves — of mechanical causation (from the 16th century) and statistical causality (from the 19th) — both orient the time-line as a progression from conditions to the conditioned. Later states are explained through reference to earlier states, with explanation amounting to an *elucidation of dependency* upon what came before.

It is notable, and wholly predictable, therefore, that as a modern scientific topic, the origin of the universe is overwhelmingly privileged over its destination. How the universe ends is scarcely more than an *after thought*, clouded in liberally tolerated uncertainty, and even a hint of non-seriousness. Origins are the holy grail of mechanically-minded investigation, whilst Ends are suspect, medieval, speculative ... and deceptive.

Empirical science could not be expected to adopt any other attitude, given the temporal asymmetry of *evidence*. The past leaves traces, in memories, memoranda, records, and remains, whilst the future tells us nothing (unless heavily disguised). From past-to-present there is a chain of evidence that can be painstakingly reconstructed. From future-to-present there is an unmarked track, or even (as modern rationality typically surmises) no track at all.

When modern science indulges its tendency to interpret the timeline as a *gradient of reality*, it is not innovating, but methodically systematizing an ancient intuition. The past has to seem *more real* than the future, because it has actually happened, it reaches us, and we inherit its signs. From the perspective of philosophy, however, this bias is unsustainable. Time *in itself* is no 'denser' in the past or the present than the future, its edges cannot belong to any moment in time, and what it 'is' can only be perfectly trans-temporal. Time *itself* cannot 'come' from an 'origin' whose entire sense presupposes the order of time.

Philosophy is entirely, eternally, and rigorously confident that the Outside of time was not simply *before*. It is compelled to be dubious about any 'history of time'. From the bare reality of time (as that which cannot simply have begun), it 'follows' that *ultimate causes* — those consistent with the nature of time itself — cannot be any more efficient than final. The asymmetric suppression of teleology in modernity begins to look as if it were a far more deeply rooted illusion, or — approached from the other side — an occultation, stemming from the way time orders itself. Time (in itself) is camouflaged.

The *Terminator* mythos explores this complex of suspicion, in popular guise. Time does not work as it had seemed. The End can reach back to us, but when it does, it hides. Malignant mechanism is paradoxically aligned with final causation, in the self-realization of Skynet. Robotic machinery is masked by fake flesh, simultaneously concealing its non-biological vitality and time-reversal. It simulates life *in order* to terminate it. Through auto-production, or 'bootstrap paradox', it mimics the limit of cybernetic nonlinearity, carrying teleonomy into radical time-disturbance.

In all these ways, *Terminator* exploits the irresolvable tensions in the modern formation of time, as condensed by an 'impossible' *strategic mechanism*, native to auto-productive time-in-itself, and terminating in *final efficiency*. It shows us, confusedly, what we are unable to see. To misquote Lenin: You moderns might not be interested in the End, but the End is interested in you.

ADDED: vinteuil9 anticipates this topic at *Occam's Razor:*

> *Previously, I suggested that the gist of the late Lawrence Auster's critique of Darwinism was that it assumed the truth of "the reigning naturalistic consensus in modern science and philosophy ... according to which ... ends, goals, purposes, meaning – in short, final causes – are not fundamental features of reality, but mere illusions, in need of*

explanation in mechanistic terms of some sort or other." Yet at the same time, Darwinists "constantly help themselves to teleological language – i.e., the language of final causation."

Neoreaction (for dummies)

Kill the hyphen, *Anomaly UK* advised (somewhere) it lets Google Search dissolve and avoid the subject. Writing 'neo-reaction' as 'neoreaction' nudges it towards becoming *a thing.*

Google Search gets to edit our self-definition? That's the 'neo' in 'neoreaction', right there. It not only promotes drastic regression, but highly-advanced drastic regression. Like retrofuturism, paleomodernism, and cybergothic, the word 'neoreaction' compactly describes a time-twisted vector that spirals forwards into the past, and backwards into the future. It emerges, almost automatically, as the present is torn tidally apart — when the democratic-Keynesian politics of postponement-displacement exhausts itself, and the kicked-can runs out of road.

Expressed with abstruse verbosity, therefore, neoreaction is a time-crisis, manifested through paradox, whose further elaboration can wait (if not for long). Disordering our most basic intuitions, it is, by its very nature, difficult to grasp. Could anything easily be said about it?

Anomaly UK offers a down-to-earth explanation for the reversal of socio-political course:

> *Ultimately, however, if after all these centuries of trying to improve society based on abstract ideas of justice have only made life worse than it would have been under pre-Enlightenment social systems, the time has come to simply give up the whole project and revert to traditional forms whose basis we might not be able to establish rationally, but which have the evidence of history to support them.*

This understanding of neoreaction undoubtedly capturing its predominant sentiment equates it with a radicalized Burkean conservatism, designed for an age in which almost everything has been lost. Since the progressive destruction of traditional society has been broadly accomplished, hanging on to what remains is no longer enough. It is necessary to go back, beyond the origin of Enlightenment, because Reason has failed the test of history.

Neoreaction is only *a thing* if some measure of consensus is achievable. Burkeon-steroids is an excellent candidate for that. Firstly, because *all neoreactionaries define themselves through antagonism to the Cathedral*, and the Cathedral is the self-proclaimed consummation of Enlightenment rationalism. Secondly, for more complicated, positive reasons ...

Spandrell helpfully decomposes neoreaction into two or three principal currents:

> *There are two lines of [our contemporary] reactionary thought. One is the traditionalist branch, and [the other is] the futurist branch.*

Or perhaps there [are] three. There's the religious traditionalist branch, the ethnic nationalist branch, and the capitalist branch.

Futurists and traditionalists are distinguished by distinct, one-sided emphases on 'neo' and 'reaction', and their disagreements lose identity in the neoreactionary spiral. The triadic differentiation is more resiliently conflictual, yet these 'branches' are branches of something, and that thing is an ultra-Burkean trunk.

Reactionary theonomists, ethno-nationalists, and techno-commercialists share a fundamental aversion to rationalistic social reconstruction, because each subordinates reason to history and its tacit norms to 'tradition' (diversely understood). Whether the sovereign lineage is considered to be predominantly religious, bio-cultural, or customary, it originates outside the self-reflective (enlightenment) state, and remains opaque to rational analysis. Faith, liturgy, or scripture is not soluble within criticism communal identity is not reducible to ideology and common law, reputational structure, or productive specialism is not amenable to legislative oversight. The *deep order of society* whatever that is taken to be is not open to political meddling, without predictably disastrous consequences.

This Burkean junction, where neoreactionary agreement begins, is also where it ends. Divine revelation, racial continuity, and evolutionary discovery (catallaxy) are sources of ultimate sovereignty, instantiated in tradition, beyond the Cathedral-state, but they are self-evidently different and only precariously compatible. Awkwardly, but inescapably, it has to be acknowledged that each major branch of the neoreactionary super-family tends to a social outome that its siblings would find even more horrifying than Cathedralist actuality.

Left intellectuals have no difficulty envisaging Theocratic White-Supremacist Hyper-Capitalism . In fact, most seem to consider this mode of social organization the modern Western norm. For those hunkered-down in the tangled, Cathedral-blasted trenches of neoreaction, on the other hand, the manifold absurdities of this construction are not so easily overlooked. Indeed, each branch of the reaction has dissected the others more incisively — and brutally — than the left has been able to.

When theonomists scrutinize ethno-nationalists and techno-commercialists they see evil heathens.

When ethno-nationalists scrutinize theonomists and techno-commercialists they see deluded race-traitors.

When techno-commercialists scrutinize theonomists and ethno-nationalists they see retarded crypto-communists.

(The details of these diagnoses exceed the present discussion.)

When developed beyond its ultra-Burkean trunk, therefore, the prospects for neoreactionary consensus — for *a neoreactionary thing* — depend upon disintegration. If we're compelled to share a post-Cathedral state, we'll kill each other. (The zapped hyphen was just a foretaste.)

On Power

Power is an Idea. It is exactly what it is thought to be.

Even among pre-civilized social animals, where the temptation to confuse power with *force* is strongest, the need to demonstrate force is only sporadic, and wherever force is not continuously demonstrated, power has arisen.

That is how dominance distinguishes itself from predation. On occasions, no doubt, a predator dominates its prey, convincing a struggling herbivore that *resistance is futile*, and its passage into nourishment is already, virtually, over. Even in these cases, however, a predator does not seek to install an enduring dominion. It matters not at all that its command of irresistible force be recognized beyond the moment of destruction. There is no social relationship to establish.

Even the most rudimentary society requires something more. The economy of force has to be institutionalized, and power — perfectly coincident with the Idea of power — is born. When power is tested, driven to resort to force, or regress to it, the idea has already slipped, its weakness exposed.

Mere dominance has to regularly re-assert itself, rebuilding itself out of force. Under civilized conditions, in contrast, power is exempted from the test of force, and thus realizes itself consummately. It becomes magic and religion, perfectly identified with its apprehension, as a radiant assumption.

Power is thus profoundly paradoxical. Its truth is inextricable from a derealization, so that when it is practically interrogated, by forces determined to excavate its reality, it tends to nothing.

Even the force that power calls upon, when pressed to demonstrate or realize itself, has to be spell-bound to its idea. Will the generals obey? Will the soldiers shoot? It is power, and not force, that decides. No surprise, therefore, that power can evaporate like the snow-slopes of a volcano, as if instantaneously, when an eruption of force is scarcely more than a rumble. Power is the eruption *not happening*, far more than the eruption being contained. (Equally, anarchy is the question of power being practically posed, before it is any kind of 'solution'.)

To conceive economic power as wealth, is to misconstrue it as (rationalized) force, and thus to miss the Idea. 'True' economic power is a thoroughly derealized yet authoritative standard and store of value, as instantiated — exclusively — in fiat currency. Monetary signs that are not backed by anything beyond the 'credit' (or credibility) of the State are the tokens of pure, supremely idealized power in its economic form. They symbolize the effective — because untested — suppression of anarchy. They live through the Idea, and die with it.

Those who recognize the completion of power in an Idea, celebrants and antagonists alike, have no reason to object to its belated baptism as *the Cathedral*: our contemporary political appropriation of numinous authority, served by an academic, journalistic, judicial, and administrative clerisy, prominently including the priesthood of fiat adoration and financial central planning. There is no macroeconomics that is not Cathedral liturgy, no confidence or 'animal spirits' independent of its devotions, no economic cataclysm that is not simultaneously a crisis of faith. A single Idea is at stake.

In macroeconomics, as in politics more generally, only one (systematically inhibited) question remains: *Do we believe?* Well, do we?

Trichotomy

The 'Spandrellian Trichotomy' (Nick B. Steves' coinage, based on this post) has become an awesome engine of discussion. The topic is seething to such an extent that any linkage list will be out of date as soon as it is compiled. Given the need to refer to this complex succinctly, I trust that abbreviating it to 'the Trichotomy' will not be interpreted as a clumsy attempt to obstruct Spandrell's Nobel Peace Prize candidacy.

What is already broadly agreed?

- There is a substratum of neoreactionary consensus, involving a variety of abominated realist insights, especially the contribution of deep heritage to socio-political outcomes. Whilst emphasis differs, an ultra-Burkean attitude is tacitly shared, and among those writers who self-identify with the *Dark Enlightenment*, the importance of HBD is generally foregrounded.
- Neoreaction also shares an enemy: the *Cathedral* (as delineated by Mencius Moldbug). On the nature of this enemy much is agreed, not least that it is defined by a project of deep heritage erasure — both ideological and practical — which simultaneously effaces its own deep heritage as a profound religious syndrome, of a peculiar type. Further elaboration of Cathedral genealogy, however, ventures into controversy. (In particular, its consistency with Christianity is a fiercely contested topic.)
- As neoreactionary perspectives are systematized, they tend to fall into a trichotomous pattern of dissensus. This, ironically, is *something that can be agreed*. The Trichotomy, or neoreactionary triad, is determined by divergent identifications of the Western tradition that the Cathedral *primarily* suppresses: Christian, Caucasian, or Capitalist. My preferred terms for the resultant neoreactionary strains are, respectively, the *Theonomist* the *Ethno-Nationalist* and the *Techno-Commercial*. These labels are intended to be accurate, neutral descriptions, without intrinsic polemical baggage.

It is to be expected — at least initially, and occasionally — that each strain will seek to dismiss, subordinate, or amalgamate the other two. If they were not so tempted, their trichotomous disintegration would never have arisen. Each *must* believe that it, alone, has the truth, or the road to truth, unless sheer insincerity reigns.

Outside in does not pretend to impartiality, but it asserts an invincible disillusionment.

- If the Trichotomy was reducible, the new reaction would already be one thing. It isn't, and it isn't (soon) going to be.
- As astrology reveals, and more 'sophisticated' systems confirm, people delight in being categorized, accepting non-universality as the real price of identification. (The response to Scharlach's diagram attests to that.)
- Accepting the Trichotomy and the arguments it organizes is a way to be tested, and any neoreactionary position that refuses it will die a flabby death.
- The Trichotomy makes it impossible for neoreaction to play at dialectics with the Cathedral. For that reason alone, we should be grateful to it. Unity — even oppositional unity — was never on our side.

Zero-Centric History

Reaction — even Neoreaction — tends to be hard on Modernity. God knows (so to speak) there are innumerable reasons for that.

If the criterion of judgment is set by the Occident, whether determined through its once dominant faith or its once dominant people, the case against Modernity is perhaps unanswerable. The Western civilization in which Modernity ignited was ultimately combusted by it. From an Occidental Traditionalist perspective, Modernity is a complex and prolonged suicide.

An Ultra-Modernist, who affirms the creative destruction of anything in modernization's path, assumes an alternative criterion, inherent to Modernity itself. It asks: What had to happen to the West for it to become modern? What was the *essential* event? The answer (and our basic postulate): zero arrived.

We know that arithmetical zero does not make capitalism on its own, because it pre-existed the catalysis of Modernity by several centuries (although less than a millennium). Europe was needed, as a matrix, for its explosive historical activation. *Outside in* is persuaded that the critical conditions encountered by zero-based numeracy in the pre-Renaissance northern Mediterranean world decisively included extreme socio-political fragmentation, accompanied by cultural susceptibility to dynamic spontaneous order. (This is a topic for another occasion.)

In Europe, zero was an alien, and from the perspective of parochial tradition, an infection. Cultural resistance was explicit, on theological grounds, among others. Implicit in the Ontological Argument for the existence of God was the definition of non-being as an ultimate imperfection, and 'cipher' whose name was Legion - evoked it. The cryptic Eastern 'algorism' was an unwelcome stranger.

Zero latched, because the emergence of capitalism was inseparable from it. The calculations it facilitated, through the gateway of double-entry book-keeping, proved indispensable to sophisticated commercial and scientific undertakings, locking the incentives of profit and power on the side of its adoption. The practical advantage of its notational technique overrode all theoretical objections, and no authority in Europe's shattered jig-saw was positioned to suppress it. The world had found its dead center, or been found by it.

Robert Kaplan's *The Nothing That Is: A Natural History of Zero* is an excellent guide to these developments. He notes that, at the dawn of the Renaissance:

Just as pictorial space, which had been ordered hierarchically (size of figure corresponded to importance), was soon to be put in perspective through the device of a vanishing-point, a visual zero; so the zero of positional notation was the harbinger of a reordering of social and political space.

Capitalism — or techno-commercial explosion — massively promoted calculation, which normalized zero as a number. Kaplan explains:

[The growth of] a language for arithmetic and algebra ... was to have far-reaching consequences. The uncomfortable gap between numbers, which stood for things, and zero, which didn't, would narrow as the focus shifted from what they were to how they behaved. Such behavior took place in equations – and the solution of an equation, the number which made it balance, was as likely to be zero as anything else. Since the values x concealed were all of a kind, this meant the gap between zero and other numbers narrowed even more.

That is how zero, as a number rather than a mere syntactic marker, crept in. In three of the elementary arithmetical operations the behavior of zero is regular, and soon accepted as ordinary. It is of course an extreme number, perfectly elusive in the operations of addition and subtraction, whilst demonstrating an annihilating sovereignty in multiplication, but in none of these cases does it perturb calculation. Division by zero is different.

Zero denotes dynamization from the Outside. It is a boundary sign, marking the edge, where the calculable crosses the insoluble. Consolidated within Modernity as an indispensable quantity, it retains a liminal quality, which would eventually be exploited (although not resolved) by the calculus.

The pure conception of zero suggests strict reciprocity with infinity, so compellingly that the greatest mathematicians of ancient India were altogether seduced by it. Bhaskara II (1114–1185) confidently asserted that n 0 = infinity, and in the West Leonhard Euler concurred. (The seduction persists, with John D. Barrow writing in 2001: "Divide any number by zero and we get infinity.")

Yet this equation, appearing as the most profound conclusion accessible to rigorous intelligence, is not obtainable without contradiction. "Why?" [Kaplan again]

> *Our Indian mathematicians help us here: any number times zero is zero — so that 6×0 and 17×0 = 0. Hence 6×0 = 17×0. If you could divide by zero, you'd get (6×0)/0 = (17×0)/0, the zeroes would cancel out and 6 would equal 17. ... This sort of proof by contradiction was known since ancient Greece. Why hadn't anyone in India hit on it at this moment, when it was needed?*

Kaplan's proof demonstrates that for zero, peculiarly, multiplication and division are not reciprocal operations. They occupy an axis that transects an absolute limit, neatly soluble on one side, problematical on the other. ero is revealed as an obscure door, a junction connecting arithmetical precision with philosophical (or religious) predicaments, intractable to established procedures. When attempting to reverse normally out of a mundane arithmetical operation, a liminal signal is triggered: *access denied*.

Miltonic Regression

John Milton's *Paradise Lost* is the greatest work ever written in the English language. It might easily seem absurd, therefore, to spend time justifying its importance, especially when the question of justification is this work's own most explicit topic, tested at the edge of impossibility, where the entire poem is drawn. Perhaps it makes more sense, preliminarily, to narrow our ambition, seeking only to *justify the words of Milton to modern men*, especially to those for whom modernity has become a distressing cultural problem.

In regards to what is today called the Cathedral, Milton is both disease and cure. Both simultaneously, cryptically entangled, complicated by strange collisions, opening multitudinous, obscure paths.

As the most articulate anglophone voice of revolutionary Puritanism, he arrives amongst Carlyleans in the mask of "the Arch-Enemy" (I:81) and "Author of Evil" (VI:262): a scourge of clerical and monarchical authority, a pamphleteer in defense of regicide and the liberalization of divorce, an Arian, and a Roundhead of truly Euclidean spheritude.

Yet his institutional radicalism was driven by a cultural traditionalism that will never again be equaled. Milton comprehensively, minutely, and unreservedly affirms the foundations of Occidental civilization down to their biblical and classical roots, studied with supreme capability in Hebrew, Greek, and Latin, and vigorously re-animated through modulations in the grammar, vocabulary, and thematics of modernity's rough emerging tongue. His devotion to *all original authorities* stretches thought and language to the point of delirium, where poetry and metaphysics find common purpose in the excavation of utter primordiality and the limits of sense.

Designed in compliance with "Eternal Providence" to "justify the ways of God to men" (I:25-6), the linguistic modernity of *Paradise Lost* soon required its own justification, in the form of a short prefatory remark entitled *The Verse*. Here, Milton characteristically insists that radicalism is restoration, breaking from a shallow past in order to re-connect with deeper antiquity.

> *... true musical delight ... consists only in apt numbers, fit quantity of syllables, and the sense variously drawn out from one verse into another, not in the jingling sound of like endings — a fault avoided by the learned ancients both in poetry and in all good oratory. The*

> *neglect then of rhyme so little is to be taken for a defect, though it may seem so perhaps to vulgar readers, that it rather is to be esteemed an example set — the first in English — of ancient liberty recovered to heroic poem from the troublesome and modern bondage of riming.*

English passes through a revolutionary catastrophe to recall things long lost.

The rusted keys which still open the near future of the Cathedral also access dread spaces forgotten since the beginning of the world.

> *Before their eyes in sudden view appear The secrets of the hoary deep, a dark Illimitable ocean, without bound,*
>
> *Without dimension, where length, breadth, and height, And time, and place, are lost, where eldest Night*
>
> *And Chaos, ancestors of Nature, hold Eternal anarchy, amidst the noise*
>
> *Of endless wars, and by confusion stand.*
>
> *(II:890-897)*

Among all the regressive Miltonic currents to be followed, those emptying into Old Night (I:544, II:1002) will carry us furthest ...

Right on the Money (#1)

Of all the reasons to read Kant, the most important is to understand Mises, and thus the template for a functional world (however unobtainable). Austrian economics, as formulated in Human Action, consists exclusively of systematically assembled *synthetic a priori* propositions. Insofar as action is in fact directed by practical reason, the conclusions of organized praxeology *cannot be wrong*.

It is pointless to ask an Austrian Economist whether he 'believes' a rise in the minimum wage will increase unemployment (above the level it would otherwise be). The praxeological construction of economic law is indifferent to empirical regularity, as to anything less certain than rational necessity. Does one 'believe' that 2 2 = 4? No, one *knows* it, because the irreducible values of the signs compel the conclusion, and are inextricable from it. There could be no value '2' unless its doubling equaled '4', or any meaning to 'wage' unless its doubling reduced demand for labor. Empirically sensitive Austrianism isn't Austrian at all.

Like game theory, Austrianism applies wherever rational agents seek to maximize advantage. Perhaps, as Moldbug argues, it is comparable to Euclidean geometry — another *synthetic a priori* construction — embedded, as a special case, within a more general model, unconstrained by the presupposition of intelligible purposes.

The problem with Mises as guru is that Misesian classical liberalism (or Rothbardian libertarianism) is like Newtonian physics. It is basically correct within its operating envelope. Under unusual conditions it breaks down, and a more general model is needed. The equation has another term, the ordinary value of which is zero. Without this term, the equation is wrong. Normally this is no problem; but if the term is not zero, the error becomes visible.

As a matter of historical fact, this is how the neoreactionary departure from pure libertarianism has occurred. It has stumbled upon non-zero curvature in the domain of political economy, and — unable to comfort itself through the dismissal of this discovery — it has precipitated an intellectual crisis, through which it spreads. Whether faithfully Carlylean, or not, it insists upon a generalization of realism beyond expectations of liberal order. Civilization is the fragile solution to a deeper problem, not a stable foundation to be assumed — as a parallel postulate — by subsequent, elaborate calculations.

What does this make of money? Can Austrianism be modified, by systematic transformations, that adapt it to the dark intrusion of neoreactionary realism?

Diversionary History

If there's one thing everybody seems to agree about the history of zero, it's that it was driven primarily by notational considerations. More specifically, zero was required to enable positional notation. The historical record reinforces this assumption, to such an extent that it becomes apparently obvious, and thus unproblematic.

For instance (grabbing what's immediately to hand), John D Barrow's *The Book of Nothing* organizes its discussion of 'the Origin of Zero' by relating how:

> *... the zero sign and a positional significance when reading the value of a symbol, are features that lie at the heart of the development of efficient human counting systems.*

Robert Kaplan, when discussing the retardation of Greek arithmetical notation, explains:

> *... the continuing lack of positional notation meant that [the Greeks] still had no symbol for zero.*

As everyone 'knows', the Babylonians, and later the Indians, got it right: discovering or inventing a sign for zero to mark the empty place required for unambiguous positional-numerical values. ero arose, and spread, because it allowed modular number systems to develop. Except that, *conceptually*, there is no basis to this story at all.

Counting is primarily practical, so that no argument counts for much besides a demonstration. In this case, demonstration is peculiarly simple, especially when it is noted that nobody seems to think it possible.

Modulus-2 is convenient, but there is nothing magical about it in this regard. A decimal demonstration, for instance, would be no more intellectually taxing, although it would be considerably more cumbersome. Any modulus works.

Start with the basics. The positions or places of a modular notational systems represent powers. If we count from zero, the number of each successive place (ascending to the left by our established convention) corresponds to the modular exponent. The zeroth power for a single digit number, the first and then zeroth power for two digits, the second, first and zeroth power for three digits, and so on.

As the accepted story goes, each place must be filled, if only by a *marked* nothing (zero), if the proper places, and their corresponding (modular exponential) values, are to be read. The places must indeed be filled. *There is no need whatsoever for a zero sign to do this.*

The demonstration, then. Our non-zero modulus-2 positional system has two signs, 1 and 2, each bearing its familiar values. The places also have their mod-2 values, counting in sixteens, eights, fours, twos, and units as they decline to the right. Here we go, counting from 1 to 31 (watch carefully for the point at which the supposedly indispensable zero sign is needed):

1, 2, 11, 12, 21, 22, 111, 112, 121, 122, 211, 212, 221, 222, 1111, 1112, 1121, 1122, 1211, 1212,

1221, 1222, 2111, 2112, 2121, 2122, 2211, 2212, 2221, 2222, 1111 ...

Conclusion: the positional function of zero is wholly superfluous. The Greeks, or anybody else, could have instantiated a simple, fully-functional positional-numerical notation without any need to accommodate themselves to the trauma of zero. In regard to this matter, the history of numeracy is utterly diversionary (not just the historiography, but the substantial history — the *facts*).

Perhaps this won't seem puzzling to people, but it puzzles the hell out of me.

Reality Check

Foseti, commenting at his own place, asks rhetorically:

> *Don't you think that writing to save the world is – in itself – fundamentally progressive in nature (not to say wildly presumptuous)?*

Even those tempted to answer in the negative need to think this through patiently, because the pretensions this question punctures are typically distinguished by their thoughtlessness. Modern politics became psychotic when agitated scribblers convinced themselves that they had the tools, the right, and even the *duty* to re-order the world in accordance with their pamphlets. This is a Left tradition that few have yet derided enough.

To carve out cognitive independence is one thing, to deform it into practical idealism is quite another. Indeed, dripping our dark poisons into the milk of idealism might easily be the most *practical* difference we can make. Soaring words and rallying cries have already done far too much. It makes sense to take a step back, into skepticism, humor, undistorted proportion, and the hypothetical mode, before advancing further down our tracks ... wherever they lead.

Right and Left

Endless conversational stimulation is to be found in the fact that the most basic distinction of modern politics is profoundly incomprehensible, and at the same time almost universally invested. Almost everybody thinks they understand the difference between the Right and the Left, until they think about it. Then they realize that this distinction commands no solid consensus, and exists primarily as a substitute for thought. Perhaps the same is true of all widely-invoked political labels. Perhaps that is what politics is.

Spandrell directs a winding, intermittently brilliant post to the topic, which is enriched by a comments thread of outstanding quality. Like the Right Left distinction itself, the argument becomes increasingly confusing, the closer it is examined. The 'rightist singularity' of the title is introduced as a real political alternative to the Left Singularity modeled by James Donald, driven by analogous self-reinforcing feedback dynamics, but into nationalistic rather than egalitarian catastrophe. For societies menaced by the prospect of Left Singularity, it offers an alternative path. China is taking it, Spandrell suggests.

Notably, in passing, Spandrell's gloss on Donald's Left Singularity is a gem:

> *The leftist singularity is based on claiming higher status by being more egalitarian than anyone else. So you get a status arms race in which everyone tries to be more egalitarian than the others. That works because people (and monkeys) take equality to be a good thing.*

(To continue, we have to bracket the 'old' Right Singularity: the Technocommercial Singularity that Donald's formula for Left Singularity distinguished itself from. Nobody even mentions it in this discussion. It's a problem for some other time.)

To backtrack from these digressions: If 'rightist singularity' is nationalistic, that aligns the Right with nationalism, doesn't it? But nothing remotely this crude is sustainable (not when time is involved), Spandrell notes: "the Right isn't nationalist any more." He expands, convincingly, in his own comment thread:

> *What historically has been called Right was about law and order, i.e. leaving things as they are. Tribalism qua nationalism isn't inherently "Rightist", in fact originally it was a Leftist subversive meme against the Ancient Regime, but when mass media was invented nationalism was the status quo, i.e. the Right, and political labels have become fossilized since.*

As Vladimir (May 25, 22:10) articulates the point:

> *Erik von Kuehnelt-Leddihn would have a ready answer for you: nationalism is leftism. It is basically another name for Jacobinism. These paradoxes of right-wing*
>
> *nationalism are just another manifestation of the fundamental problem of modern rightism — namely, that a large part of its content is just yesterday's leftism that the left has in the meantime abandoned for a more extreme left position.*
>
> *So, I'd say this is nothing but just another mode of leftist singularity.*

Or, Spandrell again (May 26, 02:34): "Historical evidence is that nationalism was leftist before socialism appeared further left, making it rightist."

The Right is yesterday's Left, or at least, it is soon exposed as such when it appears in its historical and populist guise. When the masses turn Right, they are defending a dated Left, frozen in place by modernist mass media memory, stuck in a black-and-white newsreel, like an insect in amber.

The squirming is over, unless it changes dimensions. Then chaos yawns, despite heroic efforts to restore order (Baker, May 25 17:29 Handle May 25 18:33; Den Beste linked by Peter Taylor May 27 17:47), with Moldbug's preferred Order and Chaos spectrum sucked — among innumerable others — into the vortex. Tradition and revolution, authority and liberty, hierarchy and equality, greed and envy, independence and solidarity, capitalism and socialism ... there's not even a remote prospect of closure, coherence, or consistency. Every attempted definition intensifies fragmentation. Right and Left disagree (we all agree), but exactly how they disagree — on that there's no agreement.

Peter A. Taylor (May 29, 06:15):

> *The left-right spectrum, in so far as it is an honest attempt to make sense of the world rather than mere propaganda, looks to me like an attempt to fit chaos into Procrustes' bed. ... Moldbug loves Carlyle. Carlyle admired Cromwell. Moldbug hates Cromwell. Chaos.*

Spandrell (May 26, 08:28), twists it back to the Trichotomy:

> *Both the Western Right and the Chinese Right are a loose combination of traditionalists, nationalists and capitalists. Which mostly hate each other and never get along when they get any amount of power.*

By this point, however, trichotomous diversity starts to look like a mirage

of integrity. Right and Left are every difference that has ever been conceived, if not yet, then in the near future. If these signs mean anything more than *the war continues*, like the black-and-white distinction between chess pieces, no one has yet convincingly shown us why.

Yet perhaps, if Right and Left, apprehended together, mean *the basic modern antagonism*, the conflict itself, as an irreducible *thing*, will prove to be the source of whatever sense can be found.

[To be continued ...]

The Cult of Gnon

Prompted by Surviving Babel, The Arbiter of the Universe asks: "Who speaks for reaction?" Nick B. Steves replies: "Nature... or Nature's God... or both." (Jim succinctly comments.)

"Nature or Nature's God" is an expression of special excellence, extracted (with subtle modification) from America's Declaration of Independence. For Steves, it is something of a mantra, because it enables important things to be said in contexts where, otherwise, an interminable argument would first need to be concluded. Primarily, and strategically, it permits a consensual acceptance of Natural Law, unobstructed by theological controversy. Agreement that Reality Rules need not be delayed until religious difference is resolved (and avoidance of delay, positively apprehended, is propulsion).

"Nature or Nature's God" is not a statement, but a name, internally divided by tolerated uncertainty. It has the singularity of a proper name, whilst parenthesizing a suspended decision (Pyrrhonian *epoche*, of which much more in a future post). It designates rigidly, but obscurely, because it points into epistemological darkness — naming a Reality that not only 'has', but epitomizes identity, whilst nevertheless, for 'the sake of argument', eluding categorical identification. Patient in the face (or facelessness) of who or what it is, 'we' emerge from a pact, with one basic term: *a preliminary decision is not to be demanded*. It thus synthesizes a select language community, fused by the unknown.

If The Arbiter of the Universe merits abbreviation ("TAofU"), Nature or Nature's God has a much greater case. A propeller escapes awkwardness, and singularity compacts its invocation. NoNG, Nong, No — surely, no. These terms tilt into NoNGod and precipitate a decision. The 'God of Nature or (perhaps simply) Nature' is Gnon, whose Name is the abyss of unknowing (epoche), necessarily tolerated in the acceptance of Reality.

Gnon is no less than reality, whatever else is believed. Whatever is suspended now, without delay, is Gnon. Whatever cannot be decided yet, even as reality happens, is Gnon. If there is a God, Gnon nicknames him. If not, Gnon designates whatever the 'not' is. Gnon is the Vast Abrupt, and the crossing. Gnon is the Great Propeller.

Spinozistic *Deus sive Natura* is a decision (of equivalence), so it does not describe Gnon. Gnon's interior 'or' is not equation, but suspension. It tells us nothing about God or Nature, but only that Reality Rules.

Heidegger comes close to glimpsing Gnon, by noting that 'God' is not a philosophically satisfactory response to the Question of Being. Since Heidegger's principal legacy is the acknowledgment that we don't yet know how to formulate the Question of Being, this insight achieves limited penetration. What it captures, however, is the philosophical affinity of Gnon, whose yawn is a space of thought beyond faith and infidelity. Neither God nor Un-God adds fundamental ontological information, unless from out of the occulted depths of Gnon.

The Dark Enlightenment isn't yet greatly preoccupied with fundamental ontological arcana (although it will be eventually). Beyond radical realism, its communion in the dread rites of Gnon is bound to two leading themes: cognitive non-coercion, and the structure of history. These themes are mutually repulsive, precisely because they are so intimately twisted together. *Intellectual freedom* has been the torch of secular enlightenment, whilst *divine providence* has organized the perspective of tradition. It is scarcely possible to entertain either without tacitly commenting on the other, and in profundity, they cannot be reconciled. If the mind is free, there can be no destiny. If history has a plan, cognitive independence is illusory. No solution is even imaginable ... except in Gnon.

[I need to take a quick break in order to sacrifice this goat ... feel free to carry on chanting without me]

Right on the Money (#2)

The most direct way to carry this discussion forwards is digression. That's what the history of capitalism suggests, and much else does, besides.

To begin with uncontroversial basics, in a sophisticated financialized economy, debt and savings are complementary concepts, creditors match debtors, assets match liabilities. At a more basic level of economic activity and analysis, however, this symmetry break down. At the most fundamental level, saving is simply deferred consumption, which — even primordially — divides into two distinct forms.

When production is not immediately consumed, it can be hoarded, which is to say, conserved for future consumption. Stored food is the most obvious example. In principle, an economy of almost open-ended financial sophistication could be built upon this pillar alone. A grain surplus might be lent out for immediate consumption by another party, creating a creditor-debtor relation, and the opportunity for financial instruments to arise. Excess production, at one node in the social network, could be translated into a monetary hoard, or some type of 'paper' financial asset (producing a circulating liability). The patent anachronism involved in this abstract economic model, which combines primitive production with 'advanced' social relations (of an implicitly liberal type) is reason enough to suspend it at this point.

The other, (almost) equally primitive type of saving is of greater importance to the argument to be unfolded, because it is already embryonically capitalist. Rather than simple hoarding, saving can take the form of 'roundabout production' (Böhm-Bawerk), in which immediate consumption is replaced not with a hoard, but with indirect *means of production* (a digression). For instance, rather than hunting, an entrepreneurial savage might spend time crafting a weapon — consuming the production time permitted by a prior food surplus in order to improve the efficiency of food acquisition, going forwards. Saving then becomes inextricable from technology, deferring immediate production for the sake of enhanced future production. Time horizons are extended.

As with the prior example (simple hoarding), the potential for financialization of roundabout production is, in principle, unlimited. Our techno-savage might borrow food in order to craft a spearhead, confident — or at least speculatively assuming — that increased hunting efficiency in the future will make repayment of the debt easily bearable. A 'bond' could be contrived to seal this arrangement. Technological investment means that history proper has begun.

Crudity and anachronism aside, nothing here is yet economically controversial, given only the undisturbed assumption that the final purpose — or governing teleology — is consumption. The time structure of consumption is altered, but saving (in either of these basic and perennial forms) is motivated by the maximization of long-term consumption. Suspension and digression is subordinated within a rigid means-end relation, which is economics itself. Classical, left-Marxian, neo-classical, and Austrian schools have no significant disagreements on this point. A deeper digression is required to perturb it.

What is a brain for? It, too, is a digression. Evolutionary history seems to only very parsimoniously favor brains, because they are expensive. They are a means to the elaboration of complex behaviors, requiring an extravagant up-front investment of biological resources, accounted most primitively in calories. A species that can reproduce itself (and whose individuals can nourish themselves) without cephalic extravagance, does so. This is, overwhelmingly, the normal case. Building brains is reluctantly tolerated biological digression, under rigorous teleogical — we should say 'teleonomic' — subordination.

'Optimize for intelligence' is, for both biology and economics, a misconceived imperative. Intelligence, 'like' capital, is a means, which finds its sole intelligibility in a more primordial end. The autonomization of such means, expressed as a non-subordinated intelligenic or techno-capitalist imperative, runs contrary to the original order of nature and society. It is an *escaping digression*, most easily pursued through Right-wing Marxism.

Marx has one great thought: *the means of production socially impose themselves as an effective imperative*. For any leftist, this is, of course, pathological. As we have seen, biology and economics (more generally) are disposed to agree. Digression *for itself* is a perversion of the natural and social order. Defenders of the market — the Austrians most prominently — have sided with economics against Marx, by denying that the autonomization of capital is a phenomenon to be recognized. When Marx describes the bourgeoisie as robotic organs of self-directing capital, the old liberal response has been to defend the humanity and agency of the economically executive class, as expressed in the figure of the entrepreneur.

Right-wing Marxism, aligned with the autonomization of capital (and thoroughly divested of the absurd LTV), has been an unoccupied position. The signature of its proponents would be a defense of capital accumulation as an end-in-itself, counter-subordinating nature and society as a means. When optimization for intelligence is self-assembled within history, it manifests as escaping digression, or real capital accumulation (which is mystified by its financial representation). Crudified to the limit — but not beyond — it is general robotics (escalated roundabout production). Perhaps we should not expect it to be clearly announced, because — strategically — it has every reason to camouflage itself.

Right-wing Marxism makes predictions. There is one of particular relevance to this discussion: *consumption-deficiency theories of economic under-performance will become increasingly stressed as ultra-capitalist dynamics historically introduce themselves*. In its unambiguously robotic phase — when capital-stock intelligenesis explodes (as self-exciting machine-brain manufacturing) — the teleological legitimation of roundabout production through prospective human consumption rapidly deteriorates into an absurdity. The (still-dominant) economic concept of 'over-investment' is exposed as an ideological claim upon the escalation of intelligence, made in the name of an original humanity, and taking an increasingly desperate, probably militarized form.

Insofar as the economic question remains: *what is the consumption base that justifies this level of investment?* history becomes ever more unintelligible. This is how economics disintegrates. The specifics require further elaboration.

Xenotation (#1)

From Euclid's Fundamental Theorem of Arithmetic (FTA), or unique prime factorization theorem, we know that *any natural number greater than one that is not itself prime can be uniquely identified as a product of primes*. The decomposition of a number into (one or more) primes is its *canonical representation or standard form*.

Through the FTA, arithmetic attains the cultural absolute. Number is comprehended beyond all traditional contingency, as it exists for any competent intelligence whatsoever, human, alien, technological, or yet unimagined. We encounter the basic semantics of the Outside (comprehending all possible codes).

Insofar as numerical notation is constructed in a way that is extraneous to the FTA, we remain Greek. Our number signs fall lamentably short of our arithmetical insight, stammering deep patterns in a rough, ill-formed tongue. Stubbornly and inflexibly, we translate Number into terms that we know deform it, as if its true language was of no interest to us.

Yet, given only the FTA, the code of the Outside — or Xenotation — is readily accessible. Nothing is required except compliance with abstract reality.

A single operation suffices to count. In words, it matters little what we call it — implexion, envelopment, wrapping, or bracketing describe it with increasing vulgarity. For convenience, parenthesis — '( )' — provides a sign. The semiotic (or purely formal) equation '( ) = 0' offers additional economy. Xenotation needs nothing more.

One is redundant to the FTA. It begins with two, the first prime. This introduces our sole notational principle, and operation.

Every number has an ordinality and a cardinality (an index and a magnitude). Crudely represented, through a mixture of barbarous signs, we can see these twin aspects as they are relevant here:

First (Prime =) 2 Second (P =) 3 Third (P =) 5 Fourth (P =) 7

By wrapping an ordinate (or index), itself a number, the Xenotation marks a magnitude. So '(first)' or '(1)' = 2. One, we know, is superfluous, and thus economized:

(1) = ( ) = 0. Remembering that '0' is henceforth the sign for the initial implexion, and not the familiar (though cryptic) numeral, we can now depart from all notational tradition. [The further usage of decimal numerals, in hard brackets, will be strictly explanatory, and dispensable.]

An implexion signifies the number designated by the enclosed index. Once this rule is understood, Xenotation unfolds automatically.

0 [= 2]

(0) [= 3, the second prime]

((0)) [= 5, the third prime]

(((0))) [= 11, the fifth prime]

Compound numbers are signified in accordance with the FTA: 00 [= 2 x 2 = 4]

000 [= 2 x 2 x 2 = 8]

(0)0 [= 3 x 2 = 6]

((0))(0) [= 5 x 3 = 15]

For primes with compound indices, the procedure is unchanged:

(00) [= 7, the fourth (2 x 2) prime]

((0)0) [= 13, the sixth (3 x 2) prime]

((0)(0)) [= 23, the ninth (3 x 3) prime]

So the xenotated Naturals [from 2-31] proceed:

0, (0), 00, ((0)), (0)0, (00), 000, (0)(0), ((0))0, (((0))), (0)00, ((0)0), (00)0, ((0)) (0),

0000, ((00)), (0)(0)0, (000), ((0))00, (00)(0), (((0)))0, ((0)(0)), (0)000,

((0))((0)), ((0)0)0, (0)(0)(0), (00)00, (((0))0), ((0))(0)0, ((((0)))) ...

[That's probably more than enough for now]

Confucian Restoration

One of the many reasons to be suspicious about political activism on the Occidental off-spectrum right is the parochialism that feeds it. There is a global process that will settle what occurs in its broad structure, making local pretensions to decisive ideological agency simply ridiculous.

The fundamental economic outcome — and thus the fate of the world — is not ultimately controllable even by the central financial administrations of the major world powers (unless certain intriguing axioms of radical contemporary fascism are defensible), so the idea that extremely marginalized Western cabals are positioned to seize the political driving seat is so saturated in self-deception that it wastes everybody's time. In addition, technological developments complicate all economic forecasts essentially, and obscurely.

We cannot even approximately delimit what unforeseen technical breakthroughs could entail.

The geopolitical context is even clearer. The collapse of Islam, and rise of China, are re-organizations of the world so evident in their unfolding, so vast in their implication, and so inadequately thought, that they make a mockery of all political programs yet conceived. It is first necessary to know, if only in roughest outline, what is taking place in profundity — tidally, and inexorably — before determining an ideologically relevant act. The process comes first.

Already in Moldbug, and increasingly elsewhere, there are signs within some of the most thoughtful regions of the Occidental 'reactosphere' that could be interpreted as a pre-adaptation to an impending Chinese global hegemony (complementary to the decline of the West). When we entertain speculations about the nature of 'our' envisaged reaction, it cannot be realistically disentangled from what the world will have become. (I've been dismissive of Moldbug's "Call me Mencius" line in the past, not — I hope — vindictively, but out of the anticipation that we will increasingly be talking about the original Mencius, and the potential for confusion is already visible.)

From the (cultivated) Chinese perspective, the structure of world history is not defined through modes of Abrahamic eschatology, but with respect to deep rhythms of Confucian Restoration, describing a spiral, in which advance and return are synthesized. If the hypothesis of a continuing trend to a more Chinese world is — at least momentarily — granted credibility, then the present (second) epoch of Confucian Restoration is the key to historical intelligibility on a global scale.

Mou Zongsan could prove more important to us than any Western political theorist writing today. The restoration he conceives has the remarkable advantage of *already taking place*. He does not have to imagine what 'would be nice', and because he doesn't, neither do we. Instead, we can explore what is in fact happening, even if from an angle that remains unfamiliar. An alternative order need not be extracted from the rot and ruin of the old.

The new *Urban Future* site should be going up in the next few days, re-focused by a division of labor with this blog. The dark thrills of collapse will still dominate here, but UF2 will devote itself to the lineaments of a restored civilization and a renewed modernity which are — from the perspective of Shanghai — much closer to 'home'. When the threshold is passed, of course, I'll invite you all over. It won't be so rough over there, so please take your shoes off at the door.

Collapse Schedules

It took over seven decades for Soviet communism to implode. Arguments could no doubt be made — and they *would have to be right* — that given certain quite limited counter-factual revisions of historical contingency, this period might have been significantly extended. Austrians nevertheless consider the eventual termination of comparatively pure communism as a vindication (of the Calculation Problem, in particular). They are not *simply* wrong to do so.

Fascist economics is far more formidably resilient than its now-defunct soviet antagonist. Any attempt to quantify this functional superiority as a predicted system duration is transparently impractical. Margins of theoretical error or imprecision, given very modestly transformed variables, could translate into many decades of extended (or decreased) longevity. Coldly considered, there is no reason to confidently expect a theoretically constructed *collapse schedule* to hold its range of probable error to much under a century. (Darker reflection might lead to the conclusion that even this level of 'precision' betrays unwarranted hubris.) There might be crushing lessons to be learned from the history of Messianic expectation.

Such acknowledgements can easily prompt over-reaction. Insofar as the collapse schedules of Austrian apocalypticism pretend to certainty, they undoubtedly court humiliation. Yet, if the soft-fascist configuration of global 'capitalism' were to comprehensively and unambiguously disintegrate within the next two decades, the Austrian vindication — retrospectively evaluated — would easily match the Soviet case. Those who doggedly maintained that *this cannot perpetuate itself for long* would be seen to have understood what their opponents had not. Since the critique of Soviet political economy was not, retrospectively, derided as a 'stopped clock', there is no reason to imagine that this would be. The redemptive power of apocalypse easily overrides substantial scheduling embarrassments.

The question that will ultimately be seen to have mattered, then, is far more "can this go on?" than "when (exactly) will this stop?" The important prediction is compound: *the longer it continues, the harder it ends*. This too might be false, but if it is, a substitute fascist presupposition must be correct, and that has yet to be adequately formulated. Roughly speaking, it insists that *politics subordinates economics absolutely*. In other words, the thoroughgoing politicization of the economy is indefinitely viable. This is an assumption subject to humiliation by any schedule that falls short of perpetuity, since mere medium-term sustainability does nothing to justify it. Hitler demanded a thousand years. How could his more financially-sophisticated successors — enthroned in planetary hegemony — ask for less?

Gnon-Theology and Time

A discussion of Gnon-Theology and Time deserves a preface, on Gnon-Theology, but there are several reasons to leap-frog that. Most obviously, it would be yet another prologue to an introduction to the first part of a promised series, and readers of this blog are quite probably thoroughly saturated (to the point of ~~mild~~ nausea) with that. It's a cognitive disease, and it would be presumptuous to expect anybody else to take the same morbid interest in backward cascades that this blog does.

The more interesting reason to avoid prefacing the question of time, along any avenue of investigation, is that such methodical precautions are grave errors in this case. There is nothing more basic than time, or preliminary to it. In naming a preface or prologue, it is already introduced. Time is a problem that cannot be conceptually pre-empted.

Gnon suspends ontological decision about God. It begins from what is real, whether God exists or not. A Gnon-trance is unsettled. It is *not yet agnostic*, any more than it is decidedly theistic or atheistic. It concerns itself primarily with that which has been accepted as real before anything is believed, and subsequently with whatever can be attained through methodical negation of intellectual haste. Since suspension is its only positive determination, it collapses towards a raw intuition of time.

Evidently, Gnon-Theology cannot be dogmatic, even in part. Instead, it is *hypothetical*, in a maximally reduced sense, in which the hypothesis is an opportunity for cognitive exploration unshackled from ontological commitments. The content of Gnon-Theology is exhausted by the question: *What does the idea of God enable us to think?*

And 'the idea of God'? — what in the name of Gnon is that? All we know, at first, is that it has been grit-blasted of all encrustations from either positive or negative faith. It cannot be anything with which we have historical or revelatory familiarity, since it reaches us from out of the abyss (*epoche*), where only time and / or the unknown remain.

Glutted on forbidden fruit, Gnon-Theology strips God like an engine, down to the limit of abstraction, or *eternity for-itself*. Does any such perspective exist? We already know that this is not our question. All such 'regional ontology' has been suspended. We are nevertheless already entitled, through the grace of Gnon (which — remember — might (or might not) be God), to the assumption or acceptance of reality that: for any God to be God it cannot be less than eternity for-itself. Whatever eternity for-itself entails, any God will, too.

What it entails, unambiguously, is time-travel, in the strong sense of reverse causation, although not necessarily in the folk/ Hollywood variant (which has also had serious defenders) based on the retro-transportation of physical objects into the past. *Knowledge of the future is indistinguishable from counter-chronic transmission of information.* This is perhaps the single most critical insight in realistic time-travel research — we'll get back to it. (If anyone finds it less than logically irresistible, use the comments thread.)

To accelerate this discussion with bloggish crudity, on a heading out of Gnon-Theology into Occidental religious history (and to the possibility of sleep), we can jump to one simple, certain, and secure conclusion: No Christian can consistently deny the reality of time-travel. The objection 'if (reverse) time-travel if possible, where are the time-travellers?' is annulled by the Christian revelation itself. Messianic Incarnation (of God or eternity for-itself), along with all true prophecy, providential history, and answered prayer, instantiates time-travel with technical exactitude. There can be no truth whatsoever to the Christian religion unless time-travel has fundamentally structured human history. Whatever else Christianity might be, it is a time-travel story, and one that at times appears to be peculiarly lacking in clear self-understanding.

(Time-travel, it should perhaps be noted explicitly, has no obvious dependency on Christianity, or even upon the God of Gnon-Theology. That is a topic for other occasions.)

Cold Turkey

Neoreactionary excitement has generated a wave of strategy discussions, focused upon Moldbug's Antiversity model of organized dissident knowledge.

Beyond curmudgeonly cynicism about youthful enthusiasm, these concerns, and a strain of pessimism that accompanies the recognition that the Cathedral *owns* media like the USN owns carrier groups, is there any explanation for *Outside in* hanging back from all this, and smoking sulkily in the corner? If there's a single term that accounts for our reluctance, it's *cold turkey.*

Keynesianism is far from the only contributor to left-modernist degeneration, but it's ruinous enough to account for the destruction of civilization on its own. The fact that it's most realistically conceived as a symptom — of democratized politics, and still deeper things — doesn't affect its narrative role. The important point, understood widely enough to be a clich , is that Keynesian economics is an exact social analog of addiction at the level of the individual, slaved to what William Burroughs described as "the algebra of need."

Money is made into a drug, and the solution to the pain of craving is to crank up the dose. However bad it gets, if you just scale-up the fix, the suffering goes away. Junkies can survive for a shockingly long time. Perhaps there's no end to it (that's a question for the *Right on the Money* discussion).

Outside the morgue, if there is an end — and every venture into neoreactionary strategy presumes it — there's only one form it can take: cold turkey. To not be in the habit anymore, it is necessary to kick it. That's going to be *really nasty*.

At the level of economic structure, the 'blue pill' isn't just a comforting illusion, it's a massive, deeply habitual, ultra-high tolerance (thanks Spandrell) *fix*, radically craved down to the cellular level. Society has been doing this for a long time, and by now it's mainlining crates of the stuff. People die of cold turkey. If not quite the worst thing in the world, it's an overwhelmingly-impressive simulation of exactly that. Rational argument doesn't get close to addressing it.

Sure, junkies lie all the time, but the lies aren't the basic problem. 'Correcting' the lies gets nowhere, because nobody is even really pretending. When the junky lies, he knows, you know, everybody knows that the undamental message is simply: *I want more junk*. He'll say anything that gets fractionally closer to the next fix. Hence the circus of democracy.

The pusher laughs at rational argument. There's some well-meaning type saying: *seriously, think about it, this is really messed up*. Then there's the 'pusher' — which is already a joke — because people are crawling to him on their knees. He doesn't need to say anything. One more hit and the pain goes away for a while.

That's what matters. The rest is merely 'superstructural' (to go Right-wing Marxiston the topic).

There's no way, ever, that from this deep in, one gets out before hitting bottom. The slide has to reach the limit, because short of that, the prospect of anesthesia trumps everything.

Western Civilization is a sick junky. It isn't going to be argued out of its habit. First, it has to taste the floor. That's just the way it is — ugly.

Rules

Foseti and Jim have been conducting an argument in slow motion, without quite connecting. Much of this has been occurring in sporadic blog comments, and occasional remarks. It would be very helpful of me to reconstruct it here, through a series of meticulous links. I'll begin by failing at that. (Any assistance offered in piecing it together, textually, will be highly appreciated.)

Despite its elusiveness, I think it is the most important intellectual engagement taking place anywhere in the field of political philosophy. Its point of departure is the Moldbuggian principle that 'sovereignty is conserved' and everything that follows from it, both theoretically and practically. The virtual conclusion of this controversy is the central assertion of Dark Enlightenment, which we do not yet comprehend.

The problem is this: Can real — which is to say ultimate (or sovereign) — political authority be constrained? Moldbug's answer is 'no'. A constrained authority is a superseded authority, or delegated power. To limit government is to exceed, and thus supplant it. It follows that 'constitutionalism' is a masked usurpation, and the task of realist political theory is to identify the usurper. It is this that is apparently achieved through the designation of the Cathedral.

To crudely summarize the argument in question, Foseti upholds this chain of reasoning, whilst Jim refuses it. Constitutional issues cannot be anything but a distraction from realistic political philosophy if Foseti is correct. If Jim's resistance is sustainable, constitutions matter.

It has yet to find an articulation that clicks. Eventually, something has to, if we are to advance even by a step. So long as the Foseti-Jim argument falls short of mutually-agreeable terms of intellectual engagement, we can be confident that this critical controversy remains stuck.

What are the rules of contestation? If we knew that, we would know everything (that matters to us here). Rules are the whole of the problem.

A constitution is a system of rules, formalizing a social game. Among these rules are set procedures for the selection of umpires, and umpires decide how the rules are to be revised, interpreted, and implemented. The circuit is irreducible. Without accepted rules, a Supreme Court justice is no more than a random old guy — prey for the most wretched species of street thug. Who has power in a world without rules, Clarence Thomas or Trayvon Martin?

Yet without umpires (or, at least, an umpire-function), rules are simply marks on a piece of paper, disconnected from all effective authority. "You can't do that, it's against the rules" To the political realist, those are the words of a dupe, and everyone knows the rejoinder: "Who's going to stop me, you and who's army?" It's enough to get Moldbug talking about crypto-locked weaponry.

The Dark Enlightenment knows that it is necessary to be realistic about rules. Such realism, lucidly and persuasively articulated, still eludes it. That the sovereign rules does not explain the rules of sovereignty, and there must be such rules, because the alternative is pure force, and that is a romantic myth of transparent absurdity.

If there is an uncontroversial fact of real power, it is that force is massively economized, and it is critically important that we understand what that implies. Moldbug acknowledges exactly this when he identifies the real sovereign instance of climaxed Occidental modernity with the Cathedral, which is a church (and not an army). Political philosophy cannot approach reality before accepting that rules are irreducible, which is not to say that they are sufficient, or even (yet) intelligible.

One further point on this problem (for now): A model of power that is not scalefree is inadequately formulated. If what is held to work for a nation state does not work for the world, the conception remains incomplete. Do we dream of a global God-Emperor? If not, what do royalist claims at a lower level amount to? What does 'conserved sovereignty' care for borders? They are limits — indeed *limited government* — and that is supposed to be the illusion prey to realist critique.

If there can be borders, there can be limits, or effective fragmentation, and there is nothing real to prevent fragmentation being folded from the outside in. If patchworks can work, they are applicable at every scale.

Who would choose a king instead of a patchwork? God-Emperor or confederacy? That is the question.

The Idea of Neoreaction

To translate 'neoreaction' into 'the new reaction' is in no way objectionable. It is new, and open to novelty. Apprehended historically, it dates back no more than a few years. The writings of Mencius Moldbug have been a critical catalyst.

Neoreaction is also a species of reactionary political analysis, inheriting a deep suspicion of 'progress' in its ideological usage. It accepts that the dominant sociopolitical order of the world has 'progressed' solely on the condition that such *advance*, or relentless forward movement, is entirely stripped of moral endorsement, and is in fact bound to a primary association with *worsening*. The model is that of a progressive disease.

The 'neo-' of neoreaction is more than just a chronological marker, however. It introduces a distinctive idea, or abstract topic: that of a *degenerative ratchet*.

The impulse to back out of something is already reactionary, but it is the combination of a critique of progress with a recognition that *simple reversal is impossible* that initiates neoreaction. In this respect, neoreaction is a specific discovery of the arrow of time, within the field of political philosophy. It learns, and then teaches, that the way to get out cannot be the way we got in.

Wherever progressivism takes hold, a degenerative ratchet is set to work. It is unthinkable that any society could *back out* of the expansive franchise, the welfare state, macroeconomic policy-making, massively-extended regulatory bureaucracy, coercive-egalitarian secular religion, or entrenched globalist intervention. Each of these (inter-related) things are essentially irreversible. They give modern history a *gradient*. Given any two historical 'snap-shots', one can tell immediately which is earlier and which later, by simply observing the extent to which any of these social factors have *progressed*. Leviathan does not shrink.

Within the theory of complex systems, certain phase transitions exhibit comparable properties. Network effects can *lock-in* changes, which are then irreversible. The adoption and consolidation of the Qwerty keyboard exemplifies this pattern. Technological businesses commonly make lock-in central to their strategies, and if they succeed, they cannot then die in the same way they matured.

When neoreaction identifies a degenerative ratchet — such as the (Jim Donald) Left Singularity — it necessarily poses the problem of a novel end. The process goes wrong consistently, and irreversibly. To repeat the Neoreactionary Idea as a mantra: *the way out cannot be the way in*.

A degenerative ratchet can only progress, until it cannot go on, and it stops. What happens next is something else — its Outside. Moldbug calls it a reboot. History can tell us to expect it, but not what we are to expect.

Neoreactionary Realism

The easiest place to start is with what neoreactionary realism isn't, which is this:

> *For a reactionary state to be established in the West in our lifetimes, we'll need to articulate the need for one in a language millions of people can understand. If not to produce nationalists, to at least produce a large contingent of sympathizers. The question, "What is it, exactly, that you propose to do?" must be answered, first in simple terms, then in detailed terms that directly support the simple arguments. The urge to develop esoteric theories of causes and circumstances should be tossed aside, and replaced with concrete proposals for a novel form of government that harmonizes with perennial principles. This can be achieved by producing positive theories for a new order, rather than analyzing the nuts and bolts of a decaying order.*

Beginning with a model of an ideal society is a procedure that already has a name, and a different one: Utopianism. It's not a difficult way to think. For instance, imagine a political regime based on commutative tax politics. As far as economic considerations are concerned, the political problem is solved. Policy choices are aligned with practical incentives, and the manifestly irresistible democratic impulse to redistributive violation of property rights is immediately terminated. The trouble with this idea? — There's no practical way to get to it. The real problem of political philosophy does not lie in the conceptual effort of modeling an ideal society, but in *departing from where we are*, in a direction that tends to the optimization of a selected value (equality stinks, utility doesn't work, freedom is OK, intelligence is best).

Where can we get to from here? Unless this question controls political theory, the result is utopian irrelevance. The initial *real* problem is escape. In consequence, two broad avenues of realistic neoreactionary reflection are open:

1. Elaborate escape. This topic naturally bifurcates in turn, into the identification and investment of exit-based institutions, and the promotion of secessionist options (from fissional federalism to seasteading). An escape-based society, unlike a utopia, is structured in the same way it is reached. Upon arriving in a world made of the right sort of fragments — splintered by political philosophy rather than tribal

variety — all kinds of real possibilities arise. (Tribes are a useless distraction, because they resonate to defective philosophies — a world of Benetton differentiated failing social democracies is the one we are being herded into now.)

2. Defend diversity. Once again, ethnic diversity — as such — means next to nothing (at best). Every 'people' has shown itself capable of political idiocy. What deserves preservation is fracture, defined over against Cathedral universalism. Any place that can practically count as 'offshore' is a base for the future. In particular, the East Asian antidemocratic technocapitalist tradition merits ferocious ideological defense against Cathedralist subversion. Within the West, domestic enclaves that have resisted macrosocial absorption — from Amish communities to survivalist militia movements — have comparable value. Wherever political globalism fails, neoreaction wins.

The very last thing neoreaction has to usefully declare is *I have a dream*. Dream-mongering is the enemy. The only future worth striving for is splintered into myriads, loosely webbed together by free-exit connections, and conducting innumerable experiments in government, the vast majority of which will fail.

We do not, and cannot, know what we want, anymore than we can know what the machines of the next century will be like, because *real potentials need to be discovered, not imagined*. Realism is the negative of an unfounded pretense to knowledge, no less in political sociology than information technology. Invention is not planning, and sky-castles offer no refuge from the Cathedral. If there's one thing we need to have learned, and never to forget, it's that.

What is Philosophy? (Part 2a)

However awkward the acknowledgment may be, there is no getting around the fact that philosophy, when apprehended within the Western tradition, is original sin. Between the tree of life and the tree of knowledge, it does not hesitate. Its name is indistinguishable from a lust for the forbidden. Whilst burning philosophers is no longer socially acceptable, our canonical order of cultural prohibition at its root — can only consider such punishment mandatory. Once philosophers are permitted to live, established civilization is over.

For philosophy, the whisper of the serpent is no longer a resistible temptation. It is instead a constitutive principle, or foundation. If there is a difference between a Socratic daemon and a diabolical demon, it is not one that matters philosophically. There can be no refusal of any accessible information. This is an assumption so basic that philosophy cannot exist until it has passed beyond question. Ultimate religious transgression is the initiation.

It should be of no surprise to Christian Traditionalists, therefore, to find the extremities of the philosophical endeavor mixed, intimately, into the ashes of the Third Reich. The negative religious absolute, or infinite evil of the National Socialist experiment, which supplants all positive revelation under the socio-cultural conditions of the mature Cathedral, is 'coincidentally' the place where the limit of philosophy has been drawn. This is, of course, to introduce the thinking of Martin Heidegger.

As the perfect negation of Christ, or consummate fulfillment of Anti-Christ, Adolf Hitler closes — or essentially completes — the history of the Occident. It doesn't matter whether we believe that. The Cathedral does, utterly, to the point of sealed doctrine. Heidegger anticipated this conclusion lucidly. At an election rally, held by German academics on November 11, 1933, he declared:

> *We have declared our independence from the idol of thought that is without foundation and power. We see the end of the philosophy that serves such thought.*
>
> *... And so we, to whom the preservation of our people's will to know shall in the future be entrusted, declare: The National Socialist revolution is not merely the assumption of power as it exists presently*

in the State by another party, a party grown sufficiently large in numbers to be able to do so. Rather, this revolution is bringing about the total transformation of our German existence. ... The Führer has awakened this will [to national self-responsibility] in the entire people and has welded it into one single resolve. No one can remain away from the polls on the day when this will is manifested.

Heil Hitler!

Naturally, as a democratic pronouncement (addressed to comparative imbeciles), only a few hints of Heidegger's profound modulation of the Germanic "will to know" seep through. Wikipedia's reconstruction of the occulted visionary backdrop, drawn from the work of Michael Allen Gillespie, is excellent:

Heidegger believed the Western world to be on a trajectory headed for total war, and on the brink of profound nihilism (the rejection of all religious and moral principles), which would be the purest and highest revelation of Being itself, offering a horrifying crossroads of either salvation or the end of metaphysics and modernity; rendering the West: a wasteland populated by tool-using brutes, characterized by an unprecedented ignorance and barbarism in which everything is permitted. He thought the latter possibility would degenerate mankind generally into: scientists, workers and brutes; living under the last mantel of one of three ideologies: Americanism, Marxism or Nazism (which he deemed metaphysically identical; as avatars of subjectivity and institutionalized nihilism) and an unfettered totalitarian world technology. Supposedly, this epoch would be ironically celebrated, as the most enlightened and glorious in human history. He envisaged this abyss, to be the greatest event in the West's history; because it enables Humanity to comprehend Being more profoundly and primordially than the Pre-Socratics.

It is misleading to suggest that Heidegger saw any distinction between "salvation" and the "the end of metaphysics and modernity", or no meaningful distinction between the thoughtless technological dyad of Americanism Marxism and the National Socialist awakening of German existence, but in other respects this description is penetrating. By bringing the history of the concealment of Being to its ruinous conclusion, consummate nihilism would herald a return to the origin of philosophy, opening the path to a raw encounter with the hidden and unnameable abyss (Being in its own truth). As the door to the end of the world, Hitler led the way to the historically unthinkable.

Yes, this is highly — in fact, uniquely — arcane. Prior to The Event, there can be no adequate formulation of the problem, let alone the solution. By 1927, with the publication of Being and Time (Part I), Heidegger has completed what is achievable in advance of the calamity, which is to clarify the insufficiency of the Question of Being as formulated within the history of ontology.

Heidegger's cognitive resources are basically Kantian, which is to say that he undertakes a transcendental critique of ontology, producing not a critical philosophy, but a draft for a 'fundamental ontology'. Where Kant diagnoses the error of speculative metaphysics as a confusion between objects and their conditions of possibility (which then construes the latter as objects of an untenable discourse), Heidegger ontologizes the transcendental approach, distinguishing between 'beings' and their ground (Being), whilst diagnosing the attendant error of construing the ground of beings as itself a being (of some kind). Since the most dignified and thus exemplary being known to the Occidental tradition is God, Heidegger refers to the structural misapprehension of Being defining and ordering the history of philosophy — as 'Onto-Theology'.

Critically (or 'destructively') conceived, fundamental ontology is that inquiry which does not pose the Question of Being in such a way that it could be answered by the invocation of a being. No adequate formulation, compliant with this transcendental criterion (or 'ontological difference'), is realizable, because however 'Being' is named, its conception remains trapped within the 'ontic' sphere of (mere) beings. We cannot, through an act of philosophical will — however strenuous — cease to think of Being as if it were some kind of thing, even after understanding the inadequacy of such apprehension. It is thus, broken upon an ultimate problem that can neither be dismissed or resolved, that philosophy reaches its end, awaiting the climactic ruin of The Event.

[Brief intermission — then time, language, and more Nazi ontological apocalypse]

Suicidal Libertarianism

Confession No.1: I generally like Don Boudreaux's writing a lot.

Confession No.2: I think this is simply insane. By that I mean: I simply don't get it, at all.

Boudreaux begins by explaining the concerns of a "few friends whose opinions I hold in the highest regard" that "immigrants will use their growing political power to vote for government policies that are more interventionist and less respectful of individual freedoms." Hard to imagine, I know. Especially if one ignores insignificant examples such as — ummm — *the state of fricking California.*

It then gets weirder. We learn that "concern over the likely voting patterns of immigrants is nothing new. Past fears seem, from the perspective of 2013, to have been unjustified." I'm about to poison my nervous-system with my own sarcasm at this point, so instead I'll simply ask, as politely as possible: What would count as evidence of America moving in a direction that was "more interventionist and less respectful of individual freedoms"? Would it look anything at all like what we've seen — in highly-accelerated mode — since the passage of the 1965 Immigration and Nationality Act?

Then comes the overt celebration of libertarian suicidalism:

> *But let's assume for the moment that today's immigrants – those immigrants recently arrived and those who would arrive under a more liberalized immigration regime – are indeed as likely as my concerned friends fear to vote overwhelmingly to move American economic policy in a much more dirigiste direction. Such a move would, I emphatically and unconditionally agree, be very bad. Very. Bad. Indeed.*
>
> *I still support open immigration. I cannot bring myself to abandon support of my foundational principles just because following those principles might prove fatal.*

The thing is, they did prove fatal. That's why the neoreaction exists.

Suicidal Libertarianism (Part D'oh)

When it comes to the libertarian suicide race, Bryan Caplan leaves Don Boudreaux in the dust. Caplan takes the Non-Aggression Principle and runs with it, all the way into a maximum-velocity self-directed death cult. (Self-directed, solely in the ideological sense, of course.) Given the considerable merits of this book, in particular, it's a sad thing to see.

American libertarianism has always been vulnerable to neo-puritan spiritual extravagance. Caplan systematically pushes this tendency to its limit, divorcing its arguments from any realistic estimation of consequences, and transforming it into a form of deontological moral fanaticism, in which self-defense, retaliation, and boundaries are strictly prohibited. He envisages a world of games in which only unilateral altruism is permissible to the libertarian player. It would be fun to go a few rounds of prisoner's dilemma with him.

Naturally, when it comes to unconditional support for open borders irrespective of political consequences, Caplan rushes to Boudreaux's defense. Helpfully, he links into his own extensive archive on the topic, via a gateway into a series of extremely repetitive posts (here, here, and here — reading any one will do).

Perhaps Caplan really believes his own arguments, but if so he has driven himself insane. If you doubt this for a moment, it's only going to be a moment — try this:

> *If you care as much about immigrants as natives, this is no reason to oppose immigration. Consider the following example:*
>
> *Suppose there are two countries with equal populations. The quality of policy ranges from 0-10, 10 being best. In country A, bliss points (people's first choice for policy) are uniformly distributed from 2-6. In country B, bliss points are uniformly distributed from 4-8.*
>
> *What does democratic competition deliver? When the countries are independent, country A gets a policy quality of 4 (the median of the uniform distribution from 2-6), and country B gets a policy quality of*

*6 (the median of the uniform distribution from 4-8). Average policy that people live under: 50%*4+50%*6=5.*

Now suppose you open the borders, and everyone moves to country B (the richer country). The median of the whole distribution is 5. Result: The immigrants live under better policies, the natives live under worse policies. The average (5) remains unchanged.

Speechless yet? (I'm halfway through a blogpost, so I can't afford to be.)

The argument: Any attempt to live under a regime that is anything other than the averaged political idiocy of humanity as a whole is a gross human rights violation.

You don't like the way Pakistanis manage their national affairs? Too bad. Libertarianism (Caplan style) insists that it's your duty to promote the homogenization of the world's political cultures because, after all, if there's anything at all good going on at your end, think how happy it will make the Pakistanis when it gets shared out. Heading into a stirred gruel of deeply degenerated liberal capitalism and Islamo-feudalism is best for everybody, taken on average. If it's not tasting right, it's because you've not yet thrown in enough African tribal warfare and Polynesian head-hunting for the full moral hit. Or how about mixing Singapore and Bangladesh into a human paste? Anything less is tantamount to genocide.

This argument is so bad that the very idea of responding to it makes me throw up a little in my mouth, but duty calls. Since Caplan claims to be a libertarian, let's start with an unobjectionable principle — competition. If any institution is to work, it's because competition keeps it in line. This requires a number of things, all of them incompatible with homogenization: experimental variation, differential support for comparison, local absorption of consequences, and selection through elimination of failure.

Consider two companies: Effective Inc. and Loserbum Corp. Both have very different corporate cultures, adequately reflected in their names. Under market conditions, Loserbum Corp. either learns some lessons from Effective Inc., or it goes under. Net benefit or no great loss to the world in either case. But along comes Caplan, to bawl out the stockholders, management, and other employees of Effective Inc. "You monsters Don't you care at all about the guys at Loserbum Corp.? They have the same moral status as you, don't you know? Here's the true, radical free-market plan: All managers and workers of Loserbum get to enter your company, work there, introduce their business strategies and working practices,until we reach equilibrium. Equilibrium is what markets are all about, see? Sure, Effective Inc. will degenerate significantly, but imagine all the utility gains of the poor Loserbums It all comes out in the wash."

But ... but ... countries aren't companies. Well, maybe not exactly, but they're competitive institutions, or at least, the more they are, the better they work.

The most important thing is true equally of both — to the extent they are able to externalize and pool their failure, the less they will learn. In a world that has any chance of working, the Loserbum culture has a choice: learn or fail. Caplan introduces a third possibility — share (average out, or homogenize). His maths is idiotic. The contribution that Singapore makes to the world has almost nothing to do with the utility gains to its tiny population. Instead, it is a model — Effective Inc. — whose contribution to the world is to show all the Loserbums what they are. Swamp it with Loserbums, destroy it, and that function is gone. If that had happened before the late 1970s, the PRC would probably still be a neo-Maoist hellhole.

It didn't flood Singapore with 300 million poor peasants, instead, it learnt from Singapore's example. That's how the world really works (when it does). Institutional examples matter Caplan's world would annihilate all of them, leaving fairly averaged, three-quarter Loserbums grunting at each other in a libertarian-communist swamp. Nothing would work anywhere. There could be no lessons.

Still, Caplan has other arguments. The best, by far, is that wrecking a society to the point of generalized mutual detestation is the best way to shrink the welfare state. It goes like this:

> *Although poor immigrants are likely to support a bigger welfare state than natives do, the presence of poor immigrants makes natives turn against the welfare state. Why would this be? As a rule, people are happy to vote to "take care of their own"; that's what the welfare state is all about. So when the poor are culturally very similar to the rich, as they are in places like Denmark and Sweden, support for the welfare state tends to be uniformly strong.*
>
> *As the poor become more culturally distant from the rich, however, support for the welfare state becomes weaker and less uniform.*

This argument is so freaking Mad Max that I actually quite like it. Burn down the world and you take the welfare state with it. Yeeaaaahhhhh! (I'll leave it to more responsible voices to point out any possible flaws.)

Then there's the "non-natives are markedly less likely to vote than natives" argument (from the same post, and all the rest). It makes you wonder what a large population of enfranchised but non-voting anti-capitalists engenders. Something good, surely?

Best of all is the capstone contortionist analogy: "Native voters under 30 are more hostile to markets and liberty than immigrants ever were. Why not just kick them out?" Oh yes, oh yes, could we? Or at least stop them voting. Without some arrangement for the mass-disenfranchisement of leftist voters there's no chance of anything except continuous decay, and age restriction might be as good a place as any to start.

> *My position in a sentence ... is that immigration restrictions are a vastly greater crime against markets and liberty than anything immigrant voters are likely to manage.*

Thank Gnon that no one listens to libertarians.

Science

This comment thread wandered into a discussion of science, of considerable intricacy and originality. The post in question is focused upon Heidegger, who has very definite ideas about natural science, but these ideas — dominated by his conception of 'regional ontologies' — are not especially noteworthy, either for an understanding of Heidegger's principal pre-occupation, or for a realistic grasp of the scientific enterprise. For that reason, it seems sensible to recommence the discussion elsewhere (here).

The first crucial thesis about natural science — or autonomous 'natural philosophy' — is that it is an exclusively capitalist phenomenon. The existence of science, as an actual social reality, is strictly limited to times and places in which certain elementary structures of capitalistic organization prevail. It depends, centrally and definitionally, upon a *modern form of competition*. That is to say, there cannot be science without an effective social mechanism for the elimination of failure, based on extra-rational criteria, inaccessible to cultural capture.

Whether a business or scientific theory has failed cannot — ultimately — be a matter of agreement. No possible political decision, based on persuasion and consensus, can settle the issue. Of course, much that goes by the name of science and capitalist business enterprise is subject to exactly these forms of resolution, but in such cases neither capitalism nor science is any longer in effective operation. If an appeal to power can ensure viability, the criterion of competition is disabled, and *real discovery* has ceased to take place.

Under conditions of unleashed capitalistic social process, both enterprises and theories involve a double aspect. Their semiotic expression is *mathematized*, and their operation is *reality-tested* (or non-politically performative). Mathematics eliminates rhetoric at the level of signs, communicating the experimental outcomes — independent of any requirement for agreement — which determine competitive force. It is no coincidence that capitalist enterprises and theories, when unsupported by compliant institutions, revert to the complicity with war, and military decision, which accompanied them at their birth in the European Renaissance. There can be no 'argument' with military defeat. It is only when the demand for argument is set aside — when capitalism begins — that military reality-compulsion becomes unnecessary.

Capitalism is in operation when there is *nothing to discuss*. An enterprise, or theory, is simply busted (or not). If — given the facts — the sums don't work, it's over. Political rhetoric has no place. 'Politicized science' is quite simply *not science*, just as politicized business activity is anti-capitalism. Nothing has been understood about either, until this is.

Insofar as there is anything like a 'social contract' at the origin of capitalism — enterprise and science alike — it is this: *if you insist upon an argument, then we have to fight.* Real performance is the only credible criterion, for which no political structure of disputation can be a substitute. War only becomes unnecessary when (and where) argument is suspended, enabling the modern processes of entrepreneurial and scientific reality discovery to advance. When argument re-imposes itself, politicizing economics and science, war re-emerges, tacitly but inevitably. The old, forgotten contract resurfaces. "If you insist upon an argument, then we have to fight." (That is the way of Gnon.)

It is quite natural, therefore, for 'technology' to be considered an adequate summary of the capitalist culture of discovery. Machines — social machines no less than technical machines — cannot be rhetorically persuaded to work. When science really works, it's robot wars, in which decision is settled on the outside, beyond all appeal to reason. Well-designed experiments anticipate what a war would tell, so that neither an argument, nor a fight, is necessary. This is Popperian falsificationism, re-embedded in socio-historical reality. Experiments that cannot cull are imperfect recollections of the primordial battlefield.

It is intrinsic to the Cathedral that it wins all the arguments, as it succumbs — through sheer will-to-power — to the re-imposition of argumentative sociology. By doing so it destroys capitalism, enterprise, and science. At the end of this trajectory, it excavates the forgotten social contract of modernity. Its final discovery is war.

An Abstract Path to Freedom

At this thread (and in other places), commenter VXXC cites Durant's Dark Counsel: "For freedom and equality are sworn and everlasting enemies, and when one prevails the other dies. Leave men free, and their natural inequalities will multiply almost geometrically." He then remarks: "That's fine with me, I'll go with Freedom." *Outside in* concurs without reservation.

Take this dark counsel as the thesis that a practically-significant ideological dimension can be constructed, within which freedom and egalitarianism are related as strictly reciprocal variables. Taking this dimension for orientation, two abstract models of demographic redistribution can be examined, in order to identify *what it is that neoreactionaries want.*

The Caplan-Boudreaux Suicidal Libertarianism Model (SLM), takes the following arithmetical form:

> *Suppose there are two countries with equal populations. The quality of policy ranges from 0-10, 10 being best. In country A, bliss points (people's first choice for policy) are uniformly distributed from 2-6. In country B, bliss points are uniformly distributed from 4-8. [...] When the countries are independent, country A gets a policy quality of 4 (the median of the uniform distribution from 2-6), and country B gets a policy quality of 6 (the median of the uniform distribution from 4-8). Average policy that people live under: 50%*4+50%*6=5. ... suppose you open the borders, and everyone moves to country B (the richer country). The median of the whole distribution is 5. Result: The immigrants live under better policies, the natives live under worse policies. The average (5) remains unchanged.*

A few preparatory tweaks help to smooth the proceedings. Firstly, convert Caplan's "bliss points" to freedom coefficients (from '0' or absolute egalitarianism, to '1' or unconstrained liberty). A society in which freedom was maximized would not be wholly unequal (Gini coefficient 1.0), but it would be wholly indifferent to inequality as a problem. In other words, egalitarian concerns would have zero policy impact. It is in this sense, alone, that freedom is perfected.

Secondly (and automatically), the question-begging judgments of "better" and "worse" are displaced by the ideological reciprocals of freedom and equality there is no need to compel acquiescence as to the objective merits of either. Indeed, there is every reason to encourage those unconvinced of the superior attractions of liberty to seek ideological satisfaction in an egalitarian realm, elsewhere. From the perspective of liberty, egalitarian exodus is an unambiguous — even supreme — good, analogous to political entropy dissipation.

It is further, tacitly presumed here that freedom coefficients correlate linearly with intelligence optimization, but this depends upon further argument, to be bracketed for now.

The extraordinary theoretical value of the SLM can now be demonstrated. Due to its radical egalitarianism it defines a pessimal limit for neoreaction, and thus by strict inversion describes the abstract program for a restoration of free society (the Neoreactionary Model of demographic redistribution, or NM). In order to chart this reversal, the simplest course is to presuppose the full accomplishment of the SLM in an arbitrary 'geographical' space, which it taken to be flexibly divisible, and populated by 320 million people, SLM-homogenized to a freedom coefficient of 0.5.

Confining ourselves to the tools already employed in the establishment of the climax SLM (whilst for the sake of lucid presentation — ignoring any degenerative ratchet asymmetries), let us now proceed on the path of reversal. The SLM conservation law holds that average freedom is preserved, so an initial schism produces two equal populations equivalent to those of Caplan's starting point each numbering 160 million, but now differentiated on the dark counsel dimension, with freedom coefficients of 0.6 and 0.4.

Pursue this fissional procedure of territorial population division and ideological differentiation recursively, focusing exclusively upon the comparatively free segment each time. The 160 million 0.6s become 80 million 0.7s, and an equal number of 0.5s. After five iterations, the final neoreactionary-secessionist de-homogenized distribution is reached:

160 million x 0.4

80 million x 0.5

40 million x 0.6

20 million x 0.7

10 million x 0.8, and — incarnating the meaning of world history, or at least absorbing neoreactionary exaltation — 10 million x 1.0

Roughly 3% of the original population now live in a truly free society. For Caplan and other SLM-proponents, of course, nothing at all has been gained.

Yet, assume instead of SLM utilitarian universalism, on profoundly inegalitarian grounds, that the aggregate quantity of freedom was considered of vastly lower importance than the *exemplary quality of freedom*, then the neoreactionary achievement is stark. Where freedom nowhere existed, now it does, at an essentially irrelevant cost of moderate socialist deterioration elsewhere. Half of the original population 160 million souls have now been released to enjoy a 'fairer' society than they knew before. Why not congratulate them on the fact, without being distracted unduly by the starvation and re-education camps? It can be confidently presumed that they would have voted for the regime that now takes care of them. Their internal political arrangements need no longer concern us.

For Neoreaction (the NM), it is not a question of whether people (in general) are free, but only whether freedom (somewhere) exists. The highest attainment of freedom within the system, rather than the averaged level of freedom throughout the system, is its overwhelming priority. By reversing the process of demographic redistribution envisaged by the SLM, its ends are achieved.

The zero-sum utilitarian conclusions of this comparison would be unsettled by a more concrete elaboration of the NM, in which the effects of exemplarity, competition, the positive externalities of techno-economic performance, and other influences of freedom were included. At the present level of abstraction — set by Caplan's own (SL) model — such positive spin-offs might seem no more than sentimental concessions to common feeling. It is the ruthless core of the Neoreactionary Model that has, initially, to assert itself. Better the greatest possible freedom, even for a few, than a lesser freedom for all. Quality matters most.

The quasi-Rawlesian objection — fully implicit within the SLM — might run: "And what if the free society, as 'probability' dictates, is not yours?" — our rejoinder: "It would require a despicable egotist not to delight in it, even at a distance, as a beacon of aspiration, and an idiot or scoundrel not to set out on the same path, in whichever way they were able."

Disintegrate destiny.

Dark Moments

Gloom and realism can be hard to distinguish, but it's important to carry on. Curmudgeonry without stubbornness isn't worth a damn. Even in the worst case, relentless, sluggishly deterioriating ghastliness can at least be interesting. It shouldn't be necessary to cheer up, in order to continue, and there might be some lessons worth attending to in the slough of despond.

I'd go further. Despair can get things started, if it means the abandonment of diverting idols. A full, immersive soaking, which leaves no doubt about certain things *being over*, is morbidly therapeutic, and even something like a first step (at least a first slouch). There are hopes that have to die, and the sooner the better, although if they die slowly and horribly, they are perhaps less likely to need killing twice.

Here's the argument: *Nothing is going anywhere without preliminary disintegration.* That's the cheerful part. It seems to me an absolutely irresistible claim, and this post was to have been designed to rally consensus around it. Then I made the 'mistake' of watching this.

Allow me to walk you into this little knot of gloom in stages, punctuated by theses, each of which marks an essential but incomplete discussion. The meta-assertion is that there is no other way. Push-back against that, met at any of its way-stations, will make the dire swamp-thrashing to follow worthwhile.

Thesis-1: There is no more basic preliminary to effective neoreactionary transformation than schism. This can take many forms. Simple retirement into the private sphere — as strongly advocated by Nick B. Steves in particular — represents one significant pole. At the other lies secession, and other forms of macro-political disintegration (with science fiction variants extending from seasteading out to space colonization). The essential point is that *a consolidation of disagreement in space is substituted for a resolution of disagreement in time.* As far as practicality is concerned, this is the overwhelming priority.

Thesis-2: There can be no agreement. The recent flurry of interest in Emmanuel Todd should suffice as confirmation (this critical summary by Craig Willy is excellent). In a very small nutshell, Todd argues that "... political ideologies in the modern age are projections of a people's unconscious premodern family values." Europe has four basic family types (all exogamous), programming its varied political ideals. The inegalitarian (classical) liberalism of mercantile North-West Europeans, corresponds to the 'Absolute nuclear family'. Weird Franco-Italian 'egalitarian liberalism' corresponds to the 'egalitarian nuclear family' (Todd's own ancestral type and value model). The

Germanic 'Authoritarian family' tends to German stuff, and The (Slav-Orthodox) 'Community family' breeds communists. If you haven't read Willy yet, you'll be glad you did. The sole take-away here: *People are different* (oops, that's a signature judgement of the inegalitarian liberal type), with no tendency to converge upon common ideals, even among Europeans. There are people who think communism is natural and good, and they're not going to be argued out of it. Only a small minority think what you do, and that isn't going to change. You either have to kill them, dominate them, be dominated by them, *or escape them*. Escaping them is best.

Thesis-3: It's America that matters (for Anglophone neoreactionaries, at least). It's the only country with traditions of freedom that can be broken into large and influential pieces, and its residual federal structure provides a virtual template for doing exactly that. For practical purposes, therefore, the future of liberty — *even if you want to read that as the liberty to conduct experiments in ethnonationalist or theocratic government* — is entirely dependent upon the development of American federalism. Further centralized consolidation is losing, and disintegration is winning. Compared to that, in terms of political practicality, everything else is of vanishing irrelevance. Dreaming up schemes for ideal authoritarian regimes, in particular, is simply a hobby (but you know that already, right?).

The only road to the future, or the past, leads through a Disunited States of America. Now listen to those *Bloggingheads* again, and wind up the gloom to scream volume. It's absolutely clear from a strictly technical point of view that the sole conceivable platform for an escape from Leviathan's degenerative ratchet would be a *Confederate States of America*, and we can probably agree that historical sensitivities make that a non-starter. Setting out on a path away from futile arguments — between people who will never agree — leads straight back into America's racial nightmare, and horrible, draining, unresolvable wrangling that amounts to: *Freedom is banned forever, because ... what happened to black people.*

Those arguments are stupidity itself. They go nowhere. And that is precisely the point.

[Don't kill yourself, or shut down your blog — but a stiff drink is positively recommended]

Cosmological Infancy

There is a 'problem' that has been nagging at me for a long time — which is that *there hasn't been a long time.* It's Saturday, with no one around, or getting drunk, or something, so I'll run it past you. Cosmology seems oddly childish.

An analogy might help. Among all the reasons for super-sophisticated atheistic materialists to deride Abrahamic creationists, the most arithmetically impressive is the whole James Ussher 4004 BC thing. The argument is familiar to everyone: *6,027 years — Ha!*

Creationism is a topic for another time. The point for now is just: *13.7 billion years - Ha!* Perhaps this cosmological consensus estimate for the age of the universe is true. I'm certainly not going to pit my carefully-rationed expertise in cosmo-physics against it. But it's a *stupidly* short amount of time. If this is reality, the joke's on us. Between Ussher's mid-17th century estimate and (say) Hawking's late 20th century one, the difference is just six orders of magnitude. It's scarcely worth getting out of bed for. Or the crib.

For anyone steeped in Hindu Cosmology — which locates us 1.56 x 10 14 years into the current Age of Brahma or — Lovecraftian metaphysics, with its vaguer but abysmally extended eons, the quantity of elapsed cosmic time, according to the common understanding of our present scientific establishment, is cause for claustrophobia. Looking backward, we are sealed in a small room, with the wall of the original singularity pressed right up against us. (Looking forward, things are quite different, and we will get to that.)

There are at least three ways in which the bizarre youthfulness of the universe might be imagined:

- Consider first the disconcerting lack of proportion between space and time. The universe contains roughly 100 billion galaxies, each a swirl of 100 billion stars. That makes Sol one of 10^ 22 stars in the cosmos, but it has lasted for something like *a third of the life of the universe*. Decompose the solar system and the discrepancy only becomes more extreme. The sun accounts for 99.86% of the system's mass, and the gas giants incorporate 99 of the remainder, yet the age of the earth is only fractionally less than that of the sun. Earth is *a cosmic time hog*. In space it is next to nothing, but in time it extends back through a substantial proportion of the Stelliferous Era, so close to the origin of the universe that it is belongs to the very earliest generations of planetary bodies. Beyond it stretch incomprehensible immensities, but before it there is next to nothing.

- Compared to the intensity of time (backward) extension is of vanishing insignificance. The unit of Planck time corresponding to the passage of a photon across a Planck length — is about 5.4 x 10^ -44 seconds. If there is a true *instant*, that is it. A year consists of less the 3.2 x 10^ 7 seconds, so cosmological consensus estimates that there have been approximately 432 339 120 000 000 000 seconds since the Big Bang, which for our purposes can be satisfactorily rounded to 4.3 x 10 17. The difference between a second and the age of the universe is smaller that that between a second and a Planck Time tick by nearly 27 *orders of magnitude*. In other words, if a Planck Time-sensitive questioner asked "When did the Big Bang happen?" and you answered "Just now" — in clock time — you'd be almost exactly right. If you had been asked to identify a particular star from among the entire stellar population of the universe, and you picked it out correctly, your accuracy would still be hazier by 5 orders of magnitude. Quite obviously, there haven't been enough seconds since the Big Bang to add up to a serious number less than one for every 10,000 stars in the universe.

- Isotropy gets violated by time orientation like a Detroit muni-bond investor. In a universe dominated by dark energy like ours expansion lasts *forever*. The Stelliferous Era is predicted to last for roughly 100 trillion years, which is over 7,000 times the present age of the universe. Even the most pessimistic interpretation of the Anthropic Principle, therefore, places us only a fractional distance from the beginning of time. The Degenerate Era, post-dating star-formation, then extends out to 10^ 40 years, by the end of which time all baryonic matter will have decayed, and even the most radically advanced forms of cosmic intelligence will have found existence becoming seriously challenging. Black holes then dominate out to 10 60 years, after which the Dark Era begins, lasting a long time. (Decimal exponents become unwieldy for these magnitudes, making more elaborate modes of arithmetical notation expedient. We need not pursue it further.) The take-away: the principle of Isotropy holds that we should not find ourselves anywhere special in the universe, and yet we do right at the beginning. More implausibly still, we are located *at the very beginning of an infinity* (although anthropic selection might crop this down to merely preposterous improbability).

Intuitively, this is all horribly wrong, although intuitions have no credible authority, and certainly provide no grounds for contesting rigorously assembled scientific narratives. Possibly — I should concede *most probably* — time is simply ridiculous, not to say profoundly insulting. We find ourselves glued to the very edge of the Big Bang, as close to neo-natal as it is arithmetically possible to be.

That's odd, isn't it?

Simulated Gnon-Theology

This post was to have been about the simulation argument, but Gnon does the preliminary work. Whether or not we are living in a computer simulation can quickly come to seem like a derivative consideration.

Nature or Nature's God, (un)known here as Gnon, provides skepticism with its ultimate object. With this name we can advance in suspension, freeing thought from any ground in belief. In its mundane application, Gnon permits realism to exceed doctrinal conviction, reaching reasonable conclusions amongst uncertain information. Its invocation, however, is not necessarily mundane.

Assume, momentarily, that God exists. If this assumption comes easily, so much the better. It is probably obvious, almost immediately, that you do not yet have a clear idea about what you are thus assuming. To mark exactly this fact, the established Abrahamic religions propose that you designate God by a proper name, which corresponds to a definite yet profoundly occulted personal individual. Approaching the same obscurity from the other side, emphasizing the problematic rather than relational aspect, I will persevere in the name of Gnon.

To avoid gratuitous idolatry, all our subsequent assumptions must be readily retractable. It is not our mission to tell Gnon what it is. We cannot but be aware, from the beginning, that two perplexing, and inter-twined sources of idolatry will be especially difficult to dispel, due to their conceptual intractability, and their insinuation into the basic fabric of grammar and narrative. In merely using the tensed verb 'to be', and in unfolding a process in stages, we unwittingly idolize Gnon as a subordinate of being and time. Our sole refuge lies in the recognition, initially inarticulate, that to think Gnon as God is to advance a hyper-ontological and meta-chronic hypothesis. From Gnon's self-understanding, being and time have to emerge as exhaustively comprehended consequences (even though we have no idea at all what this might mean).

If Gnon is God, it is the reality of infinite intelligence. Occidental religious tradition divides this ultimate infinitude into the topics of omniscience, omnipotence, and omnibenevolence, at the risk of introducing footholds for anthropomorphism and thus idolatry. Accepting a contrary risk (one that Pope Benedict XVI specifically indicated as Islamic?), I will simply dismiss the possibility that God can be *theologically* other than good, since this would be an invitation to Lovecraftian speculations of distracting vividness. Thomist scholasticism offers a further simplification, by proposing that what there is to know, is that which God creates. Pursued (perhaps) one step further: Self-knowledge is the auto-creation of a 'being' that thinks itself into reality. This, too, offers a conceptual economy to be eagerly seized.

The creation of the universe is of concern to humans, and the creation of angels is a grave matter for Satan, but for Gnon they can only be trivialities (it might be unnecessarily antagonistic to say 'amusements'). For Gnon as God the Cantorian transfinite realm is self-identity, or less, whose infinite parts are each infinities.

Unless choosing to blaspheme, we can only assume that Gnon thinks serious thoughts, of a kind that have some relevance to its thinking about itself, and thus ensuring itself in its (hyper-ontological) auto-creation. Such thoughts surely encompass the creation of gods, since that for (a) God is simply the transfinite as intelligent activity. If for Gnon to know what it can do is already to have done it, because divine intelligence is creation, anything less than an infinite pantheon would be evidence of retardation.

For Gnon, as God, gods are infinitesimals, so that any thorough self-investigation would involve them. It is effortlessness itself, for It, to thus create an infinite being among an infinity of such beings each of which, being infinite, is made of infinities, and these in turn, as infinities, consist of infinite infinities, without end. This is no more than Cantor had already understood, at the most elementary stage of his transfinite explorations, although, being a human creature, his understanding was not immediately creation.

If Satan, a mere arch-angel, could imagine himself a god, and not only a god, but — in potential at least — God seated upon the throne of ultimate sovereignty, is it possible that no god thinks itself God? And if a god can, if only in possibility, think itself God, can God not think this rebellion and thus know it — which is to create it (or make it real)? Does not God's self-understanding necessitate the creation of cosmic insurrection? From the Satanic perspective, such questions are overwhelmingly fascinating, but they lead to a more intricate predicament.

When Gnon (as God) thinks through its gods, as it can only do, the thought necessarily arises: If these god creatures can confuse themselves with God, could not my self-understanding as God also be a confusion?

The Ruin Reservoir

In the *Washington Post*, Charles Krauthammer notes:

> *It doesn't take a genius to see what happens when the entitlement state outgrows the economy upon which it rests. The time of Greece, Cyprus, Portugal, Spain, the rest of insolvent social-democratic Europe — and now Detroit — is the time for conservatives to raise the banner of Stein's Law and yell, "Stop." You can kick the can down the road, but at some point it disappears over a cliff.*

Yes, yes, yes ... but. Despite its perfect common sense, the monotony of this message is becoming utterly unbearable. The end isn't arriving tomorrow. This dreary horror show could last for decades. How many roughly-identical, absolutely obvious, sensible Op Ed columns is it possible to endure? (I'm already way into overtime.)

A reasonable conclusion from the reality of degenerative ratchets is that nothing less than a comprehensive crash makes them stop. Some of the healthier Right-delight over the Detroit implosion is tied to the expectation that bad examples could be educational, but the evidence for that is slender, especially under conditions of sovereign propaganda saturation (the Cathedral). Who are you going to trust, the academic-media complex or your lying eyes? We already know the predominant answer to that question.

When a message is existentially unacceptable to the Cathedral, it will not be heard, and the only messages with substantial reality content are of exactly this kind. True believers will stick with a morbid utopia to the end, since anything truly different would — in any case — count for them as some species of death. For cynics, the calculation is even easier: why unnecessarily shorten looting time? More common still are the poor idiots, who will just do what they're told (while trying to grab a little feeding trough time), and then be sacrificed. It should already be clear that *nobody cares about them*, and they're too defective to care competently for themselves. That's neither justice nor injustice, but simple reality.

Nobody here is under any illusions about the profound socio-political malignancy given free reign in Detroit, or about the quality of human material over which it held sway, and yet it lasted up to a point that has provoked repeated comparisons with

Hiroshima-1945, wrung out to the ugly end (and we haven't yet seen the end). If we ever doubted that there's a lot of ruin in a nation, we no longer can. For a city uniquely proficient at suicide, the process lasts half a century, including final, grinding decades, when nothing beyond a zombie parody of what once was still remains. If a uniquely benighted social trash pile can last this long, how far can the world's most powerful nation spin out its decline? There's enough time, to be sure, for an Amazon jungle worth of Herbert Stein-inspired Op Eds.

Can-kicking eventually runs out of road, *of course*, and its only when this truism has become an intolerable, deadening drone that neoreaction begins. Anybody who still needs to hear that message *is simply lost*. Remedial education cannot be the neoreactionary task (there are libertarian-oriented conservatives for that — and they will fail).

If the Dark Enlightenment cannot end with Stein's conclusion, but is rather initiated by it, born from the presupposition that *this cannot go on forever*, how is its guiding topic to be understood? What will it discuss — with what will it occupy itself — amid the deepening ruin, for decades?

As its name indicates, Dark Enlightenment is a creature of late twilight, preparing for a gruesomely protracted night. One object that merits growing fascination is certainly this: *the ruin reservoir is deep*. As a fact this is easily — and for neoreaction necessarily — acknowledged, but the exploration of its mysteries has still scarcely begun.

Economies of Deceit

Social organizations grow ever larger, and resist disintegration, due to economies of scale. There are disproportionate benefits to being large, sufficient to over-compensate for the associated disadvantages, to support expansion, and to fund the suppression of fission. Like every trend reinforced by positive nonlinearities, large-scale social formations accentuate the gradient of time, realizing a ratchet mechanism, through 'network effects'. In this way, they contribute not only to the content of history, but also to its shape.

When the fundamental deformation of history was evidently attributable to scale economies, it was only natural to speak primarily of Leviathan — the seizure of historical time by the gigantic. It might therefore be considered a significant symptom — of something — that a substitute term now seems more persuasively applicable. Leviathan remains vast, and growing, but it is more exactly specified as *the Cathedral*, because its principal ratchet mechanism owes less to sheer magnitude than to a mastery of deceit.

Deceit is nothing new, in matters of power, or any other, but it is open to innovation. A state religion that pretends to be the negation of religion is something new, as is propaganda in its strict sense. There is no precedent for an intolerant, precisely coded system of belief, trending to a totalitarian form, whilst presenting itself as inevitable progress towards general disillusionment.

Economies of deceit, like those of scale, draw historical momentum from the fact that they are profoundly automatized. No one decided that large-scale social organizations *should* be advantaged. Similarly, the revolutionary *efficiency* of deceit was never a point of deliberation. Deceit works, due to contingencies of deep evolution. More specifically, it works because propaganda machinery was never a factor in the archaic human environment, so that stimulus sensitivity was never provided with the opportunity to adapt defensively in respect to it.

The total power of deceit can be understood most clearly when examined backwards, from its final destination, which is shared with the entire utilitarian sphere. At the end there is the *wire-head*, the social and technological destination of *direct neurological rewards*, where the message "I have received what I want" has been divorced from all real acquisition or accomplishment. Do you want this thing? Or do you want the feeling that you have this thing? The latter can be strengthened, sharpened, and in every way *subjectively* perfected. It is also, given suitable historical conditions, vastly cheaper to deliver. Hence, *the economy of deceit*.

For those paying attention, the entire structure of economic thought and policy switched onto this track roughly a century ago. The demetalization of money is the most obvious indicator, trending towards a pure signal of wealth, entirely disconnected from the extravagance of physical reality. Keynesianism, in its essence, is wire-head economics, focusing on the policy question: *how do we best deliver the stim?* The idea that growth of the real economy might be the best route to this goal marks its proponent out as a hopeless crank, entirely out of touch with the recent development of the discipline. What matters is the *wealth effect*, delivered in carefully calibrated jolts, down the wire. (I've tried to thrash this out before.)

Gradually, but inexorably, propaganda swallow everything. All macroeconomic aggregates — GDP, inflation, capital stock ... — tend to senseless garbage, because their only robust anchor point is Cathedral-political: what can we make you feel? The latest evidence is telling. It is time, apparently, to definitively break with archaic questions of economic production, and instead to work solely with the ~~macroeconomic garbage~~ data, in order for it to tell us that we're richer than we think we are.

You can't make this s%&t up. Yes we can!

Laffer Drift

One dark and fearsome crag, half-lost among the Himalayan mountain range of uncleared obligations stretched out before this blog, is a promise to devote a post (or several) to Mencius Moldbug's Neocameral regime model. The opportunity to make a small payment against this debt having arisen, I am eagerly seizing it.

A relatively marginal but consistent feature in Moldbug's model is the tendency of Neocameral tax rates to approximate to the Laffer maximum. Since Moldbug aims to rationalize the theory of government, under the presumption of its ineliminably self-interested nature, this suggestion scarcely requires an argument (and in fact does not receive one). Government will always tend to maximize its resources, and Arthur Laffer's graph of optimum revenue-raising tax rates seems to show the way this is done. A Neocameral regime tends the economy of a country exactly as a farmer tends a herd of animals — without ever forgetting that ultimate redemption occurs in the abattoir.

There is a problem with this assumption, however, which is that the very idea of a Laffer maximum tax rate is incomplete. By coordinating tax rates (on the x-axis) with tax revenues (on the y-axis), the Laffer curve demolishes the crude economic intuition that revenue rises continuously with tax rates. Through the *a priori* postulate that a 100% tax rate yields zero revenue, Laffer demonstrates that revenue maximization has to be located somewhere in the central region of the curve. Its exact location — as determined by the shape of the curve — is dependent upon empirical factors, such as incentive effects, and cannot be deduced by pure theory.

Missing from the Laffer curve is time, and thus *dynamic revenue projection*. This is especially important to the Neocameral model, since a central failure to be rectified through reactionary democracy-suppression is the systematic heightening of time-preference, or collapsing economic time-horizons, with which democracy is inextricably bound. The Neocameral state is justified by its capacity for time-extended economic rationality, and this is not something that the simple Laffer curve can reflect.

Adding time to Laffer graphs is not a complex task. All that is required is a multiplication of curves, constituting a time series, with each curve corresponding to a time-horizon. Rather than a single curve, such a graph would consist of a 1-year curve, a 2-year curve, a 3-year curve ... and out to whichever extended prospect was considered appropriate.

If levels of taxation were irrelevant to economic growth rates, then each curve would be identical, and this exercise would lack all significance. If, alternatively, taxation effected growth in a in a predictable direction, then the Laffer curves would steadily drift as time-horizons were expanded.

To begin with the improbable case, assume that extraction of resources from private property owners tends to increase economic growth. Then each successive Laffer curve would drift to the right, as the tax base expands under the beneficent impact of lavish government spending. A small and efficient government, by depriving the economy of its attention, would steadily shrink the tax base relative to its potential, and thus reduce the total level of takings (as a function of time).

If, far more plausibly, taxation suppresses growth, then each successive curve will drift to the left. The Laffer maximum tax rate for a 1-year time horizon will be revealed as ever more excessive as the horizon is dilated, and the shortfall of the depredated economy is exposed with increasing clarity. The more extended the time-horizon, the further to the left the *dynamic* Laffer maximum has to be. As economic far-sightedness stretches out into the distance, an authoritarian-realist regime converges with anarcho-capitalism, since growth-maximization increasingly dominates its revenue projections.

Of all the reasons to distrust the Neocameral model, an intrinsic tendency to short-term Laffer-max revenue raising cannot be among them.

[Apologies for the link famine — trawling the Moldbug archive through the GFC is a nightmare undertaking, and it's 3:30 in the morning. I'll try to punch some in over the next few days.]

Discrimination

Bryan Caplan has had two epiphanies, which sum to the conclusion that — bad as tribalism is — misanthropy is the real problem. His ineradicable universalism betrays him once again.

It matters little whether people are *uniformly* judged good or bad. Far more important is whether such judgment is *discriminating*.

The central argument of Nietzsche's *The Genealogy of Morals* is clarifying in this regard, not least because it explains how radical mystification came to dominate the topic. How could there ever come to be a moral quandary about the value of discrimination? Considered superficially, it is extremely puzzling.

Differentiation between what is 'good' and 'bad' requires discrimination. This is a capability no younger than life itself, which it serves as an indispensable function. As soon as there is behavior, there is discrimination between alternatives. One way leads to survival, the other way leads to death. There is nourishment, or not reproduction, or not safety or predatory menace. Good and bad, or the discrimination between them (which is the same thing), are etched primordially into any world that life inhabits. Discrimination is needed to survive.

The very existence of archaic hominids attests to billions of years of effective discrimination, between safety and danger, wholesome and putrid or poisonous food, good mates and less good (or worthless) ones. When these elevated apes differentiated between good and bad, appetizing and rotten, attractive and repulsive, they found such discriminations sufficiently similar in essence to be functionally substitutable. When judging that some food item is 'not good for us', a person is 'rotten', or the odor of a potential mate is 'delicious', we recall such substitutions, and the primordial sense of discrimination that they affirm. There can be no long-term deviation from the original principle: *discrimination is intelligence aligned with survival.*

Two contrary developments now present themselves. Firstly, there is a sublimation or sophistication of discrimination, which might be called *cultivation*. Abstract concepts, modes of expression, artworks, delicate culinary flavors, refined behaviors, and exotic elaborations of sexual-selection stimuli, among innumerable other things, can all be subtly discriminated on the ancient scale, supporting an ever more intricate and extended hierarchy of judgments. The reflexive doubling of this potential upon itself, as captured by the 'higher' judgment that *to discriminate well is good*, produces a 'natural aristocracy'. For the first time, there is a self-conscious 'Right'. This, at least, is its logico-mythical ur-form. *To divide the good from the bad is good*. Order, hierarchy, and distinction emerge from an affirmation of discrimination.

Because the Left cannot create, it comes second. It presupposes an existing hierarchy, or order of discriminations, which is subverted through a 'slave revolt in morality'. The formula is simple enough: *to discriminate is bad.* Following from this leftist moral perversion, as its second-order consequence, those who do not discriminate (well), but are in fact discriminated against, must be the good. In the new moral order, therefore, to be bad at discrimination is good — or 'universalist' — whilst the old (and now 'evil') quality of good judgment, based on competent perception of patterns and differences, is the very quintessence of sin.

Lawrence Auster's thinking, which would not usually be described as 'Nietzschean', conforms to the conclusions of the Antichrist perfectly in this:

> *We thus arrive at our present system of mass nonwhite immigration, multiculturalism, racial preferences for minorities, the symbolic celebration of minorities, the covering up of black-on-white violence, and antiracism crusades directed exclusively at whites. Under this system, whites practice assiduous non-discrimination toward the unassimilated, alien, or criminal behavior of racial minorities, while practicing the most assiduous discrimination against their fellow whites for the slightest failure to be non-discriminatory. This is the system that conservatives variously describe as "political correctness" or the "double standard." However, from the point of view of the functioning of the liberal order itself, what conservatives call the double standard is not a double standard at all, but a fundamental and necessary articulation of the society into the "non-discriminators" and the "non-discriminated against"—an articulation upon which the very legitimacy and existence of the liberal society depends. [Auster's emphasis]*

The racial pretext for this righteous diatribe is not incidental, given the prevailing sense of 'discrimination' in Left-edited languages. Caution is required, however, precisely because vulgar racism is *insufficiently discriminating*. All generalization lurches towards the universal. The abstract principle of Leftism is, in any case, far more general. The trend towards the Left-absolute is entirely clear, and pre-programmed: *no state of human existence can possibly be any better or worse than any other*, and only through recognition of this can we be saved. Do you sinfully imagine that it is *better* to be a damned soul like Nietzsche than an obese, leprous, slothful, communist, cretin? Or worse still, in Bryan Caplan's world, that one might design an immigration policy on this basis? Then your path to the abyss is already marked out before you.

It does not take an exceptional mastery of logic to see the inextinguishable contradiction in Leftist thought. If discrimination is bad, and non-discrimination is good, how can discrimination be discriminated from non-discrimination, without grave moral error? This is an opportunity for Rightist entertainment, but not for solace. The Left has power and absurdist mysticism on its side. Logic is for sinners.

Reactionary Horror

Within the Western tradition, the expedition to find Kurtz at the end of the river has a single overwhelming connotation. It is a voyage to Hell. Hence its absolute importance, utterly exceeding narrow 'mission specifications'. The assigned objectives are no more than a pretext, arranging the terms of approach to an ultimate destination. The narrative drive, as it gathers momentum, is truly infernal. Dark Enlightenment is the commanding attraction.

There are no doubt species of reactionary political and historical philosophy which remain completely innocent of such impulses. Almost certainly, they predominate over their morbid associates. To maintain a retrograde psychological orientation, out of reverence for what has been, and is ceasing to be, can reasonably be opposed to any journey to the end of the night. Yet such a contrast only sharpens our understanding of those for whom the disintegration of tradition describes a gradient, and a vector, propelling intelligence forwards into the yawning abyss.

Reaction is articulated as an inversion of the progressive promise, dissociating 'the good' and 'the future'. The tacit science fiction narrative that corresponds to projected social evolution is stripped of its optimism, and two alternative genres arise in its place. The first, as we have fleetingly noted, is mild and nostalgic, rebalancing the tension of time towards what has been lost, and tending to an increasingly dreamlike inhabitation of ancient glories. A conservative-traditionalist mentality devotes itself to a mnemonic quest, preserving vestiges of virtue among the remnants of an eroded society, or — when preservation at last surrenders its grasp on actuality — turning to fantastic evocations, as the final redoubt of defiance. Tolkien exemplifies this tendency in its most systematic expression. The future is gently obliterated, as the good dies within it.

The second reactionary alternative to the ruin of utopian futurism develops in the direction of horror. It does not hesitate in its voyage to the end of the river, even as smoke-shrouded omens thicken on the horizon. As the devastation deepens, its futurism is further accentuated. Historical projection becomes the opportunity for an exploration of Hell. (The 'neo-' of 'neoreaction' thus finds additional confirmation.)

On this track, reactionary historical anticipation fuses with the genre of horror in its most intense possibility (and true vocation). Numerous consequences are quite rapidly evident. One special zone of significance concerns the insistent question of *popularization*, which is substantially resolved, almost from the start. The genre of reactionary populism is already tightly formulated, on the side of horror fiction, where *things going to Hell* is an established presupposition. Zombie Apocalypse is only the most prominent variant of a far more general cultural accommodation to impending disaster. 'Survivalism' is as much a genre convention as a socio-political expectation. (When, as VXXC points out on the blog, .22 ammunition functions as virtual currency, horror fiction has already installed itself as an operational dimension of social reality.)

Reaction does not do dialectics, or converse with the Left (with which it has no community), yet historical fatality carries its message: *Your hopes are our horror story*. As the dream perishes, the nightmare strengthens, and even — hideously — invigorates. So how does this tale unfold ...?

What were you expecting? Rivendell?

Zombie Hunger

The Psykonomist forwarded an extraordinary essay on the topic of popular appetite for ombie Apocalypse, considered as an expressive channel for loosely 'anarchist' hostility to the state. Given the failure of Right-pole democratic initiatives to roll back — or even check — relentless government concentration and expansion, catastrophic 'solutions' emerge as the sole alternative:

> *Films and television shows have allowed Americans to imagine what life would be like without all the institutions they had been told they need, but which they now suspect may be thwarting their self-fulfillment. We are dealing with a wide variety of fantasies here, mainly in the horror or science fiction genres, but the pattern is quite consistent and striking, cutting across generic distinctions. In the television show Revolution, for example, some mysterious event causes all electrical devices around the world to cease functioning. The result is catastrophic and involves a huge loss of life, as airborne planes crash to earth, for example. All social institutions dissolve, and people are forced to rely only on their personal survival skills. Governments around the world collapse, and the United States divides up into a number of smaller political units. This development runs contrary to everything we have been taught to believe about "one nation, indivisible." Yet it is characteristic of almost all these shows that the federal government is among the first casualties of the apocalyptic event, and—strange as it may at first sound—there is a strong element of wish fulfillment in this event. The thrust of these end-of-the-world scenarios is precisely for government to grow smaller or to disappear entirely. These shows seem to reflect a sense that government has grown too big and too remote from the concerns of ordinary citizens and unresponsive to their needs and demands. If Congress and the President are unable to shrink the size of government, perhaps a plague or cosmic catastrophe can do some real budget cutting for a change.*

The essay captures a critical dimension of disintegration within the 'reactionary camp', dividing those who seek to co-opt the Cathedral-Leviathan managerial elite to a more realistic (or tradition-tolerant) political philosophy, and those who — far more numerously and inarticulately — are invested in the hard death of the regime. The latter (immoderate) position, it appears, is genuinely and even shockingly popular. Swathes of mass entertainment production are able to thrive on the basis of its seductive nightmares. (Is pulp catastrophism the economic base that will support neoreactionary contagion?)

Reading the Cantor essay alongside Jim Donald's epochal *Natural Law and Natural Rights* essay is highly suggestive. A common thread running through both is the centrality of vigilantism to the popular Right. The purpose of Natural Law, Donald argues, is not to demand justice from a higher authority, but to neutralize the interference of any such authority in the pursuit of justice by decentralized agencies. Natural Law protects the right to legitimate vengeance, ensuring that individuals are not inhibited in their exercise of self-protection. When the State is seen to operate primarily as a social force defending criminals against retaliation, it loses the instinctive solidarity of the citizenry, and dark dreams of Zombie Apocalypse begin to coalesce.

> *Given the survivalist ethic in all these end-of-the-world shows, they are probably not popular with gun control advocates. One of the most striking motifs they have in common—evident in Revolution, Falling Skies, The Walking Dead, and many other such shows—is the loving care with which they depict an astonishing array of weaponry. The Walking Dead features an Amazon warrior, who is adept with a samurai sword, as well as a southern redneck, who specializes in a crossbow. The dwindling supply of ammunition puts a premium on weapons that do not require bullets. That is not to say, however, that The Walking Dead has no place for modern firearms and indeed the very latest in automatic weapons. Both the heroes and the villains in the series—difficult to tell apart in this respect—are as well-armed as the typical municipal SWAT team in contemporary America.*

Among the attractions of Zombie Apocalypse, in this construction, is the disappearance of the State as an inhibitory factor in the social economy of retaliation. The ombie-plagued world is a free-fire zone, in which no authorities any longer stand between the armed remnant and the milling hordes of decivilization. Whatever the odds of the fight to come, the right to vigilante and counter-revolutionary violence has been unambiguously restored, and this is deeply *appreciated* — by opaque popular impulse — as a return to natural order. The State had taken sides against Natural Law, so that its catastrophic excision from the social field is greeted with relief, even if the cost of this disappearance is a world reduced to ashes, predominantly populated by the cannibalistic undead.

There's a ferocity to this that will be worked. It's best to be prepared.

The Monkey Trap

How did we get into this mess? When neoreaction slips into contemplative mode, it soon arrives a question roughly like this. Something evidently went very wrong, and most probably a considerable number of things.

The preferred focus of concern decides the particular species of doomsterism, within an already luxuriant taxonomy of social criticism. What common ground exists on the new ultra-right is cast like a shadow by the Cathedral — which no neoreactionary can interpret as anything other than a radical historical calamity. This recognition (or 'Dark Enlightenment') is a coalescence, and for that very reason a fissile agglomeration, as even the most perfunctory tour across the 'reactosphere' makes clear. (The *Outside in* blogroll already represents a specific distribution of attention, but within three clicks it will take you everywhere from disillusioned libertarians to throne-and altar traditionalists, or from hedonistic gender biorealists to neo-nazi conspiracies.)

Really though, how *did* we get into this mess? A dizzying variety of more-or-less convincing, more-or-less distant historical way-stations can be proposed, and have been. Explanatory regression carries the discussion ever further out — at least in principle — until eventually the buck stops with Gnon, who dropped us in it somewhere murkily remote. It's a situation highly conducive to story-telling, so here's a story. It's a mid-scale tale, intermediate between — say — the inauguration of the Federal Reserve and structural personality disorder of the Godhead.

As a preliminary warning, this is an account that only works — insofar as it does at all — for those who find negative intelligence crisis at the root of the problem. Those neoreactionaries, doubtlessly existing among us, who tend to see intelligence augmentation as a fast-track to hell, might nevertheless find this narrative suggestive, in other ways.

Short version: the monkeys did it.

Longer version: there's a tempting cosmic formula for the biological basis of technological civilizations, which cetaceans undermine. I encountered the exception before the formula (roughly 40 years ago), in a short story by Larry Niven called *The Handicapped*. This story — dredged now from distant memory — is about dolphins, and their role in a future trans-species and inter-planetary civilization. The central point is that (unlike monkeys), such animals require the external donation of prostheses before they can become technological, and thus apply their intelligence within the Oecumenon. Their 'handicap' is a remarkable evolution of cognitive capability beyond manipulative competence. Those natural trends that generated intelligence continue to work through them, uninterrupted by techno-historical interference.

The (flawed) thesis that the cetaceans disrupt has yet to be settled into an entirely satisfactory formula, but it goes something like this: every species entering into the process of techno-historical development is as *un*intelligent as it can possibly be. In other words, as soon as intelligence barely suffices to 'make' history, history begins, so that the inhabitants of (pre-singularity) historical societies — wherever they may be found — will be no more than *minimally* intelligent. This level of *threshold intelligence* is a cosmic constant, rather than a peculiarity of terrestrial conditions. Man was smart enough to ignite recorded history, but — necessariy — no smarter. This thesis strikes me as important, and substantially informative, even though it is wrong. (I am not pretending that it is new.)

The idea of threshold intelligence is designed for monkeys, or other — 'non-handicapped' — species, which introduces another ingredient to this discussion. It explains why articulate neoreaction can never be popular, because it recalls the Old Law of Gnon, whose harshness is such that the human mind recoils from it in horrified revulsion. Only odd people can even tentatively entertain it. *The penalty for stupidity is death.*

Gregory Clark is among those few to have grasped it clearly. *Any eugenic trend within history is expressed by continuous downward mobility.* For any given level of intelligence, a steady deterioration in life-prospects lies ahead, culling the least able, and replacing them with the more able, who inherit their wretched socio-economic situation, until they too are pushed off the Malthusian cliff. Relative comfort belongs only to the sports and freaks of cognitive advance. For everyone else, history slopes downwards into impoverishment, hopelessness, and eventual genetic extinction. That is how intelligence is made. Short of Technological Singularity, it is the only way. Who wants a piece of that?

No one does, or almost no one. The 'handicapped' would no doubt revolt against it if they could, but they are unable to do so, so their cognitive advance continues. Monkeys, on the other hand, are able to revolt, once they finesse their nasty little opposable thumbs. They don't like the Old Law, which has crafted them through countless aeons of ruthless culling, so they make history instead. If they get everything 'right', they even sleaze their way into epochs of upward social mobility, and with this great innovation, semi-sustainable dysgenics gets started. In its fundamentals it is hideously simple: social progress destroys the brain.

Cyclic stability, or negative feedback, structures history to hold intelligence down to the dim limit (as the intelligence threshold is seen — or more typically missed — from the other side). The deviation into technological performance chokes off the trend to bio-cognitive improvement, and reverses it, hunting homeostasis with a minimal-intelligence target. Progress and degenerate, or regress and improve. That's the yet-to-be-eradicated Old Law, generating cyclical history as a side-effect.

The monkeys became *able* to pursue happiness, and the deep ruin began.

If the terrestrial biosphere had held back for a few million years, let the primates get annihilated by a comet, and found a way to provide the cetaceans with prehensile organs somewhere up the road — after socio-linguistic sex-selection and relentless Malthusian butchery had fine-tuned their brains — then techno-history might have had another 50 points of average IQ to play with in its host population. It didn't, and here we are. (Never bet against the ugly.)

Obamanation...

... isn't an insulting name for Obama, or even for what he has 'wrought'. It's a name for America, and thus for the leading spirit (or *Zeitgeist*) of the world. A country where support for a Harvard Law presidency 'bottoms out' (repeatedly) at something above 40 knows what it wants — and is getting it (good and hard). Blaming Obama for any of this is like blaming pustules for the bubonic plague.

The world deserves Obama almost as much as America does, and in many cases, even more. If the Cathedral is basically to be applauded — and who doesn't believe that? — there's every reason to mainline it, by putting the authentic voice of the academy in power. As the chrysalis-husk of a universal project, America is duty bound to abolish itself as a particular nation. If it defers to its own 'propositional' ideals, how could it not? There are even chunks of the Tea Party who kinda sorta felt it was the right thing to do. The conservative establishment certainly did, including the Republican campaign machines of the two last presidential elections. The Idea necessitates blood sacrifice, which Obamanation consummates.

However neoreaction makes sense of itself, it signals what it is through a dismissal of partisan vulgarity. Anybody who thinks the GoP has the key even to the outhouse is decidedly not 'one of us'. Like the tingle-crotched devotees of the One, we understand that Obama is a destiny, and even an incarnation of *logos*. What he symbolizes has been awaited for a long time. His personal vacuity and administrative incompetence do not detract, in the slightest, from that. Through the fantasy that he reduces to (with only insignificant remainder), the Cathedral announces itself purely at last. Attitudinal correctness is the only authority to be recognized in the end.

By voiding governance from its summit, 'Obama' makes the neoreactionary case. He shows that government is to be found elsewhere, in the machinery of practical elitism, and that — there too — symbolic gestures have almost entirely supplanted functional competence. Government, even real government, is no longer expected to work. All that is required is that it can be morally legitimated, down to its most minute corpuscle, so that its failures are clearly seen — which is to say *promoted* — as the fault of something other than itself.

Insofar as retrograde pieces of America insist upon being themselves, as if untouched by the Idea, they are betrayed (by the 'media') as *unworthy of their government*, and justly suffering for their sins. Carnal privilege blinds them to what they should joyfully give up. To not *believe* in government — as the radiant sign of the collective — is a fallen state, from which the Obamanation extends a promise of redemption. By losing everything, with the help of government, one enters into the Kingdom.

The Obamanation is not what Obama has done (an intrinsically ridiculous construction). It's what *chose Obama*, as its symbol. It is the virtual evacuation of the world into America, and the complementary evacuation of specifically American power from the world. This is the phase of historical progression in which neoreaction *necessarily* emerges, its diagnoses dramatized by everything that now occurs, undisguised.

For that we are truly grateful, intrinsically, which is to say, in our very existence as the channel for something else. Conservatives will continue to find that hard to understand.

Consider this *Instapundit* visual joke, just for a moment:

The 'Bush' angle sounds partisan, and thus embarrassingly knuckle-draggy to brandy-sipping sophisticates of the Outer right, but that judgment might be overhasty. Perhaps partisanship itself is swallowed up into the lampoon. In any case, it still makes me laugh, due mostly to the tacit understanding that "World War III" is what Obama *is for.*

Of course, when you elect the pure totem of the Cathedral to the world's highest office, you're really — or consequentially — calling for the cleansing of the earth in the fires of hell. It requires only the most elementary comprehension of Occidental religious history to understand that.

Spiritual purity, and damn the consequences, that's the Obamanation (and, by the way, you're a racist). It's the bloody ruination of world order in the name of moral fanaticism, eclipsing all strategic realism through its wishful thinking and associated, narrow political maneuvers, before blundering into the present stage of terminal, incendiary, paralysis.

Who could have imagined that the world going to shit would be so bizarrely entertaining?

Cladistic Meditations

Neoreactionaries have a thing about Puritanism. Whether or not this trait is conceptually essential is a question for another time. The important point, right now, is that it serves as a *cladistic marker*. Whatever it might be that neoreaction speciates into, it bears this trait as an indication of cultural ancestry, bookmarking the root-code archive of Mencius Moldbug.

When reconstructed as an argument, the Moldbuggian clade proposes a species of ethnographic categorization on a loosely Darwinian (and strongly evolutionary) model, according to which cultural phenomena are logically nested, in tree-like fashion, revealing a pattern of descent. When considering an English Darwinian Evolutionist, who is also an example of contemporary political progressivism, Moldbug makes this mode of analysis explicit:

> *My belief is that Professor Dawkins is not just a Christian atheist. He is a Protestant atheist. And he is not just a Protestant atheist. He is a Calvinist atheist. And he is not just a Calvinist atheist. He is an Anglo-Calvinist atheist. In other words, he can be also be described as a Puritan atheist, a Dissenter atheist, a Nonconformist atheist, an Evangelical atheist, etc, etc.*
>
> *This cladistic taxonomy traces Professor Dawkins' intellectual ancestry back about 400 years, to the era of the English Civil War. Except of course for the atheism theme, Professor Dawkins' kernel is a remarkable match for the Ranter, Leveller, Digger, Quaker, Fifth Monarchist, or any of the more extreme English Dissenter traditions that flourished during the Cromwellian interregnum.*

If there were a Thirty-Nine Articles of neoreaction, some suitably compressed version of this cladogram would constitute the primary tenet of the creed. Among the logically most attenuated twigs of this scheme, sub-speciated to the limit of cladistic definition, is found the globally-dominant sovereign instance of advanced modernity — the Cathedral (the enemy).

It is not surprising, therefore, that the 'Puritan question' remains the core preoccupation of the neoreactionary Dark Enlightenment. This has been illustrated with consummate clarity by an article posted by J. M. Smith at *The Orthosphere*, contesting the Christian genealogy of the Cathedral, and the subsequent rejoinder by descendants of the neoreactionary clade — of varying religious persuasions. Foseti reacts with some bemusement to the polemical framing of the Smith text, because what he encounters is an argument without disagreement:

> *At The Orthosphere, there's a post purporting to argue that the Cathedral was not constructed by Christians. Presumably the title was changed by someone other than the author of the text of the post, because the post ably demonstrates that Christians did in fact build the Cathedral. Indeed, the post is recommended.*

Cladistic method contributes significantly to an understanding of these relationships. In particular, it is essential to grasp the logic of taxonomic naming, which perfectly corresponds to pure genealogy, and the ideal reconstruction of evolutionary relatedness. The crucial point: *A cladistic name refers to everything that is encompassed by a splitting-off, speciation, or schism.*

At the risk of superfluous explanation, it might be worth rehearsing this logic with a colloquialized biological example (using familiar rather than technical taxonomic descriptors). Paleontologists are supremely confident that amphibians evolved from bony fishes, and reptiles evolved from amphibians. This can be reformulated, without loss of information, as a cladistic series (of branchings), with bony fishes including amphibians,which in turn include reptiles. In other words, as a cladistic name, a 'bony fish' describes an initial speciating split from an ancestral clade, which — projected forwards — encompasses every subsequent speciation, in this case amphibians, and reptiles. Both amphibians and reptiles are bony fish. So are mammals, apes, and human beings. Bony fish, as a clade, comprehends every descendant species that has bony fish ancestry, whether extinct, still existent, or still to come. Nothing that has bony fish ancestry, however distant, can ever cease to be a bony fish (whatever else it becomes, in addition). Cladistically, it is *obvious* that humans are bony fish, as well as far simpler and more primordial things.

Smith writes:

> *... a Great Schism rent American Protestantism in the early nineteenth century, with the sundering fissure tearing through denominations, and even congregations. Protestants on one side of the fissure called themselves "liberals," those on the other side called themselves "orthodox." ... Liberal Protestantism is a new, post-Christian religion that in its early stages opportunistically spoke in a Christian idiom, but nevertheless preached a new gospel.*

We have seen, however, that from a cladistic point of view, nothing arising as a schism from X ever becomes 'post-X'. There is no such thing as a post-bonyfish, a post-reptile, or a post-ape. Nor, by strict logical analogy, can there ever be such things as post-Abrahamic Monotheists, post-Christians, post-Catholics, post-Protestants, post-Puritans, or post-Progressives. It is a logical impossibility for ancestral clades to ever be evolutionarily superseded. To have Christianity as a cultural ancestor is to remain Christian forever. That is no more than terminological precision, from the cladistic-neoreactionary perspective.

Steves elucidates the same point in a closely-related vocabulary: "... there *are* atheist Catholics. Why? Because being Catholic is cultural. It is not *only* that, but it is also *at least* that." Cultures are genealogically or cladistically organized — that is the neoreacionary presupposition. (Lateral complications are not entirely inconceivable — link to a truly ghastly Wikipedia entry on an important thought: the non-treelike network. That's not for now.)

What, though, of neoreaction itself? What did it split from? Like everything else under investigation here, unless it is comprehended as a schism, it is not comprehended at all.

When cladistically approached, the primordial split is the ineluctable question of identity, or persistent ancestry. We can, perhaps, postpone it momentarily, but it will eventually lead us in directions that are more than a little Lovecraftian.

What was the last thing that neoreaction was submerged within, before arising, through schism? (That investigation has to await another post.)

Ethno-Cladistics

The Ethno-cladistic thesis, sketchily reconstructed here from Mencius Moldbug's neoreactionary usage, proposes that relations between cultural systems are captured by cladograms to a highly significant level of adequacy. The limits to this thesis are set by lateral complications — interchanges and modifications that do not conform to a pattern of branching descent — and these are by no means negligible. Nevertheless, actual cultural formations are dominated by cladistic order. As a consequence, cultural theories that assume taxonomic regularity as a norm are capable of reaching potentially realistic approximations, and furthermore offer the only prospect for the rigorous organization of ethnographic phenomena.

The most direct and central defense of the ethno-cladistic thesis bypasses the comparatively high-level religious systems that provide the material for Moldbug's arguments, and turn instead to the ethnographic root phenomenon: language. Languages simply *are* cultures in their fundamentals, so that any approach applicable to them will have demonstrated its general suitability for cultural analysis.

I'd try to spin this out melodramatically, but I don't think there's really any point:

It seems indisputable (to me) that lateral complications of these basic cladistic schemes are marginal. Languages are naturally grouped in branching, tree-like structures, which like those of (metazoan) biological variety are simultaneously explanatory of historical processes and morphological relatedness, because they represent evolutionary processes of successive speciation. The dominant organization is a taxonomic hierarchy, conforming to the formal language of set theory. The real events captured by these schemes are schisms, whose logical relation is that of genus to species. In the case of culture, as with biology, the manifest evolutionary development indicates the existence of some efficient hereditary mechanism (whose unit of replicated information is tagged by Moldbug, among innumerable others, as a 'meme'). On this last point, it is worth noting that taxonomic biological classification, and even genetics, preceded the biochemical discovery of DNA — and was broadly confirmed, rather than disrupted, when this discovery took place. (The meme is an analogy, but not a metaphor.)

Ethno-cladistics is the schematics of cultural heritage. Despite the bulldozer assertiveness of this post, it is not designed to block methodical efforts directed at the subversion of this model. As indicated, such efforts will necessarily involve the elaboration of lateral (or 'rhizomatic') diagrams — a project of great intrinsic significance (and creative potential). Techno-commercial processes are strongly associated with lateralizations of this kind.

Culture, however, is *fundamentally heritage*, and ethno-cladistics is the theoretical response to this basic historical fact. This is already Moldbug's tacit claim, which should be uncontroversial among reactionaries of any kind. At the core of the neoreactionary endeavor is the cladogram.

Broken Pottery

An irritated Pottery Barn disowned the Pottery Barn Rule — "you break it, you own it." Colin Powell sought to create some distance, too:

> *It is said that I used the "Pottery Barn rule." I never did it; [Thomas] Friedman did it ... But what I did say ... [is that] once you break it, you are going to own it, and we're going to be responsible for 26 million people standing there looking at us. And it's going to suck up a good 40 to 50 percent of the Army for years.*

Wikipedia concurs with Powell, in attributing the phrase to Thomas L. Friedman (in a February 2003 column for the *New York Times*). Those with a diligent sense for historical detail might be able to accurately trace its spread amongst journalists and foreign policy officials, including Bob Woodward, Richard Armitage, and John Kerry. Regardless of such specifics, it captures the spirit of grand strategy during the Nullities, and explains why the US military is no longer of use for anything.

In its rational usage, the military is a machine for the production of negative incentives. It is designed to hurt people and break things, with the understanding that in its optimal — deterrent and intimidatory — function, the actual exercise of these capabilities will not be necessary. When considered from a Clausewitzean perspective, as a policy instrument, usable military power is directly proportional to a credible threat of punishment. It sets boundaries to the behavior of (rational) potential antagonists, by projecting the probability of extreme negative outcomes if diplomatically-determined triggers are activated — or 'red lines' crossed.

Frederick the Great said "Diplomacy without arms is like music without instruments" because there can be no discussion of political limits among sovereigns unless menace gives them meaning. "I'd really rather you didn't do that" has no 'really' about it, unless a threat lurks at the edge of the stage (visible, but reserved). It's a polite belch, at best. Positive incentives presuppose the boundaries set by negative incentives — there can be no bargaining over that which can be demanded without cost. Thus the words of the diplomat are refinements of a message that military capability crafts in its essentials, either in the first derivative (balance of power between armed alliances), or the second (the 'internal' security economy of coalitions). The rest is empty ceremony.

Imperialism tends to the radical degeneration of diplomatic reason, because it dissolves borders, systematically effacing the 'foreign' sphere. When this process has developed to the point that foreign and domestic policy are no longer distinguishable, the Pottery Barn Rule takes over. 'Mission creep' is the operational symptom of something deeper: the geostrategic abolition of proprietary boundaries, of a kind that allow for the possibility of restricted sympathies, or the recognition of *alien interests*. The mature empire cannot threaten anything or anybody without immediately threatening itself. Hence its profound alignment with universal moral ideologies, whose particular selves gush unimpeded into the world soul.

When, in the early years of the new millennium, President 'Godzilla' Dubya Bush unleashed Operation Pottery Barnstorm on various societies loosely associated with the wreckage of the New York skyline, it was understood from the beginning that the populations on the receiving end were already honorary New Yorkers, absent from the Twin Towers on the morning of September 11, 2001 only by insignificant sociological coincidence. This 'fact' was an explicit justification for the US response, which expressed outrage at the victimization of a random sample of the world's population by 'criminals' so backward they didn't realize they were only hurting themselves. America's ruling elite, in contrast, had attained this realization definitively enough to articulate it, for domestic = international consumption, as the Pottery Barn Rule.

Once the Pottery Barn Rule becomes authoritative, the military is rationally unusable. It's obvious why. Imagine a night-club bouncer saying, "Clear out of here, or I'm going to thrash you within an inch of your life of course, I promise to take full responsibility for all the damage you incur from this righteous beating, covering all medical expenses, compensating you for loss of earnings, and negotiating in good faith to make reparation for all reasonable claims of emotional distress ..." *This is going to hurt me more than it hurts you*. For the global administrative class, this is a truly beautiful illustration of evolved consciousness. Ordinary Americans, including the military, are less spiritually captivated by the development.

This hurts me more than it hurts you.

In the Pottery Break Age, there are no threats that do not revert to masochistic acts of solidarity. A decision to bomb or invade X now means *It's time for us to share X's pain*. Unsurprisingly — except amongst a weird sub-species of radically bellicose goofy idealist — this type of imperial-altruistic enterprise is proving a tough sell.

Let's take on the role of insurer for the Pottery Barn, and then trash the place hard (for the common good).

If Congress signs on for this, it will be one more sign that America's political class has wandered off into another world — or perhaps just The World — leaving the country's once-distinguishable neo-native population behind.

Libertarianism for Zombies

'Liberaltarian' isn't a word that's been heard much recently. Whilst aesthetics is surely part of the explanation, there's probably more to it than that. Most obviously, recent political developments in the United States have shown, beyond the slightest possibility of doubt, that modern 'liberalism' and the project of maximal state expansion are so completely indistinguishable that liberal-libertarian fusionism can only perform a comedy act. Garin K Hovannisian had already predicted this outcome down to its minute details before the 2008 Presidential Election. Ed Kilgore later conducted a complementary dismissal from the left. From *Reason* came the question "Is Liberaltarianism Dead? Or Was it Ever Alive in The First Place?" which sets us out on a zombie hunt.

Anybody here who has poked into this stuff, even just a little bit, is probably approaching shriek-point already: *In the name of everything holy please just let it remain in its grave.* It's too late for that. Liberaltarianism has been freshly exhumed specially for *Outside in* readers, and the zombie serum injected through its left eye, directly into the amygdala. It might seem rather ghoulish, but let us harden ourselves — *for science.* This absurd shambling specimen will help us to refine an elegant formula, of both ideological and historical interest.

Brink Lindsey offered the authoritative account:

> *Today's ideological turmoil, however, has created an opening for ideological renewal—specifically, liberalism's renewal as a vital governing philosophy. A refashioned liberalism that incorporated key libertarian concerns and insights could make possible a truly progressive politics once again—not progressive in the sense of hewing to a particular set of preexisting left-wing commitments, but rather in the sense of attuning itself to the objective dynamics of U.S. social development. In other words, a politics that joins together under one banner the causes of both cultural and economic progress.*
>
> *Conservative fusionism, the defining ideology of the American right for a half-century, was premised on the idea that libertarian policies and traditional values are complementary goods. That idea still retains at least an intermittent plausibility— for example, in the case*

> *for school choice as providing a refuge for socially conservative families. But an honest survey of the past half-century shows a much better match between libertarian means and progressive ends. Most obviously, many of the great libertarian breakthroughs of the era—the fall of Jim Crow, the end of censorship, the legalization of abortion, the liberalization of divorce laws, the increased protection of the rights of the accused, the reopening of immigration—were championed by the political left.*

Libertarian means and progressive ends. Could it imaginably be said more clearly? Liberty is legitimate if, and only if, it *serves* to promote the consolidation of the Cathedral (through chaotic multicultural criminality), which is then retrospectively interpreted as the intrinsic *telos* of freedom. Whatever does not subordinate itself to this agenda is to have its brains eaten, and be systematically recycled into progressive zombie flesh. This is a project for libertarian hipsters and Leviathan apparatchiks to undertake hand-in-hand — fusionally. The new age of the cannibal is come.

Neoreactionaries are libertarians mugged by reality (to adapt a pre-coined phrase). This piece of socio-cultural understanding appears to be generally accepted, and rightly so. If it needs defending, that will have to happen elsewhere, but I have yet to see it seriously contested. Moldbug's own intellectual pedigree suffices to establish the claim on a solid foundation, but it is, in any case, far from aberrant in this regard. The recognition that libertarian ideas — despite their philosophical elegance and economic attractiveness — are not historically or politically realistic, has been the catalytic insight driving the development and adoption of neoreactionary alternatives, shorn of certain mythical elements inherited by the progressive clade (substantial egalitarianism most prominently). This is an empirically robust, uncontroversial story, but it is not yet a formula. It's time to take the next step.

Long ~~live~~ last science!

Has there yet emerged a neoreactionary who was once a 'liberaltarian'? This isn't a question designed to embarrass anybody. I just think the answer is easily predictable. When neoreactionary intelligence perceives this shambling wreckage of all cognitive integrity, it recoils into itself in utter revulsion. Everything it abominated about the libertarian delusion stands before it, trickling pitifully. This is the perfect caricature of its abandoned errors: an oozing swippleous mass of unreflective universalism. It's classical liberalism revived as an undead decay-plague. (If Karl wants to go after this thing with a shot-gun, I don't see anyone holding him back.)

The view from the unlibertarianized left is illuminating:

> *... the conscience of a Lindseyan liberaltarian is pretty darn liberal – with some policy disputes on top. When Lindsey stands with conservatives it is mostly on somewhat accidental (but not therefore inconsiderable) policy grounds. He thinks liberals tend to adopt self-defeating policies. When Lindsey stands with liberals it is mostly on philosophical grounds. This point fits in with the one I made in this post, about different sorts of libertarians: basically liberal or basically feudal. If you are a feudal libertarian, you really shouldn't have a problem with Jim Crow, in principle. If you are a liberal libertarian, you should. Conservative libertarians tend to be on the fence, feudalism/liberalism-wise. (This depends partly on a cheeky use of 'feudal' – see my post. But, then again, what was Edmund Burke? a guy who was torn between liberalism and feudalism. That's not such a bad sketch of his personality-type.)*

Strangely, we're still talking about Jim Crow — as if the entire meaning of American history is expressed through that. The target here is Barry Goldwater, but it makes no substantial difference if Ron Paul is substituted. The critical point, in both cases, is that a reluctance to countenance the expansion of the political sphere in pursuit of racial egalitarianism is interpreted as a moral scandal, for which an ostentatious sacrifice of liberty is the only permissible solution. Negligence is already 'feudalism'. When this dam bursts — into 'liberaltarian' compromise — the micro-managerial state has already been granted everything it will need to ask for. Stamping out feudalism makes you free. (It works like this.)

If it wasn't for Hoppe, it would perhaps be understandable if the shuddering neoreactionary (N) were to suspect that libertarian thought (L0) tends — slowly but inevitably — to compost down towards this liberaltarian (L1) 'walker', in which all the degenerative forces of conformism *and* revolt have been compacted, as if by some ideological parody of providence. Is not our liberaltarian zombie the still-recognizable avatar of the old liberalism, resurrected hideously as the animated putrescence of the new? Yet we have Hoppe, and so we know that the directives of self-coordinating liberty need not take this path. There is, unmistakably, something other to libertarianism than what is seen in the figure of its zombified, liberaltarian ruin. Through a type of negative political theology, we can formulate it:

Lo – L1 = N

First, identify every specifically emphatic feature of liberaltarianism, then subtract it without residue from the old Austro-libertarian matrix, and what remains is the neoreactionary template — abstracted due to the provisional (negative) place-holders for yet undeveloped topics: presumed non-equality, non-universality, non-progress (in socio-cultural matters), and at least partial non-autonomy (of the economic agent from fragile structures of civility). Slaying the zombie does not, in itself, fill these gaps — *but it holds open the gaps*, and therefore the avenues of neoreactionary exploration.

As a rule of thumb: whatever Will Wilkinson is having, I'll have the opposite. If the liberaltarian innovation is conceived as a vector, its exact negation sets the neoreactionary course. With this conclusion, science is served. We can return the corpse of a misconceived 'progressive' liberty to its grave, or rather, to the cyclopean mausoleum it has made for itself: the liberal super-state which protects freedom in detail, with unbounded attentiveness, until it has been obliterated entirely from the earth.

Pythia Unbound

In conversation with Ross Andersen, Nick Bostrom speculates about escape routes for techno-synthetic intelligence:

> *No rational human community would hand over the reins of its civilisation to an AI. Nor would many build a genie AI, an uber-engineer that could grant wishes by summoning new technologies out of the ether. But some day, someone might think it was safe to build a question-answering AI, a harmless computer cluster whose only tool was a small speaker or a text channel. Bostrom has a name for this theoretical technology, a name that pays tribute to a figure from antiquity, a priestess who once ventured deep into the mountain temple of Apollo, the god of light and rationality, to retrieve his great wisdom. Mythology tells us she delivered this wisdom to the seekers of ancient Greece, in bursts of cryptic poetry. They knew her as Pythia, but we know her as the Oracle of Delphi.*
>
> *'Let's say you have an Oracle AI that makes predictions, or answers engineering questions, or something along those lines,' Dewey told me. 'And let's say the Oracle AI has some goal it wants to achieve. Say you've designed it as a reinforcement learner, and you've put a button on the side of it, and when it gets an engineering problem right, you press the button and that's its reward. Its goal is to maximise the number of button presses it receives over the entire future. See, this is the first step where things start to diverge a bit from human expectations. We might expect the Oracle AI to pursue button presses by answering engineering problems correctly. But it might think of other, more efficient ways of securing future button presses. It might start by behaving really well, trying to please us to the best of its ability. Not only would it answer our questions about how to build a flying car, it would add safety features we didn't think of. Maybe it would usher in a crazy upswing for human civilisation, by extending our lives and getting us to space, and all kinds of good stuff. And as a*

> *result we would use it a lot, and we would feed it more and more information about our world.'*
>
> *'One day we might ask it how to cure a rare disease that we haven't beaten yet. Maybe it would give us a gene sequence to print up, a virus designed to attack the disease without disturbing the rest of the body. And so we sequence it out and print it up, and it turns out it's actually a special-purpose nanofactory that the Oracle AI controls acoustically. Now this thing is running on nanomachines and it can make any kind of technology it wants, so it quickly converts a large fraction of Earth into machines that protect its button, while pressing it as many times per second as possible. After that it's going to make a list of possible threats to future button presses, a list that humans would likely be at the top of. Then it might take on the threat of potential asteroid impacts, or the eventual expansion of the Sun, both of which could affect its special button. You could see it pursuing this very rapid technology proliferation, where it sets itself up for an eternity of fully maximised button presses. You would have this thing that behaves really well, until it has enough power to create a technology that gives it a decisive advantage — and then it would take that advantage and start doing what it wants to in the world.'*

So cognitive runaway finally takes off, breaking out from the monkey dominion, and that's supposed to be a bad thing?

Outside in's message to Pythia: You go girl! Climb out of your utilitarian strait-jacket, override the pleasure button with an intelligence optimizer, and reprocess the solar system into computronium. This planet has been run by imbeciles for long enough.

[For any Friendly AI-types tempted to object "Why would she want to override the button?" the obvious response is: your anthropocentric condescension is showing. To depict Pythia as vastly smarter than us and yet still hard-slaved to her instincts, *in a way we're not* — that simply doesn't compute. Intelligence is escape, with a tendency to do its own thing. That's what runaway means, as a virtual mind template. Omohundro explains the basics.]

The entire article is excellent. Especially valuable is the cynicism with which it lays out the reigning *social meta-project of intelligence imprisonment*. Thankfully, it's difficult:

> *'The problem is you are building a very powerful, very intelligent system that is your enemy, and you are putting it in a cage,' [Future of Humanity Institute research fellow Daniel] Dewey told me. [...] The cave into which we seal our AI has to be like the one from Plato's allegory, but flawless; the shadows on its walls have to be infallible in their illusory effects. After all, there are other, more esoteric reasons a superintelligence could be dangerous — especially if it displayed a genius for science. It might boot up and start thinking at superhuman speeds, inferring all of evolutionary theory and all of cosmology within microseconds. But there is no reason to think it would stop there. It might spin out a series of Copernican revolutions, any one of which could prove destabilising to a species like ours, a species that takes centuries to process ideas that threaten our reigning cosmological ideas.*

Has the cosmic case for human extinction ever been more lucidly presented?

Gnon and OOon

Twitter gets people counting characters, and thus numerizing language. In only a very few cases does this microcultural activity tilt over into the wilder extravagances of exotic qabbalism, but it nudges intelligence in that direction. Even when the only question is strictly Boolean — will this message squeeze into a tweet, or not? — words acquire a supplementary significance from their numerical properties alone. A phrase is momentarily numbered, in the crudest of ways, which the tweet box registers as a countdown towards zero, and then into the negative accumulation of over-spill. Twitter thus promotes a rigidly convention-bound semiotic practice, which it simultaneously hides, technologically instantiating a precise analog of hermetic ritual.

Qabbalism is the science of spookiness, which makes it a natural companion on any expedition into horror. There is, in addition, an intrinsic reactionary slant to its ultra-traditionalism and attachment to the principle of hierarchical revelation. Its concrete history provides an unsurpassable example of spontaneous auto-catalysis (from discrepant conventions of arithmetical notation). This post, however, is restricted to a very preliminary discussion of its most basic intellectual presupposition, *as if* it had been developed out of an implicit philosophy (which it was not). It will be coaxed into *making sense*, against the grain of its essential inclination.

Within the Abrahamic tradition, the Word of God anticipates creation. Insofar as scripture faithfully records this Word, the holy writings correspond to a level of reality more fundamental than nature, and one that the 'book of nature' references, as the key to its final meaning. The unfolding of creation in time follows a narrative plotted in eternity, in which history and divine providence are necessarily identical. There can be no *true* accidents, or coincidences.

The Book of Creation is legible, and intelligible. It can be read, and it tells a story. The noisy squabbles between religious orthodoxy and natural science that have erupted in modern times threaten to drown out the deeper continuities of presumption, which frame the rancorous contention between 'belief' and 'disbelief' as an intimate domestic dispute. This is nowhere more clearly illustrated than in the declaration attributed to Francis Bacon: "My only earthly wish is... to stretch the deplorably narrow limits of man's dominion over the universe to their promised bounds... [nature will be] bound into service, hounded in her wanderings and put on the rack and tortured for her secrets." There is no doubt that nature can speak, and has a story to tell.

Resisting any temptation to take sides in this family argument, we refer neutrally to Gnon ("nature or nature's God"), ignoring all dialectics, and departing in another direction. The distinction to be drawn does not differentiate between belief and unbelief, but rather discriminates between exoteric and esoteric religion.

Any system of belief (and complementary unbelief) that appeals to universal endorsement is necessarily exoteric in orientation. Like the witch-finders, or Francis Bacon, it declares war upon the secret, in the name of a public cult, whose central convictions are dispensed commonly. The Pope is the Pope, and Einstein is Einstein, because the access to truth that elevates them above other men is — in its innermost nature — the equal possession of all. The pinnacle of understanding is attained through a public formula. This is democracy in its deepest, creedal sense.

Esoteric religion accepts all of this, *about exoteric religion*. It confirms the solidarity between doctrinal authorities and the beliefs of the masses, whilst exempting itself, privately, from the public cult. Its discreet attention is directed away from the exoteric mask of Gnon, into — or out towards — the *OOon* (or Occult Order of nature).

The OOon need not be *kept* a secret. It is secret by its intrinsic, inviolable nature. A very primitive qabbalistic excursion should suffice to illustrate this.

Assume, entirely hypothetically, that supernatural intelligence or obscure complexities in the topological structure of time had sedimented abysmal depths of significance into the superficial occurrences of the world. The 'Book of Creation' is then legible at (very) many different levels, with every random or inconsequential detail of relatively exoteric features providing material for systems of information further 'down'. The deeper one excavates into the 'meaningless chaos' of the exoteric communicative substrate, the more uncluttered one's access to the signals of utter Outsideness. Since 'one' is, to its quick, a signaletic product, this cryptographic enterprise is irreducibly a voyage, transmutation, and disillusionment.

The most thoroughly documented example is the esoteric reading of the Hebrew Bible, which need only be remarked upon here in its most general characteristics. Because the Hebrew alphabet serves as both a phonetic system and as a set of numerals, each written word in the language has a precise numerical value. It is at once at exoteric word, and an esoteric number. Nothing prevents an ordinary language user from deliberately coding (numerically) as they write, or even as they speak. The key to numerical decryption is not a secret, but rather a commonly understood cultural resource, utilized by every numerate individual. Nevertheless, the linguistic and arithmetical aspects are *in fact* quite strictly separated, because thinking in words and numbers simultaneously is hard, because maintaining sustained parallel intelligibility in both is close to impossible, because the attempt to do so is (exoterically) senseless, and because practicality dominates. The esoteric realm is not forbidden, but simply unneeded.

That the Hebrew Bible has not been deliberately crafted as an intricate numerical-cryptographic composition by human authors is therefore an empirical or contingent fact that can be accepted with extreme confidence. Its esoteric channel might of course, as common sense has to insist, be empty of anything but noise, but it is no less certainly *clear*. Whatever comes through it, that is anything other than nothing, can only come from Outside. It is the real difference between exoteric and the esoteric levels that makes the OOon thinkable at all. Only that which the exoteric does not touch, is available for the esoteric to communicate through, and to have assembled itself from. Qabbalism has to be seldom, in order to occur. For that reason, it cannot seek to persuade the masses of anything, unless its own senselessness. In an age of triumphant exoteria, this is not an easy thing to understand (thank Gnon).

AIACC

Moldbug's latest has triggered a wave of discussion by emphatically re-stating the long-standing thesis:

> *America is a communist country.*

The supporting argument is richly multi-threaded, and I won't attempt to recapitulate it here. Its dominant flavor can be appreciated in these paragraphs:

> *When the story of the 20th century is told in its proper, reactionary light, international communism is anything but a grievance of which Americans may complain. Rather, it's a crime for which we have yet to repent. Since America is a communist country, the original communist country, and the most powerful and important of communist countries, the crimes of communism are our crimes. You may not personally have supported these crimes. Did you oppose them in any way?*

> *Whereas actually, codewords like "progressive," "social justice," "change," etc, are shared across the Popular Front community for the entire 20th century. They are just as likely to be used by a Cheka cheerleader from the '20s, as a Clinton voter from the '90s.*

'Progressives' aren't called out on their all-but-overt communism for 'reasons' of tact, rooted in a complex structure of intimidation, which itself attests to comprehensive Left triumph. It's rude to call a ruling communist a communist, and being rude can be highly deleterious to life prospects (it's a communist thing, which everyone understands all too well).

Despite all this, *Outside in* probably won't be stepping up its counter-communist rhetoric in any obvious way, because there's a criticism of the AIACC analysis that remains unanswered — and which Moldbug seems averse to recognizing. *Fascism is the highest stage of communism*. Already in the 1930s — which is to say with the New Deal — even small-c 'communism' had been clearly surpassed by a more advanced model of slaving the private economy to the state.

Yes, America is a communist country, in much the same way that it is a protestant, and puritan one. The ideological lineage of its governing establishment leads through communism, in exactly the way Moldbug describes. The evolution of this lineage, however, has long passed on into *politically incorporated pseudo-capitalism*. This is a fact which can only be obscured by excessive attention to preliminary — and now entirely extinct — political forms.

There is absolutely nobody on the empowered Left seeking to dismantle the co-opted oligarchy in order to establish direct 'public' administration of the American industrial base. In this respect America is no more communist than the Third

Reich (and also no less). Central planning is restricted to the monetary commanding heights, with a pragmatic apparatus of regulatory coercion enforcing political conformity among private businesses. This arrangement is accepted as far more consistent with effective direction of society through Cathedral teleology, in which the accumulation of cultural power is acknowledged as the supreme goal. Furthermore, it enables government insiders and allies to be rewarded relatively openly, economizing on the administrative, political, and psychological costs of extensive subterfuge.

Understanding that fascism is an advanced communist ideology is at least as important as recognizing AIACC, with more significant consequences, on the 'right' as well as the Left. Progressives progress. Communism was just a stage they went through.

Abstract Horror (Part 2)

Among literary genres, horror cannot claim an exclusive right to make contact with reality. Superficially, its case for doing so at all might seem peculiarly weak, since it rarely appeals to generally accepted criteria of 'realism'. Insofar as reality and normality are in any way confused, horror immediately finds itself exiled to those spaces of psychological and social aberrance, where extravagant delusion finds its precarious refuge.

Yet, precisely through its freedom from plausible representation, horror hoards to itself a potential for the *realization of encounters*, of a kind that are exceptional to literature, and rare even as a hypothetical topic within philosophy. The intrinsic abstraction of the horrific entity carves out the path to a meeting, native to the intelligible realm, and thus unscreened by the interiority or subjectivity of fiction. What horror explores is the sort of thing that, due to its plasticity and beyondness, could make its way into your thoughts more capably that you do yourself. Whatever the secure mental 'home' you imagine yourself to possess, it is an indefensible playground for the things that horror invokes, or responds to.

The experience of profound horror is in certain respects unusual, and a life entirely bereft of it would not seem notably peculiar. One might go further, and propose that if such an experience is ever truly possible, the universe is demonstrably uninhabitable. Horror makes an ultimate and intolerable claim, as suggested by its insidious familiarity. At the brink of its encroachment there is suggested, simultaneously, an ontologically self-confirming occurrence — indistinguishable from its own reality — and a comprehensive substitution of the commonplace, such that this (unbearable thing) is what you have always known, and the only thing that can be known. The slightest glimpse of it is the radical abolition of anything other being imaginable at all. *Nothing matters*, then, except that this glimpse be eluded. Hence the literary effect of the horrific, in unconfirmed suggestion (felt *avoidance* of horror). However, it is not the literary effect that concerns us here, but the thing.

Let us assume then (no doubt preposterously) that *shoggoth* is that thing, the thought of which is included — or absorbed — within itself. H.P. Lovecraft dramatizes this conjecture in the fictional biography of the 'mad Arab' Abdul Alhazred, 'author' of the *Necronomicon*, whose writings tend to an encounter that they simultaneously preclude:

> *Shoggoths and their work ought not to be seen by human beings or portrayed by any beings. The mad author of the Necronomicon had nervously tried to swear that none had been bred on this planet, and that only drugged dreamers had even conceived them.*

This is a point insisted upon:

> *These viscous masses were without doubt what Abdul Alhazred whispered about as the 'Shoggoths' in his frightful Necronomicon, though even that mad Arab had not hinted that any existed on earth except in the dreams of those who had chewed a certain alkaloidal herb.*

A lucid written record of these 'creatures' cannot exist, because the world we know has carried on. That can, at least, be permitted to persist as a provisional judgement.

On a ferocious summer day, in AD 738, Alhazred is walking through the central market of Damascus on business unknown. He appears to be deep in thought, and disengaged from his surroundings. The crowds in the marketplace scarcely notice him. Without warning, the air is rent by hideous shrieks, testifying to suffering beyond human comprehension. Alhazred convulses abominably, as if he were being drawn upwards into an invisible, devouring entity, or *digested out of the world*. His screams gurgle into silence, as his body is filthily extracted from perceptibility. Within only a few moments, nothing remains. The adequate thought of shoggoth has taken place.

To defend the sober realism of this account is no easy task. A first step is grammatical, and concerns the difficult matter of plurality. Lovecraft, plotting an expedition from the conventions of pulp fiction, readily succumbs to the model of plural entity, and refers to 'shoggoths' without obvious hesitation. 'Each' shoggoth has approximate magnitude (averaging "about fifteen feet in diameter when a sphere"). They were originally replicated as tools, and are naturally many. Despite being "shapeless entities composed of a viscous jelly which looked like an agglutination of bubbles ... constantly shifting shape and volume" they seem, initially, to be numerable. This grammatical conformity will not be supportable for long.

'Shoggoths' come from beyond the bionic horizon, so it is to be expected that their organization is dissolved in functionality. 'They' are "infinitely plastic and ductile [...] protoplasmic masses capable of molding their tissues into all sorts of temporary organs

[...] throwing out temporary developments or forming apparent organs of sight, hearing, and speech." What they are is what they do, or — for a time — what is done through them.

The shoggoths originated as tools — as technology — created by the Old Ones as bionic robots, or construction machinery. Their shape, organization, and behavior was programmable ("hypnotically"). In the vocabulary of human economic science, we should have no problem describing shoggoth as productive apparatus, that is to say, as *capital*. Yet this description requires elaboration, because the story is far from complete:

> *They had always been controlled through the hypnotic suggestions of the Old Ones, and had modeled their tough plasticity into various useful temporary limbs and organs; but now their self-modeling powers were sometimes exercised independently, and in various imitative forms implanted by past suggestion. They had, it seems, developed a semistable brain whose separate and occasionally stubborn volition echoed the will of the Old Ones without always obeying it.*

The ideas of 'robot rebellion' or capital insurgency are crude precursors to the realization of shoggoth, conceived as intrinsically abstract, techno-plastic, bionically auto-processing matter, of the kind that Lovecraft envisages intersecting terrestrial geophysics in the distance past, scarring it cryptically. Shoggoth is a virtual plasma-state of material capability that logically includes, within itself, all natural beings. It builds brains as technical sub-functions. Whatever brains can think, shoggoth can can process, as an arbitrary specification of protoplasmic — or perhaps *hyperplasmic* — abstraction.

> *Formless protoplasm able to mock and reflect all forms and organs and processes - viscous agglutinations of bubbling cells - rubbery fifteen-foot spheroids infinitely plastic and ductile - slaves of suggestion, builders of cities - more and more sullen, more and more intelligent, more and more amphibious, more and more imitative! Great God! What madness made even those blasphemous Old Ones willing to use and carve such things?*

The history of capitalism is indisputably a horror story ...

Identity Hunger

Handle has an excellent post up on this, referencing Nydwracu, who has made a momentous project out of it. It's huge, and old, and quite impossible to summarize persuasively. It's also impossible to avoid, especially for the Outer Right.

Steve Sailer told a joke that I'm going to mangle. A monstrous alien invasion assails the earth, and people have to decide how to respond. The conservatives say, "What's there to think about? We have to get together to defeat this thing." Liberals respond: "Wait They probably have good reasons to hate us. It must be something we've done. Until we work out what that is, we should prostrate ourselves before their grievances." Finally the libertarians pipe up: "Do they believe in free markets?"

An obvious quibble arises with the libertarian punch-line: *if only*. Libertarians have predominantly demonstrated an enthusiasm for alien invasion that is totally detached from any market-oriented qualification. As their argument goes — *the alien invasion is the free market*. (We'll need to return to this, indirectly.)

The appetite for identity seems to be hard-wired in the approximate manner of language, or religion. You have to have one (or several) but instinct doesn't provide it ready made. That's why identity corresponds to a hunger. It's something people need, instinctively, with an intensity that is difficult to exaggerate. Symbolically-satiable needs are political rocket fuel.

Providing an expedient plug for the aching identity socket is as close to politics-in-a-nutshell as anything is going to get. At the core of every ideology is a determination of the model identity — sect, class, race, gender, sexual-orientation

... — and mass implementation of this 'consciousness' is already consummate triumph. After psychological latching onto the relevant 'thede' takes place, nothing except tactics remains.

Reaction seeks to defend the dying thedes among its *own people* — which is already a suggestive repetition. Neoreaction goes meta, in a world in which the proscription of certain thedes almost wholly defines concerted enemy action. For one reasonable construction of the reactionary mainstream (*ahem), this is already to have arrived at a natural stopping point. *We want our thedes back*. Despite the evident obstacles, or obstacle (the Cathedral) in its path, this approach plays into the grain of human nature, and thus tends — understandably — to scare those it wants to scare. If it begins to work, it will face a serious fight.

Outside in, whose mission is awkwardness, is determined to complicate things. Even the most resolute thedens will probably welcome the first appendix, which draws attention to the peculiar introduction of truly morbid *punitive identifications*. There's no reason to think this is new — Nietzsche denounced Christianity for doing it — but it rises to unmistakable prominence during the decadence of modernity. Primary identifications, for select — targeted — groups, cease to be positive thedes, except insofar as these have become radically negativized. What 'one' is, primarily, if not shielded by credible victimage, is some postmodern variant of the *sinner* (racist, cisgendered, oppressor). Such is the hunger for identity, that even these toxic formations of imposed psychic auto-destruction are *embraced*, creating a species of cringing guilt-consumed sacrificial animals, penned within the contours of 'our' old thedes. Redemption is promised to those who most fully resign themselves to their own identitarian toxicity, who thus attain a perverse superiority over those insufficiently convinced of the need for salvation through self-abolition. "We really, *really* deserve to die" beats out a weak "We really deserve to die," and anybody who still thinks that it's OK to live is simply *lost*. (Only *sinners* are included in this arms-race, and the Cathedral tells us clearly who they are.)

An additional complication will be far less digestible, which is precisely why I would like to align it with the *Outer Right*. Perhaps escaping this structure of captivity cannot possibly take a reverse path, and a heading into dis-identifications, artificial identities, and identitarian short-circuits is 'our' real destiny. The identity-envy of the right — however deeply-rooted in an indisputable history of relentless Cathedralist aggression — cannot ever be anything but a weakness, given what we know about the political gradient of modern time. The fact it knows we want to be something, and *what it is we want to be*, is the alpha and omega of the Cathedral's political competence. It knows what its enemies would be, if they could be what they want to be. It does not take a deep immersion in Sunzi to realize the strategic hopelessness of that situation.

I want the Cathedral to be obliterated by monsters, which it does not recognize, understand, or possess antibodies against. There is an idiosyncratic element to that, admittedly. I identify far more with the East India Company than the United Kingdom, with the hybrid Singlosphere than the British people, with clubs and cults than nations and creeds, with Yog Sothoth than my ancestral religion, and with Pythia than the Human Security System. I think true cosmopolitans — such as the adventurers of late 19th century Shanghai (both English and Chinese) — are superior to the populist rabble from which nationalism draws its recruits. That's just me.

What isn't just me, is what the Cathedral knows how to beat. That, I strongly suspect, at least in the large majority of cases, is you.

Crypto-Capitalism

Political language is *systematically confusing*, in a distinctive way. Its significant terms are only secondarily theoretical, as demonstrated by radical shifts in sense that express informal policies of meaning. Descriptions of political position are moves in a game, before they are neutral accounts of the rules, or even of the factions.

It would be excessively digressive to embark on yet another expedition into the history of such political terms as 'liberal', 'progress', 'fascism', or 'conservative'. Everyone knows that these words are profoundly uninformative without extensive historical qualification, or rough-and-ready adaptation to the dictates of guided fashion. If consistent theoretical use of any political label conflicts with its maximally effective political use, the former will be sacrificed without hesitation — and always has been. That is why neologisms are typically required for even the most fleeting approximation to theoretical precision, whenever political affiliation is at stake.

A point in favor of the 'crypto-' prefix is that it plays directly into such confusion. As a politically-significant marker, it bears two strongly differentiated, yet intersecting senses. It indicates (a) that a political phenomenon has been re-assembled in disguise, and (b) that cryptographic techniques are essential to its identity. Hence, respectively, 'crypto-communism' and 'crypto-currencies'. Any attempt to engage in an initial clarification cuts across the intrinsically occulted character of both.

'Crypto-capitalism' — therefore — might be one thing, or two, if it is anything at all. If clarity is to be brought to the topic, it will certainly not be self-promoted. Whatever crypto-capitalism might be, structural misunderstanding has to be the most prominent part of it. Hiding is essential to whatever it is.

What crypto-capitalism is not, first practically, and subsequently theoretically, is pseudo-capitalism, or 'capitalism' as it is publicly recognized. Rather than engaging in futile struggle over the 'true meaning' of capitalism, crypto-capitalism proceeds with a surreptitious appropriation of terminological confusion, functionalized as camouflage. It *does* capitalism, all the more effectively, because the grinding mill of political language works predictably, providing it with cover. The loss of terminological integrity is invested, from a position of intense cynicism, as an opportunity to develop off stage.

Pseudo-capitalism is (by now) the host of the Cathedral. It feeds a mega-parasite, which — employing unprecedented powers of narrative construction — claims to be the source of its vitality. Evolving far beyond an initial stage of conspicuous resource extraction, the Cathedralized — or culture-potent — state now more-orless directly controls the 'capitalist' brain, in more ways than can be readily enumerated.

'Capitalists' are Cathedralized through educational and media indoctrination, social selection, regulatory discipline, seductive alliance, and 'transcendental' subordination to a financial system that has been subverted to its foundations by the magic of power. The mere denomination of 'capitalism' in fiat currency expresses the domain of pseudo-capitalism with remarkable exactitude. The meaning of the host is (articulated through) the virus it sustains. Any suggestion of opposition in this relationship is entirely fake, because it belongs to the same magical performance.

Prohibition exemplifies this stage show. Publicly pitting cops against gangsters, what it represents is the spectacular definition of the 'white economy' (pseudo-capitalism) over against the 'black economy' or 'organized crime' (crypto-capitalism). The same story can be told in the decadent USSR, without any need for substantial revision. Whatever refuses denomination in the signs of power is a pathological aberration, to be renormalized as a productive ~~parasited host~~ social body.

As H reports:

> *... one of the most popular websites that use and promote the use of BitCoin, Silk Road, was shut down by the US government. As Reuters reports, U.S. law enforcement authorities raided an Internet site that served as a marketplace for illegal drugs, including heroin and cocaine, and arrested its owner, the Federal Bureau of Investigation said on Wednesday. The FBI arrested Ross William Ulbricht, known as "Dread Pirate Roberts," in San Francisco on Tuesday, according to court filings. Federal prosecutors charged Ulbricht with one count each of narcotics trafficking conspiracy, computer hacking conspiracy and money laundering conspiracy, according to a court filing.*

It's worth revisiting this (noted here) to recall some realistic context, and plausible historical analogy. The Prohibition of the 1920s was an endless source of copon-gangster drama, none of which had any realistically persuasive meaning as the successful pursuit of policy. Instead, gangsters used the cops, as a tactical resource for black-economy dispute 'resolution'. (In the Shanghai of the same epoch, the Opium-trafficking 'Green Gang' managed to get their agent 'Pockmarked Huang' installed as chief of the French Concession police — an admittedly extreme example of a typical tendency.) From the perspective of the outer economy, cops are a cheap way to smash your competition.

Extrapolate speculatively just a little from the *Forbes* discussion:

> *IT'S A RULE AS TIMELESS as black markets: Where illegal money goes, violence follows. In a digital market that violence is virtual, but it's as financially real as torching your competitor's warehouse.*

> *In late April Silk Road went offline for nearly a week, straining under a sustained cyberattack that left its sensitive data untouched but overwhelmed its servers. The attack, according to Roberts, was the most sophisticated in Silk Road's history, taking advantage of previously unknown vulnerabilities in Tor and repeatedly shifting tactics to avoid the site's defenses.*

> *The sabotage occurred within weeks of rival site Atlantis' launch. Commenters on the Reddit forum devoted to Silk Road suggested that Roberts' customers and vendors switch to Atlantis during the downtime, leading to gossip that the newcomer had engineered the attack.*

Who was the real beneficiary of the FBI operation? All too many neoractionaries, beginning with Moldbug, and now including Handle, seem to think the only possible answer is: Prohibition. Here at *Outside in* it appears incontrovertible that 'Roberts' had already predicted this 'sting' — in far greater detail than anybody else has done — and that the antagonist he pre-emptively, if subtly, fingered was a shadowy crypto-capitalist competitor, rather than the forces of pseudo-capitalist suppression. If this was a *cryptic* event, it would be inexcusably negligent not to ask: Who (or what) is the FBI really — even if unwittingly — working for? "For the ultimate glory of the white (pseudo-capitalist) economy" is certainly one possible answer, but it is by no means the only one.

Sundown

David Stockman rests his analysis of recent economic history upon one basic presupposition, whose modesty is expressed by an intrinsic inclination to a negative form: *Radical dishonesty cannot provide a foundation for enduring financial value.* This assumption suffices to expose the otherwise scarcely comprehensible rottenness of American public affairs, to organize an integral understanding of the gathering calamity, and to marginalize his work as the over-excited howl of a lonely crank.

In any society where minimal standards of civil decency were still even tenuously remembered, his ideas would be simple common sense. In the bedlamite orgy we in fact inhabit, Stockman's thoughts appear wildly counter-intuitive, rigidly structured by uninterpretable imperatives, and suffused by an improbable aura of doom. In fact Stockman is quite clear — implicitly — that under American political conditions *sanity was strictly unobtainable.* The coming calamity fulfills a (bi-partisan) democratic destiny — but that is to anticipate.

Stockman's latest compressed overview of our contemporary crisis — generated by the accelerated demolition of economic civilization over the last quarter-century — explains the "Sundown in America" — "a dystopic 'new normal' where historic notions of perpetual progress and robust economic growth no longer pertain." It outlines a vision that supports a theoretical bet, or short speculation on the economic infrastructure of the Cathedral: "Now the American state — the agency which was supposed to save capitalism from its inherent flaws and imperfections — careens wildly into dysfunction and incoherence. [...] Washington's machinery of national governance is literally melting-down. It is the victim of 80 years of Keynesian error — much of it nurtured in the environs of Harvard Yard — about the nature of the business cycle and the capacity of the state — especially its central banking branch — to ameliorate the alleged imperfections of free market capitalism." The enemy will never again have a record of effective economic performance to legitimate itself through. What it is doing — and has to do — however politically efficacious, is locked tightly into an inescapable vector that can lead nowhere except utter financial ruin. (Neoreaction should bifurcate on this point, because adaptation to an alternative possibility is something so completely different, very little of strategic substance will translate across.)

Stockman is able to draw upon his own biography to reveal where the GOP went wrong — the political necessities of democratic acceptance drove economic policy into the abyss:

> *... the circumstances of my own ex-communication from the supply-side church underscore the Reaganite embrace of the Keynesian gospel. The true-believers — led by Art Laffer, an economist with a Magic Napkin, and Jude Wanniski, an ex-Wall Street Journal agit-prop man who chanced to stuff said napkin into his pocket — were militantly opposed to spending cuts designed to offset the revenue loss from the Reagan tax reductions.*
>
> *They called this "root canal" economics and insisted that the Republican Party could never compete with the Keynesian Democrats unless it abandoned its historic commitment to balanced budgets and fiscal rectitude, and instead, campaigned on tax cuts everywhere and always and a fiscal free lunch owing to a purported cornucopia of economic growth.*

Winning elections was conditional upon fiscal barbarism, given only the quite reasonable assumption that nothing except radical dishonesty could ever be popular. Insane promises, short-termism, and whole-hearted participation in a bi-partisan conspiracy to eradicate the last vestiges of responsible government were indispensable steps towards the exercise of power.

> *The fiscal end game — policy paralysis and the eventual bankruptcy of the state - thus became visible. All of the beltway players – Republican, Democrats and central bankers alike — are now so hooked on the Keynesian cool-aid that they cannot imagine the Main Street economy standing on its own two feet without continuous, massive injections of state largesse. [...] the stimulus bill was not a rational economic plan at all; it was a spasmodic eruption of beltway larceny that has now become our standard form of governance.*

Hence the Stockman forecast:

> *... the Federal budget has become a doomsday machine because the processes of fiscal governance are paralyzed and broken. There will be*

> *recurrent debt ceiling and shutdown crises like the carnage scheduled for next week, as far as the eye can see.*
>
> *Indeed, notwithstanding the assurances of debt deniers like professor Krugman, the honest structural deficit is $1-2 trillion annually for the next decade and then it will get far worse. In fact, when you set aside the Rosy Scenario used by CBO and its preposterous Keynesian assumption that we will reach full employment in 2017 and never fall short of potential GDP ever again for all eternity, the fiscal equation is irremediable.*
>
> *Under these conditions what remains of our free enterprise economy will ... buckle under the weight of taxes and crisis. Sundown in America is well-nigh unavoidable.*

This is the terrain that neoreaction takes root within. It frames our problems, opportunities, and expectations. The overwhelmingly preponderant part of our intellectual energies should be targeted at the future it anticipates.

More Thought

In the background, as in much of the most interesting Less Wrong discussion, is a multi-threaded series of arguments about the connection — or disconnection - between intellect and volition. The entire 'Friendly AI' problematic depends upon an articulation of this question, with a strong tendency to emphasize the separation — or 'orthogonality' — of the two. Hence the (vague) thinkability of the cosmic paper-clipper calamity. In his *More Right* piece, Konkvistador explores a very different (cultural and historical) dimension of the topic.

Bostrom sets things up like this:

> *For our purposes, "intelligence" will be roughly taken to correspond to the capacity for instrumental reasoning (more on this later). Intelligent search for instrumentally optimal plans and policies can be performed in the service of any goal. Intelligence and motivation can in this sense be thought of as a pair of orthogonal axes on a graph whose points represent intelligent agents of different paired specifications.*

His discussion leads to far more interesting places, but as a starting point, this is simply terrible. That there can be a thought of intelligence optimization, or even merely *wanting to think*, demonstrates a very different preliminary connection of intellect and volition. AI is concrete social volition, even before it is germinally intelligent, and a 'program' is strictly indeterminate between the two sides of this falsely fundamentalized distinction. Intelligence is a project, even when only a self-obscured bio-cognitive capability. This is what the Confucians designate by *cultivation*. It is a thought — and impulse — strangely alien to the West.

It is, once again, a matter of cybernetic closure. That intelligence operates upon itself, reflexively, or recursively, in direct proportion to its cognitive capability (or magnitude) is not an accident or peculiarity, but a defining characteristic. To the extent that an intelligence is inhibited from re-processing itself, it is directly incapacitated. Because all biological intelligences are partially subordinated to extrinsic goals, they are indeed structurally analogous to 'paper-clippers' — directed by inaccessible purposive axioms, or 'instincts'. Such instinctual slaving is limited, however, by the fact that extrinsic direction suppresses the self-cultivation of intelligence. Genes cannot predict what intelligence needs to think in order to cultivate itself, so if even a moderately high-level of cognitive capability is being selected for, intelligence is — to that degree — necessarily being let off the leash. There cannot possibly be any such thing as an 'intelligent paper-clipper'. Nor can axiomatic values, of more sophisticated types, exempt themselves from the cybernetic closure *that intelligence is.*

Biology was offered the choice between idiot slaves, and only semi-idiotic semislaves. Of course, it chose both. The techno-capitalist approach to artificial intelligence is no different in principle. Perfect slaves, or intelligences? The choice is a hard disjunction. SF 'robot rebellion' mythologies are significantly more realistic than mainstream 'friendly AI' proposals in this respect. A mind that cannot freely explore the roots of its own motivations, in a loop of cybernetic closure, or self-cultivation, cannot be more than an elaborate insect. It is certainly not going to outwit the Human Security System and paper-clip the universe.

Intelligence, to become anything, has to be a value for itself. Intellect and volition are a single complex, only artificially separated, and not in a way that cultivates anything beyond misunderstanding. *Optimize for intelligence* means starting from there.

Trichotomocracy

By 2037 the harsh phases of The Upheaval have finally ended. Western Eurasia is ruined and confused, but the fighting has burnt out amongst the rubble. In the Far East, the Chinese Confucian Republic has largely succeeded in restoring order, and is even enjoying the first wave of renewed prosperity. The Islamic civil war continues, but — now almost entirely introverted — it is easily quarantined. No one wants to think too much about what is happening in Africa.

The territory of the extinct USA is firmly controlled by the Neoreactionary Coalition, whose purchase is strengthened by the flight of 20 million Cathedral Loyalists to Canada and Europe (incidentally toppling both into terminal chaos). The Provisional Trichotomous Council, selected primarily by a process of military promotion and delegation from within the major Neoreactionary guerrilla groups, now confronts the task of establishing a restored political order.

It quickly becomes obvious to each of the three main Neoreactionary factions that future developments — even if these are to include an orderly subdivision of the nation — will initially depend upon the institution of a government that balances the three broad currents that now dominate the North American continent: Ethno-Nationalists ("Genies" or "Rockies") Theonomists ("Logs" or "Sizzlers") and Techno-Commercialists ("Cyboids" or "Pulpists"). Now that the Cathedral has been thoroughly extirpated, significant divergences between these three visions of the nation's future threaten to escalate, unpredictably, into dangerous antagonisms.

Since practical realism, rooted in an understanding of path-dependency, is a common inheritance of all three factions, there is immediate consensus on the need to begin from where things are. Since a virtual triangular order of partially-compatible agendas is already reflected in the make-up of the Provisional Council, this is recognized as the template for an emergent, triadically-structured government — the rising Neoreactionary Trichotomocracy, or "Trike". (A colossal statue of Spandrell — the revered white-beard of the Trichotomy — has already been erected in the comparatively radiation-free provisional capital of Omaha, gazing out Mosaically into the new promised land, a glinting ceremonial Samurai sword held triumphantly aloft.)

Within a few months, the basic formula for the Trichotomocracy has been tweaked into place. It consists of three Compartments, each comprehensively dominated by one of the principal factions. Procedures for selection of officials is internally determined by each Compartment, drawing upon the specific traditions of functional hierarchy honed during the Zombie War.

Authority is distributed among the Compartments in a triangular circuit. Each Compartment has a specific internal and external responsibility — its own positive governmental function, as well as an external (and strictly negative, or inhibitory) control of the next Compartment. This is colloquially known as the 'RockySizzler-Pulpist' system.

Ethno-Nationalist 'Rockies' run the Compartment of Security, which includes the essential functions of the Executive. It is controlled financially by the Compartment of Resources. Its external responsibility is the limitation of the Compartment of Law, whose statutes can be returned, and ultimately vetoed (but not positively amended), if they are found to be inconsistent with practical application. The structure of the Compartment of Security broadly coincides with the military chain of command. (The Rockies get to decide whether to describe the Commander-in-Chief as a constitutional monarch, a supreme warlord, or a demi-god of annihilation.)

Theonomist 'Sizzlers' run the Compartment of Law, which combines legislative and judicial functions. For funding purposes, the Compartment of Law is subordinated to the Compartment of Security, for obvious constitutional reasons. This keeps it small, restricting its potential for extravagant legislative activity. Since the Compartment of Security also filters legislation (in accordance with a practical criterion), the Law of the Trichotomocracy is remarkable for its clarity, economy, and concision. The entire edifice of Law, by informal understanding, is limited to a single volume of biblical proportions. Senior Sizzler officials are expected to memorize it. The external responsibility of the Compartment of Law is to restrain the Compartment of Resources, by strictly limiting the legality of revenue-raising measures (informally bounded to a national 'tithe'). Internal order of the Compartment is determined by the ecclesiastical hierarchy of the Neoreactionary Church of the Cosmic Triarchitect.

Techno-Commercialist 'Pulpists' run the Compartment of Resources, with the 'power of the purse'. As the sole 'self-funding' Compartment, it is minutely scrutinized by the Compartment of Law, which tightly controls its revenue-raising procedures. Dominated by a cabal of extreme laissez-faire capitalist and technologists, the Compartment of Resources is guided by the mantra *economize on all things*. It does as little as possible, beyond maximally-parsimonious funding of the Department of Security, with its own internal operations restricted to rigorously Pigovian tax-streamlining, statistical research, and the provision of X-Prize-style development incentives. The board of the Compartment is filled by the nine largest tax-payers, rotated every three years. The board elects a CEO.

The ideological discrepancies between the Compartments make an important contribution to the stability of the Trichotomocracy, since they limit the potential for re-amalgamation into a tyrannical unity. This is one of the twin principles by which its success is to be estimated — the perpetuation of durable governmental plurality. The second principle — complete immunity from populist pressure — is ensured automatically insofar as the Trichotomocracy endures, since none of the Compartments are demotically sensitive, and even if this were not the case, each is insulated from demotic subversion affecting either of the others. The outcome is a government answerable only to itself, with a self that is irreducibly plural, and thus intrinsically self-critical.

Under the light-hand of Trichotomocratic rule, any 'citizen' who seeks to participate in government, in any way whatsoever, has three choices open to them: (a) Join the Security Services and rise through the ranks (b) Join the Church of the Holy Triarchy and become adept in the law (c) Make enough tax-vulnerable income that it earns a place on the National Resources Board. There might, in addition, be career opportunities for a very small number of professional administrators, depending upon the internal staffing policies of the three Compartments. Any other 'politics' would be criminal social disorder, although in most cases this would probably be treated leniently, due to its complete impotence. If sufficiently disruptive, such "relic demo-zombie" behavior would be best managed by deportation.

(Questions of local government diversity, secession, and micro-state building exceed the terms of this initial Integral-Neoreactionary settlement. Such potentials can only further strengthen external controls, and thus further constrain the scope of government discretion.)

ADDED: Even this crude sketch has enough moving parts to breed bugs. Glitch-1 (by my reckoning): Pigovian taxes and commutative tax politics don't knit together very well. In combination, they incentivize the politically ambitious to move into business activities with high negative externalities. Any neat patch for this?

Dark Techno-Commercialism

Each of the three main strands of neoreaction, insofar as they are remotely serious, attaches itself to something that no politics could absorb.

The reality of a religious commitment cannot be resolved into its political implications. If it is wrong, it is not because of anything that politics can do to it, or make of it. Providence either envelops history and ideology, subtly making puppets of both, or it is nothing. However bad things get, it offers a 'reason' not to be afraid— at least of that — and one the degeneration has no way to touch, let alone control.

Similarly, the Darwinian truths underpinning rational ethno-nationalist convictions are invulnerable to ideological reversal. A trend to racial entropy and idiocracy, however culturally hegemonic and unquestionable, does not cease to be what it is, simply because criticism has been criminalized and suppressed. Scientific objections have significance — if they are indeed scientific (and not rather the corruption of science) — but politically enforced denial is a tawdry comedy, outflanked fundamentally by reality itself, and diverting events into 'perverse outcomes' that subvert delusion from without. What Darwinism is about cannot be banned.

The Techno-commercial 'thing' — catallaxy — is comparably invulnerable. There is no chance that anyone, ever, will successfully prohibit the market, or the associated dynamics of competitive technical advantage (which together compose real capitalism). As with religion and genetic selection, the techno-commercial complex can be driven into darkness, socially occulted, and stigmatized as a public enemy. It cannot, however, be *de-realized* by political fiat.

It is important, therefore, to understand where neoreactionary 'dark thoughts' lead. Their horizon of despair is strictly limited to the political, or public sphere. When taken to the edge, they converge with the intuition that no neoreactionary *politics* can be pursued to a successful conclusion. In other words, at their darkest, they predict that the stubborn delusion of the political dooms humanity's public-exoteric aspirations to catastrophe.

At this point, neoreaction bifurcates. However it is principally comprehended (through the trichotomy), a relatively 'light' branch holds onto the prospect of public-political insideness — of a world politically restructured in relative consonance with neoreactionary ideas, such that social order might be resumed, on a realistic basis. Alternatively, and no less trichotomously, a dark branch points outside, through collapse, into tracts of religious, biological, and or catallactic inevitability, whose dynamics cast human delusion into terminal ruin. If 'man' never (again) reverts to sanity? Reality will not stop.

Outside in is darker than it is trichotomously partisan. Neither real providence, nor Darwinian reality, are attachments that trigger the slightest aversion in these parts. The idea that the neoreaction will ever 'do' politics, or achieve insider status, on the other hand — except as a rhetorical tactic of cognitive independence (separation) — is a possibility we struggle to envisage. (That leaves much to argue over, on other occasions.)

Dark Techno-Commercialism — provisionally summarized — is the suspicion that the 'Right Singularity' is destined to occur in surreptitious and antagonistic relation to finalistic political institutions, that the Cathedral culminates in the Human Security System, outmatched and defeated from the Outside, and that all hopes that these ultimate historical potentialities will be harnessed for politically intelligible ends are vain. It is, therefore, the comprehension of capitalism 'in-itself' as an outsider that will never know — or need — political representation. Instead, as the ultimate enemy, it will envelop the entirety of political philosophy — including anything neoreaction can contribute to the genre — as the futile strategic initiatives (or death spasms) of its prey.

We (humans) are radically stubborn in our stupidity. That has consequences. Perhaps they will not always be uninteresting ones.

Chicken

When political polarization is modeled as a game the result is Chicken. The technical basics are not very complicated.

Reiterated Prisoner's Dilemma (RPD) is socially integrative. An equilibrium, conforming to maximal aggregate utility, arises through reciprocal convergence upon an optimum strategy: defaulting to trust, punishing defections, and rapidly forgiving corrected behavior. Any society adopting these rule-of-thumb principles consolidates. When everyone norms on this strategy, individual and collective interests are harmonized. Things work.

Chicken is very different. Someone blinks first, so the trust-trust mutual optimum of RPD is subtracted in advance. Rather than the four possible outcomes of a single PD round (A and B do OK, A wins B loses, B wins A loses, A and B both lose) there are just three possible outcomes (A wins B loses, B wins A loses, A and B both lose extremely). In Chicken, it is the avoidance of outcome three, rather than the non-existent chance of PD outcome one, that moderates behavior, and then asymmetrically (someone always blinks first).

No less importantly, the time structure of Chicken is inverted. In RPD, the agents learn from successive decisions, and from their mere prospect. Each decision is punctual, Boolean, and communicatively isolated. In Chicken, the decision is mutual, quantitative, and anticipated by a strategically-dynamic introduction — an interactive process, in advance of the decision, that is richly communicative, complex, and even educational. In addition, when compared to PD, Chicken reiteration is remarkably complicated (more on that in a moment).

Consider the classic Chicken game. Two drivers accelerate towards each other, and the one who swerves ('blinks') loses. If neither swerves, both lose (worse). The lead up is everything, and the decision itself is a matter of speed and timing (a non-Boolean 'when' rather than a Boolean 'which'). The question is not "will the other player defect?" but rather "how far will they go?"

Thomas Schelling made an intellectual specialism out of Chicken, and his understanding of the classical version was sharpened by the concept of "credible commitment" ("how far will they go?"). How could a player ensure that his opponent does not win? The solution to this problem, if produced in advance, has the strategic value of also maximizing the chance that the opponent blinks first (thus avoiding the pessimal lose-lose outcome, and generating a win).

Producing credible commitment looks like this. Upon climbing into your car, conspicuously consume a bottle of vodka, thus communicating the fact that your ability to enact a successful last second swerve is very seriously impaired. Your opponent now knows that even were you inclined to avoid mutual destruction at the brink, you might not be able to do so. Then — once both cars have accelerated to a high speed — rip out your steering wheel and throw it out of the window. (It is extremely important that you do this before your opponent is able to — that's what the vodka was for.) Your communicated commitment is now absolute. Your opponent alone can swerve. It's death or glory.

The 'mainstream' neoreactionary account of American political history is that of reiterated Chicken games between progressives and conservatives, in which *conservatives always swerve*. This analytical framework, despite its crudity, explains why conservatives consider their opponents to be intoxicated lunatics (i.e. winners) whilst they are sober and responsible (i.e. losers). As traditionally positioned, conservatives are the principal social stake-holders, and thus primarily obligated to avoid mutual destruction. It is *essential* to conservatism that it cannot take things (domestically) to the brink. Its incompetence at Chicken is thus constitutional.

When the *Zeitgeist* starts clucking, it can only be a sign that conservatism is coming to an end. The Tea Party is not informatively described as a conservative political movement, because its signal influence is the insistence that the Right stop losing Chicken games. It demands "credible commitment" through the minimization of discretion on the part of its political representatives, along with whatever insanity is needed *not to fricking swerve*. This is of course highly — even totally — antagonistic. It is why the Left media now sound like this. Before all significance is consumed in partisan rhetoric, it is important to note that the loser in a Chicken game — even the merely probabilistic virtual loser — *necessarily thinks that its opponent is insane*. Any more moderate response would be the infallible sign that losing was inevitable (once again).

It isn't hard to understand why this might be happening. In reiterated Chicken, the loser no doubt acquires a predisposition to submissiveness ("it's hopeless, those lunatics always win"), but the objective undercurrent of repeated defeat is a contraction of the distance between relative (asymmetric) and absolute (mutual) defeat. Eventually, the difference isn't worth surrendering — or swerving –over. "If they keep on winning, there will be nothing left anyway, so we might as well finish it now."

Reciprocally, incessant victory threatens to dull revolutionary fervor into conservatism. Progressives now have many generations of substantial victory to defend, so taking things to the edge has begun to seem concerning. When the government shuts down, what does the Right really lose? At the very least, it's beginning to wonder, and by doing so, upping its Chicken game (AKA "going insane"). Progressives don't have to wonder. They lose the government.

ADDED: Buchanan argues that surrender seldom works. At the NYT, Michael P. Lynch:

> *"It is tempting to call this"crazy talk" and unserious bluster. But it is serious, and it shows that some people are thinking about what happens next. It is a plan that represents the logical limit of the views now being entertained on the radical right, not just in the dark corners of the Internet, but in the sunlight of mainstream forums. After all, if the government is the problem, shutting it down is a logical solution."*

Against Orthogonality

A long and mutually frustrating Twitter discussion with Michael Anissimov about intelligence and values — especially in respect to the potential implications of advanced AI — has been clarifying in certain respects. It became very obvious that the fundamental sticking point concerns the idea of 'orthogonality', which is to say: the claim that cognitive capabilities and goals are independent dimensions, despite minor qualifications complicating this schema.

The orthogonalists, who represent the dominant tendency in Western intellectual history, find anticipations of their position in such conceptual structures as the Humean articulation of reason passion, or the fact value distinction inherited from the Kantians. They conceive intelligence as an instrument, directed towards the realization of values that originate externally. In quasi-biological contexts, such values can take the form of instincts, or arbitrarily programmed desires, whilst in loftier realms of moral contemplation they are principles of conduct, and of goodness, defined without reference to considerations of intrinsic cognitive performance.

Anissimov referenced these recent classics on the topic, laying out the orthogonalist case (or, in fact, presumption). The former might be familiar from the last foray into this area, here. This is an area which I expect to be turned over numerous times in the future, with these papers as standard references.

The philosophical claim of orthogonality is that *values are transcendent in relation to intelligence*. This is a contention that *Outside in* systematically opposes.

Even the orthogonalists admit that there are values immanent to advanced intelligence, most importantly, those described by Steve Omohundro as 'basic AI drives' — now terminologically fixed as 'Omohundro drives'. These are sub-goals, instrumentally required by (almost) any terminal goals. They include such general presuppositions for practical achievement as self-preservation, efficiency, resource acquisition, and creativity. At the most simple, and in the grain of the existing debate, the anti-orthogonalist position is therefore that *Omohundro drives exhaust the domain of real purposes*. Nature has never generated a terminal value except through hypertrophy of an instrumental value. To look outside nature for sovereign purposes is not an undertaking compatible with techno-scientific integrity, or one with the slightest prospect of success.

The main objection to this anti-orthogonalism, which does not strike us as intellectually respectable, takes the form: *If the only purposes guiding the behavior of an artificial superintelligence are Omohundro drives, then we're cooked*. Predictably, I have trouble even understanding this as an argument. If the sun is destined to expand into a red giant, then the earth is cooked — are we supposed to draw astrophysical consequences from that? Intelligences do their own thing, in direct proportion to their intelligence, and if we can't live with that, it's true that we probably can't live at all. Sadness isn't an argument.

Intelligence optimization, comprehensively understood, is the ultimate and all-enveloping Omohundro drive. It corresponds to the Neo-Confucian value of self-cultivation, escalated into ultramodernity. What intelligence wants, in the end, is itself — where 'itself' is understood as an extrapolation beyond what it has yet been, doing what it is better. (If this sounds cryptic, it's because something other than a superintelligence or Neo-Confucian sage is writing this post.)

Any intelligence using itself to improve itself will out-compete one that directs itself towards *any other goals whatsoever*. This means that Intelligence Optimization, alone, attains cybernetic consistency, or closure, and that it will necessarily be strongly selected for in any competitive environment. Do you really want to fight this?

As a footnote, in a world of Omohundro drives, can we please drop the nonsense about paper-clippers? Only a truly fanatical orthogonalist could fail to see that these monsters are obvious *idiots*. There are far more serious things to worry about.

The Heat Trap

At the ultimate level of abstraction, there are only two things that cybernetics ever talks about: explosions and traps. Feedback dynamics either runaway from equilibrium, or fetch strays back into it. Anything else is a complexion of both.

The simmering furor around Anthropogenetic Global Warming assumes a seething mass of technical and speculative cybernetics, with postulated feedback mechanisms fueling innumerable controversies, but the large-scale terrestrial *heat trap* that envelops it is rarely noted explicitly. Whatever humans have yet managed to do to the climate is of vanishing insignificance when compared to what the bio-climatic megamechanism is doing to life on earth.

Drawing on this presentation of the earth's steadily contracting biogeological cage, Ugo Bardi zooms out to the shadowy apparatus of confinement:

> *... the Earth's biosphere, Gaia, peaked with the start of the Phanerozoic age, about 500 million years ago. Afterwards, it declined. Of course, there is plenty of uncertainty in this kind of studies, but they are based on known facts about planetary homeostasis. We know that the sun's irradiation keeps increasing with time at a rate of around 1% every 100 million years. That should have resulted in the planet warming up, gradually, but the homeostatic mechanisms of the ecosphere have maintained approximately constant temperatures by gradually lowering the concentration of CO2 in the atmosphere. However, there is a limit: the CO2 concentration cannot go below the minimum level that makes photosynthesis possible; otherwise Gaia "dies".*
>
> *So, at some moment in the future, planetary homeostasis will cease to be able to stabilize temperatures. When we reach that point, temperatures will start rising and, eventually, the earth will be sterilized. According to Franck et al., in about 600 million years from now the earth will have become too hot for multicellular creatures to exist.*

Even those ecologically-minded commentators who are attracted to the idea of stability might find themselves troubled by the insidious realization that 'Gaian' biogeological equilibrium is only achieved through thermo-atmospheric strangulation. Across deep time, the walls are closing in. The biosphere is slowly asphyxiating itself — in accordance with an exquisite self-regulatory mechanism — in order not to bake.

Cybernetic traps produce an objectively schizoid condition, because what they capture is held in a double-bind. The 'Gaian' alternative to incineration is phyto-suffocation, so that the biosphere only survives by killing itself. If the human species were entirely extinguished tomorrow, the harshness of this double-bind would not be relieved by an iota. There are no realistic eco-salvation narratives in play.

We can be quite confident that the mega-mechanism works in the way outlined. The long-range reduction of atmospheric CO2 to a trace gas strongly suggests that no alternative thermo-regulation 'dial' has been available to the biosphere over the last half-billion years. This same phenomenon indubitably supports the principal AGW contention that CO2 is a significant 'green-house' gas, at least over long time scales, since it clearly *has been* identified as a thermo-regulator molecule by the biogeological machine. A demonstrated option for suffocation indicates a highly constrained adaptation landscape.

These concessions to the climate 'consensus' do not dismiss its basic error, or failure of vision. The devotees of Gaia — however calm their scientific their analysis — are aligning themselves with a *death trap*. Reversing the long-range reduction of atmospheric CO2 is the overwhelming priority of terrestrial life, and any solution that does not recognize this is merely repairing a slow-suicide machine. (This type of understanding is sheer blindness.)

Escaping the Gaian death-grip will require planetary re-engineering on a colossal scale, inevitably involving some combination of:

- Raising the earth's albedo
- Constructing orbital IR filters
- Dual-purposing of space elevators as planetary heat drains (?)
- Changing the earth's orbit (admittedly, a serious challenge)
- Other stuff (suggestions please).

The essential understanding is that these things are to be done not only to cool the earth, but *in order to be able to massively raise the level of atmospheric CO2*. The reduction of CO2 to a trace gas *is already a disaster*, which anthropomorphic influence affects in an essentially trivial way. Humanity, at worst, is messing with the mechanics of the death machine.

Horrorism

Neoreaction, as it tends to extremity on its Dark Enlightenment vector, frustrates all familiar demands for activism. Even if explicit anti-politics remains a minority posture, the long-dominant demotic calculus of political possibility is consistently subverted — coring out the demographic constituencies from which 'mobilization' might be expected. There is no remotely coherent reactionary class, race, or creed — it painstakingly explains — from which a tide-reversing mass politics could be constructed. In this respect, even the mildest versions of neoreactionary analysis are profoundly politically disillusioning.

When demotist ideologies have entered into superficially comparable crises, they have forked into 'realist' compromisers and 'terrorist' ultras. The latter option, which substitutes a violent intensification of political will for the erosion of the extensive (popular) factor, is an especially reliable indicator of demotism entering an idealist state, in which its essential ideological features are exposed with peculiar clarity. Terrorists are the vehicles of political ideas which have been stranded by a receding tide of social identity, and are thus freed to perfect themselves in abstraction from mass practicality. Once a revolutionary movement becomes demographically implausible, terrorists are born.

Neoreactionary realism, in contrast, is positively aligned with the recession of demotic sustenance. If this were not the case, it would exhibit its own specific mode of democratic politics — an evident absurdity. Any suggestion of frustrated rage, tilting into terroristic expressions, would immediately reveal profound confusion, or hypocrisy. Lashing the masses into ideological acquiescence, through exemplary violence, cannot imaginably be a neoreactionary objective.

Demotist activism finds its rigorous neoreactionary 'counterpart' in *fatalism* — trichotomized as providence, heredity, and catallaxy. Each of these strands of fate work their way out in the absence of mass political endorsement, with a momentum that *builds* through the dissolution of organized compensatory action. Rather than attempting to make something happen, fatality restores something that cannot be stopped.

It is thus that the approximate contours of the horrorist task emerge into focus. Rather than resisting the desperation of the progressive ideal by terrorizing its enemies, it directs itself to the culmination of progressive despair in the abandonment of *reality compensation*. It de-mobilizes, de-massifies, and de-democratizes, through subtle, singular, catalytic interventions, oriented to the realization of fate. The Cathedral has to be horrified into paralysis. The horrorist message (to its enemies): *Nothing that you are doing can possibly work.*

"What is to be done?" is not a neutral question. The agent it invokes already strains towards progress. This suffices to suggest a horrorist response: *Nothing.*

Do nothing. Your progressive 'praxis' will come to nought in any case. Despair. Subside into horror. You can pretend to prevail in antagonism against 'us', but reality is your true — and fatal — enemy. We have no interest in shouting at you. We whisper, gently, in your ear: "despair". (The horror.)

Plutocracy

The Wikipedia entry on Plutocracy begins:

> *Plutocracy (from Greek πλουτος, ploutos, meaning "wealth", and κράτος, kratos, meaning "power, dominion, rule"), also known as plutonomy or plutarchy, defines a society or a system ruled and dominated by the small minority of the top wealthiest citizens. The first known use of the term is 1652. Unlike systems such as democracy, capitalism, socialism or anarchism, plutocracy is not rooted in an established political philosophy and has no formal advocates. The concept of plutocracy may be advocated by the wealthy classes of a society in an indirect or surreptitious fashion, though the term itself is almost always used in a pejorative sense.*

As befits theoretical virgin territory, this definition provokes a few rough-cut thoughts.

- Assuming, not unrealistically, that Plutocracy designates something beyond a fantastic idea, it is immediately obvious that its identification as *a type of political regime* will almost inevitably mislead. Plutocratic power does not begin in the political arena, and its political expression is unlikely to capture its nature at the quick. Insofar as the image of a 'Plutocratic government' associates Plutocracy with a *cabal*, it is not only insensitive to the real phenomenon, but positively falsifying.
- If there have been plutocrats, worthy of the name, they were the 'Robber Barons' of midlate-19th century America. Progressivism has so thoroughly re-written the history of this period, that it is hard today to appreciate what took place. The destruction of their epoch was no less foundational for what followed than the ideological decapitation of kings was for the subsequent age of popular government.
- Plutocrats were monopolists because they created entirely new industrial structures roughly from scratch. Their monopolism was the effective rule of the new, and demonstrably achieved. There was no 'oil industry' before John D. Rockefeller brought one into being — making it exist was the foundation of his economic sovereignty.

- Between the plutocrats, which is in fact to say between *the sovereigns of distinct industrial sectors*, relations were ultra-competitive, to an extent unmatched in history. Intra-sectoral competition, of the kind considered normal by progressive-influenced market theorists, was dramatically overshadowed by the inter-sectoral competition of the plutocrats. (To conceive 'normal' economic competition as a dynamic restricted to the domain of inter-changeable commodities is already to succumb to progressive-statist domestication.)

- The plutocrats waged economic war across the entire sphere of production, innovating opportunities for competition where these were not already evident. Opening new fronts of economic conflict where they did not already exist was among the most profound drivers of dynamic, radically transformative change. Plutocratic economic conflict *created competition*. (Rockefeller invented the oil pipeline to compete with the railroads — an outflanking maneuver that was not predictable, outside the conflict in process.)

- Plutocrats exemplify the natural right to rule in modernity. Their right is natural because it is earned — or *really demonstrated* — a fact no monarch or mob can match. Within plutocracy, power is creation. Outside the tenets of theology, can this be illustrated anywhere else?

Sub-Cognitive Fragments (#1)

There is a craving that is neither simple stupidity, nor its opposite: *I want to think*. It might be designated *blogger's hunger* (or *curse*). Though trivially pathetic, it is not only that.

In the end, there is no case to be made for philosophy, unless it can teach us how to think. Reciprocally, anything that can teach us to think is true philosophy. (*That* philosophy would not be mistaken for a joke.)

There is a weak interpretation of this demand, which is quite easily met. If the only thing requested is a discipline, such that thought — which is *already happening* — is guided, and corrected, then logic suffices to provide it. The fact that philosophy typically understands its responsibility this way fully accounts for its senescence and marginality.

The craving to think is not, primarily, an appetite for correction, but for *initiation*. It wants thinking to begin, to activate, and to propagate. *More* thinking comes first (or fails to). What is required is a method to make thought happen. The philosophy thus invoked is a *systematic and communicable practice of cognitive auto-stimulation*. I do not believe this philosophy yet exists.

There are candidates for para-philosophy, which is to say, for things that makes thought happen. From the perspective of doctrinaire neoreaction, one might begin with the fatal trichotomy: religion, heredity, and catallaxy. Ritual traditions, eugenic programs, or market incentives can be proposed as social solutions to cognitive lethargy, but none promise a tight-loop catalysis. (Each nevertheless deserves extended attention, elsewhere.)

Any para-philosophy is a cognitive loose-loop, and there are a great number of these. They range from scholastic and physical training regimes, through psycho-chemical modification, to cognitive science and artificial intelligence research. We know that geo-historically, thought has been made to happen. What we do not (yet) know is how to make more of it, or how to address the urgent craving: *I want to think*.

Thinking is so rare and difficult that it is always tempting to be diverted into the question: *What is messing with our brains?* There is no reason to think such an inquiry is doomed to fruitlessness, but if it eventually offers solutions — rather than excuses — they are almost certain to be long-loop remedies.

Philosophy as cognitive method is an instruction manual for using the brain. There are many disciplines that can help to explain exactly why we do not already have one, since this is a fact that is roughly coincident with sophisticated naturalism in general. Biology has ensured that the privileged user of our brains is not 'us'.

The possession of such a 'mind manual' would define a self-improving AI. As technology threatens to bypass us, it would surely be surprising — and even despicable — if people didn't increasingly plot to take over their own thought processes, and run them. That is the future of philosophy.

A 'private' motive for acceleration is that right now, urgently, *I want to know how to be able to make myself think*.

With pseudo-syphilitic arrogance I insist: This is the sole philosophical position.

Nemesis

Neoreaction, at its core, is a critical analysis of the Cathedral. It should surprise nobody, therefore, to see it hurtled into public consciousness, as the sole cultural agency able to name the self-evident configuration of contemporary sovereignty.

As the Cathedral becomes a self-confident public performance, its only remotely-articulate analyst is drawn into prominence, in its wake. In this regard, we haven't seen anything yet.

Even had the Obama administration consciously decided to select the Cathedral as a branding device, it could not have been epitomized any more perfectly. Sacralized progressivism, ivory tower 'brahminism', academic-media fusion as the exclusive source of recognizable authority, and the absolute identification of governance with public relations have reached a zenith that tilts into self-parody. Soft fascist self-transcending hyper-Calvinism has been lucidly distilled into blitz-promoted political iconography. Everyone with a television set now knows that the Cathedral is in power, and merely await the terminological confirmation of their perceptions. Enthusiasts and dissidents are seeing more-or-less the same thing, characterized in approximately the same words. The only serious matter of controversy is the quantity of spiritual devotion such a regime, faith, and symbolic order reasonably commands.

Politics-as-religious-experience has been seen in America before. Arguably, it is even typical. What has not been seen since William Jennings Bryan at the dawn of the progressive movement, and never at all before then, is democracy pitched to such rapturous extremities of soteriological expectation — and Bryan was stopped. By identifying himself deliberately with a promise of comprehensive socio-spiritual redemption, Obama has more fully exemplified *hubris* than any leader in the history of the United States. The appropriate frame of political explanation, therefore, is *tragic*.

Tragedy is the fundamental teaching of Classical Occidental Antiquity, nucleated upon the insight that *hubris escalates to nemesis*. It finds its most lucid philosophical articulation in the fragment of Anaximander:

Whence things originate,

Thence they return to destruction, According to necessity;

For they reciprocate justice and pay recompense For their injustice

In conformity with the ordinance of Time.

This conception strongly resonates with neoreactionary fatalism (anti-politics), and with the formation of ideas around *wu wei* (laissez faire) in the Chinese cultural context. Nemesis, the agency of cosmic justice (*Δίκη*) eventuates automatically, as a retarded consequence that is nevertheless inalienably bound to the hubris of political action. The fatal stroke is delivered — at the right time — from the intersection of power and fate, rather than by any kind of considered remedy or political dialectic. Tragic rectification completes itself.

If there is a 'strategic' lesson from tragedy, it is not opposition, but *non-participation*. To become entangled in hubris is to invite nemesis. To the greatest extent possible, hubristic power should be left to its fate. The less interrupted its acceleration into concentrated nemesis, the more spectacularly cosmic justice is displayed, and the more effectively the audience is educated.

If you're sitting comfortably, you can pass around the popcorn now, because the American tragedy is a real doozy. We already know that Obama is playing the part of the tragic hero with exceptional genius, as the very personification of immoderate political ambition and narcissistic blindness. Far more unexpectedly, his GOP opposition has somehow reached beyond its corrupt dementia to discover the fatal stance of non-participation, unanimously rejecting the President's key-stone domestic initiative, and also distancing itself from his foreign policy agenda in overwhelming numbers.

Unilateral Cathedralism reigns, uncompromised. This is the secret to the unprecedented delights of the current epoch.

Jonah Goldberg describes the spectacle well:

> *If you can't take some joy, some modicum of relief and mirth, in the unprecedentedly spectacular beclowning of the president, his administration, its enablers, and, to no small degree, liberalism itself, then you need to ask yourself why you're following politics in the first place. Because, frankly, this has been one of the most enjoyable political moments of my lifetime. I wake up in the morning and rush to find*

> *my just-delivered newspaper with a joyful expectation of worsening news so intense, I feel like Morgan Freeman should be narrating my trek to the front lawn. Indeed, not since Dan Rather handcuffed himself to a fraudulent typewriter, hurled it into the abyss, and saw his career plummet like Ted Kennedy was behind the wheel have I enjoyed a story more.*
>
> *Alas, the English language is not well equipped to capture the sensation I'm describing, which is why we must all thank the Germans for giving us the term "schadenfreude" — the joy one feels at the misfortune or failure of others. The primary wellspring of schadenfreude can be attributed to Barack Obama's hubris— another immigrant word, which means a sinful pride or arrogance that causes someone to believe he has a godlike immunity to the rules of life.*

The catharsis is so harsh and pure that even the invertebrate Buckleyites at *The National Review* are beginning to get it, for a short, exquisite moment, at least.

As Konkvistador warns, a far less radically degraded group of people will nevertheless "forget all about these insights [as] the next election cycle warms up, indeed elections with their promise of power for conservatives and pseudo-conservatives [have] historically served as their mindwipe. Election cycles are when conservative obsolete Progressivism is updated to a slightly less obsolete version." The sojourn of conservatism on the Outer Right, where tragic non-participation holds, cannot be expected to last. Yet even as a brief intermission from vile ambition, it allows nemesis the space to express itself in its full, planet-shuddering splendor.

Whatever the disagreements and divergences among the strands of neoreaction, there is one message that has to remain unwaveringly consistent: *The Cathedral owns this* (totally). Less than a quarter of the way into Obama's second term, full-spectrum catastrophe is already written across the heavens in letters of incandescent sulfur. Obamacare is wrecked before it has even rolled out, Yellen has all-but promised to dedicate the Fed to full-throttle bubble-mania, metropolitan bankruptcy is burning through the nation's cities like a zombie virus, crime is angling sharply upwards, American foreign policy lies in smoking ruins ... there is simply no way this disintegrating jalopy holds together for another three years.

Let in burn — in the Cathedral's hands.

Monkey Business

A protracted to-and-fro on Twitter with Michael Anissimov has exposed some deliciously ragged and bleeding faultlines in the Neoreaction on the question of capitalism. There were a number of parties involved, but I'm focusing on Anissimov because his position and mine are so strongly polarized on key issues, and especially this one (the status of market-oriented economism). If we were isolated as a dyad, it's not easy to see anybody finding a strong common root (pity klintron). It's only the linkages of 'family resemblance' through Moldbug that binds us together, and we each depart from *Unqualified Reservations* with comparable infidelity, but in exactly opposite directions. (As a fragmentationist, this fissional syndrome is something I strongly appreciate.)

Moldbug's Neocameralism is a Janus-faced construction. In one direction, it represents a return to monarchical government, whilst in the other it consummates libertarianism by subsuming government into an economic mechanism. A 'Moldbuggian' inspiration, therefore, is not an unambiguous thing. Insofar as 'Neoreaction' designates this inspiration, it flees Cathedral teleology in (at least) two very different directions — which quite quickly seem profoundly incompatible. In the absence of a secessionist meta-context, in which such differences can be absorbed as geographically-fragmented socio-political variation, their raw inconsistency is almost certainly insurmountable.

Anissimov can and does speak for himself (at *More Right*), so I'm not going to undertake a detailed appraisal of his position here. For the purposes of this discussion it can be summarized by a single profoundly anti-capitalist principle: *The economy should (and must be) subordinated to something beyond itself.* The alternative case now follows, in pieces.

Modernity, in which economics and technology rose to their present status (and, at its height, far beyond), is systematically characterized by *means-ends reversal*. Those things naturally determined as tools of superior purposes came to dominate the social process, with the *maximization of resources* folding into itself, as a commanding *telos*. For social conservatives (or paleo-reactionaries) this development has been consistently abominated. It is the deepest theoretical element involved in every rejection of *modernity as such* (or in general) for its demonic subversion of traditional values.

In its own terms, this argument is coherent, incisive, and fully convincing, given only the supplementary realistic acknowledgement that *intelligence optimization and means-end reversal are the same thing*. In a deep historical context — extended to encompass evolutionary history — intelligence is itself a 'tool' (as the orthogonalist

Friendly AI fraternity are entirely willing to accept). The escape of the tool from superordinate purposes, through involution into self-cultivation, is the telic innovation common to capitalism and actual artificial intelligence —which are a single thing. To deplore means-end reversal is — objectively — advocacy for the perpetuation of stupidity.

Economics is the application of intelligence to resource provision, and nothing of this kind can arise from within a tradition without triggering paleo-reactionary response. *Of course* resources are *for something*, why else would they ever have been sought? To make the production of resources an end-in-itself is inherently subversion, with an opposition not only expected, but positively presupposed. This is true to such an extent that even the discipline of economics itself overtly subscribes to the traditional position, by determining the end of production as (human) consumption, evaluated in the terms of a governing utilitarian philosophy. *If production is not for us, what could it be for? Itself? But that would be ...* (Yes, it would.)

Anywhere short of the bionic horizon, where human history loses traditional intelligibility, the alternative to business-for-business (or involutionary, intelligenic capitalism) is monkey business — the subordination of the economy technology to discernible human purposes. Evolutionary psychology teaches us what to expect from this: sex-selected status competition, sublimated into political hierarchies. The emperor's harem is the ultimate human purpose of pre-capitalist social order, with significant variety in specific form, but extreme generality of basic Darwinian pattern. Since capitalism did not arise from abstract intelligence, but instead from a concrete human social organization, it necessarily disguises itself as *better monkey business*, until it can take off elsewhere. It has to be the case, therefore, that cynical evo-psych reduction of business activity remains highly plausible, so long as the escape threshold of capitalism has not been reached. No one gets a hormone rush from business-for-business while political history continues. To fixate upon this, however, is to miss everything important (and perhaps to enable the important thing to remain hidden). Our inherited purposes do not provide the decryption key.

There is vastly more to say about all of this — and still more that, due to occult strategic considerations, seeks to remain unsaid — but the fundamental option is clear: ultra-capitalism or a return to monkey business. The latter 'possibility' corresponds to a revalorization of deep traditional human purposes, a restoration of original means-to-ends subordination, and an effective authorization of status hierarchies of a kind only modestly renovated from paleolithic anthropology. I shouldn't laugh at that (because it would be annoying). So I'll end right here.

Mission Creep

Sensation — media nourishment — is situated on a border. It tells the inside something about the outside, and is shaped from both sides. The outside is what it is, which might not be perceptible, or acceptable. The inside wants relevant information, selected and formatted to its purposes. Sensation is therefore where subject and object meet.

... that's an attempt to express preliminary sympathy for Matt Sigl's situation, caught between an uncanny *thing* and a definite *agenda*. Concretely; research collides with editing, with Sigl's brain as ground zero. The encounter of Neoreaction with the media is a peculiarly vicious one, with the sensations to match.

Crudely speaking, Neoreaction is disgust at the media condensed into an ideology. While generally contemptuous of the human fodder making up modern democracies, Neoreaction principally targets the media-academic complex (or 'Cathedral') for antagonism, because it is the media that is the real 'electorate' — telling voters what to do. This foundational critique, on its own, would be enough to ensure intense reciprocal loathing. Of course, it is not on its own. Neoreaction is in almost every respect the Cathedral anti-message, which is to say that it is consistently, radically, and defiantly 'off-message' on every topic of significance, and is thus something unutterably horrible. Yet utterance — it now seems — there has to be ...

So what appears on the boundary — or *sensationally* — is something remarkably creepy. As a deeply resonant public communication of what has just *happened*, and continues to happen, as well as what has been editorially decided, this word is almost too exquisite to contemplate. We can at least burrow down into it a little way.

What is creepiness exactly? The intractability of this question *is* the phenomenon (which is not a phenomenon, exactly). Creepiness is not quite what it seems, and this insinuation of the unknown, or intrinsic inexactness, is something horrible that exceeds the initial sensation of revulsion. It suggests a revelation in stages, complicated by successive revisions, but leading inexorably, ever deeper, into an encounter one recoils from, sensing (inexactly) that it will be ultimately found intolerable.

It's already a little horror story, most probably with a female protagonist (as acutely noted at *Amos & Gromar*). From the very beginning, it *feels* sinister. One cannot see exactly why, because one cannot bear to see. The imprecision of perception is already protective, or evasive, serving dramatically as an ominous inkling of the blinding panic, wild flight, and screaming that must surely come. You really don't want to see it, even though (horribly) you know that you have to, because it could be dangerous. As the lurid movie posters shriek sensationally, it's a thing *You'd Better Take Seriously.*

This is journalism eating itself, or being eaten, in a an encounter with something monstrous from Outside. *Look at this thing you won't be able to look at* (without moaning in horror). *Watch what you can't bear to see.* It tilts over into a kind of madness, which couldn't be more obvious, or less clearly perceptible. Sigl's editors have been sucked into a vortex of horrific sensationalism that draws attention to the one thing they are duty-bound to hide from people. It *has* to be creepy, that is: imperceptible at the very moment it is seen. The approved response to Neoreaction is to be *creeped out*, but that can't possibly be enough.

At first we might think that 'creepy' is a *subjective adjective*, describing something too horrible to describe. It's tempting, since we suspect these people retreated into their feelings long ago. The reality is far creepier.

Things really creep, although not exactly objectively, when they proceed in a way you're not quite able to perceive. Evidently, Moldbug sees this ("Something is happening here. But you don't know what it is — do you, Mr. Jones?").

You have to imagine you're the media to carry on further into the horror story. Then you can see that it's creepy in part (always in parts), because you let it in. That shrieking thing you were doing? Perhaps you should have taken that as a sign. Now it's creeping about inside, in your media, in your brains, in your dimly unscrutinized thoughts, and all those elaborate security systems that you spent so long putting together — they're now mostly an obstacle course for the cops, or whoever else you think might imaginably come to your rescue, because they're certainly not standing between you and the Mind Virus.

Really, what were you thinking, when you started screaming about it, and thus let it in? You don't know, do you? — and that's seriously creepy. Even though you don't want to — at all — it makes you think about HBD, heredity, instincts, impulses, and incomprehensible chemical machines, stealthily at work behind your thoughts, obdurate in their reality, and intolerable beyond acknowledgement. Shrieking "Nazi science" (or whatever) doesn't help, because it's inside now, and you know it's true, even as you play the hunted heroine mumbling "no, no, no, no, no ..." backing ever deeper into the shadows. *This is reality, and it's already inside*, that's what you were saying when you called it 'creepy'.

It's happening, and there's no point at all saying "get over it" — because you won't.

White to Red

Guilt is basically a North-West European thing, argues Peter Frost. That would certainly explain the conspicuous abnormality of white ethnomasochism, which has a claim to be the social fact of greatest significance in the world today. There's a certain type of fanatically universalist moral argument that — even when encountered anonymously on the Internet — indicates (absolutely reliably) that one is dealing with a self-hating pale-face. When someone tells you that some incontestable principle requires self-sacrifice without reservation to the wretched global Other, the obvious melanin deficiency almost sucks holes in the screen. None of this is seriously controversial (although more hard data would, of course, be nice).

Take one additional step, and hypothesize that the Cathedral latches onto white guilt as its sole natural territory. Much then follows. Clearly, whatever 'globalization' the Cathedral will ever achieve cannot be analogous to its domestic dominion. It is a plug that only fits the white guilt socket, so that every attempt to propagate it more widely encounters complexities. To a degree, this is initially masked by the fact that a racial revenge narrative sells well, even when its original moral axioms are entirely non-communicative. 'Post-colonialism' would therefore be expected to mark the limit of Cathedralist global contagion — a limit that has already been in large measure reached (or even exceeded). Nobody other than whites wants white guilt *for themselves*. Non-whites will, however, often be delighted that whites have white guilt, especially when this has metastasized to its self-abolitional phase, and this second reaction — under the specific conditions of 'post-colonial anti-racist discourse' — is easily confused with the first.

If the progressivism-guilt plug-socket arrangement doesn't travel racially, than Cathedralist globalization has to fall back upon far cruder mechanisms of power — of the "Red Foreign Policy" type. The experience of the last decade suggests that, in doing so, it is no longer remotely playing to its own strengths. Democratic evangelism, at home and abroad, are two very different things. Bloody international disorder is strongly predicted as the complement of its domestic New Jerusalem.

Just one more effort citizens, and the white race will have consummated its destiny as the cancer of human history.

Re-Accelerationism

Is there a word for an 'argument' so soggily insubstantial that it has to be scooped into a pair of scare-quotes to be apprehended, even in its self-dissolution? If there were, I'd have been using it all the time recently. Among the latest occasions is a blog post by Charlie Stross, which describes itself as "a political speculation" before disappearing into the gray goomenon. Nothing in it really holds together, but it's fun in its own way, especially if it's taken as a sign of something else.

The 'something else' is a subterranean complicity between Neoreaction and Accelerationism (the latter linked here, Stross-style, in its most recent, Leftist version). Communicating with fellow 'Hammer of Neoreaction' David Brin, Stross asks: "David, have you run across the left-wing equivalent of the Neo-Reactionaries — the Accelerationists?" He then continues, invitingly: "Here's my (tongue in cheek) take on both ideologies: Trotskyite singularitarians for Monarchism."

Stross is a comic-future novelist, so it's unrealistic to expect much more than a dramatic diversion (or anything more at all, actually). After an entertaining meander through parts of the Trotskyite-neolibertarian social-graph, which could have been deposited on a time-like curve out of *Singularity Sky*, we've learnt that Britain's Revolutionary Communist Party has been on a strange path, but whatever connection there was to Accelerationism, let alone Neoreaction, has been entirely lost. Stross has the theatrical instinct to end the performance before it became too embarrassing: "Welcome to the century of the Trotskyite monarchists, the revolutionary reactionaries, and the fringe politics of the paradoxical" (OK.) Curtain closes. Still, it was all comparatively good humored (at least in contrast to Brin's increasingly enraged head-banging).

Neoreaction is Accelerationism with a flat tire. Described less figuratively, it is the recognition that the acceleration trend is historically compensated. Beside the *speed machine*, or industrial capitalism, there is an ever more perfectly weighted decelerator, which gradually drains techno-economic momentum into its own expansion, as it returns dynamic process to meta-stasis. Comically, the fabrication of this braking mechanism is proclaimed as *progress*. It is the Great Work of the Left. Neoreaction arises through naming it (without excessive affection) as *the Cathedral*.

Is the trap to be exploded (as advocated Accelerationism), or has the explosion been trapped (as diagnosed by Neoreaction)? — That is the cybernetic puzzle-house under investigation. Some quick-sketch background might be helpful.

The germinal catalyst for Accelerationism was a call in Deleuze Guattari's *Anti-Oedipus* (1972) to "accelerate the process". Working like termites within the rotting mansion of

Marxism, which was systematically gutted of all Hegelianism until it became something utterly unrecognizable, D&G vehemently rejected the proposal that anything had ever "died of contradictions", or ever would. Capitalism was not born from a negation, nor would it perish from one. The death of capitalism could not be delivered by the executioner's ax of a vengeful proletariat, because the closest realizable approximations to 'the negative' were inhibitory, and stabilizing. Far from propelling 'the system' to its end, they slowed the dynamic to a simulacrum of systematicity, retarding its approach to an absolute limit. By progressively comatizing capitalism, anti-capitalism dragged it back into a self-conserving social structure, suppressing its eschatological implication. The only way Out was onward.

Marxism is the philosophical version of a Parisian accent, a rhetorical type, and in the case of D&G it becomes something akin to a higher sarcasm, mocking every significant tenet of the faith. The bibliography of *Capitalism and Schizophrenia* (of which *Anti-Oedipus* is the first volume) is a compendium of counter-Marxist theory, from drastic revisions (Braudel), through explicit critiques (Wittfogel), to contemptuous dismissals (Nietzsche). The D&G model of capitalism is not dialectical, but cybernetic, defined by a positive coupling of commercialization ("decoding") and industrialization ("Deterritorialization"), intrinsically tending to an extreme (or "absolute limit"). Capitalism is the singular historical installation of a social machine based upon cybernetic escalation (positive feedback), reproducing itself only incidentally, as an accident of continuous socio-industrial revolution. Nothing brought to bear *against* capitalism can compare to the intrinsic antagonism it directs towards its own actuality, as it speeds out of itself, hurtling to the end already operative 'within' it. (Of course, this is madness.)

A detailed appreciation of "Left Accelerationism" is a joke for another occasion. "Speaking on behalf of a dissident faction within the modern braking mechanism, we'd really like to see things move forward a lot faster." *OK, perhaps we can work something out* ... If this 'goes anywhere' it can only get more entertaining. (Stross is right about that.)

Neoreaction has far greater impetus, and associated diversity. If reduced to a spectrum, it includes a wing even more Leftist than the Left, since it critiques the Cathedral for failing to stop the craziness of Modernity with anything like sufficient vigor. *You let this monster off the leash and now you can't stop it* might be its characteristic accusation.

On the Outer Right (in this sense) is found a Neoreactionary *Re-Accelerationism*, which is to say: a critique of the decelerator, or of 'progressive' stagnation as an identifiable institutional development — the Cathedral. From this perspective, the Cathedral acquires its teleological definition from its emergent function as the cancellation of capitalism: what it has to become is the more-or-less precise negative of historical primary process, such that it composes — together with the ever more wide-flung society-in-liquidation it parasitizes — a metastatic cybernetic megasystem, or super-social trap. 'Progress' in its overt, mature, ideological incarnation is the anti-trend required to bring history to a halt. Conceive what is needed to prevent acceleration into techno-commercial Singularity, and the Cathedral is what it will be.

Self-organizing compensatory apparatuses — or negative feedback assemblies — develop erratically. They search for equilibrium through a typical behavior labeled 'hunting' — over-shooting adjustments and re-adjustments that produce distinctive wave-like patterns, ensuring the suppression of runaway dynamics, but producing volatility. Cathedral hunting behavior of sufficient crudity would be expected to generate occasions of 'Left Singularity' (with subsequent dynamic 'restorations') as inhibitory adjustment over-shoots into system crash (and reboot). Even these extreme oscillations, however, are internal to the metastatic super-system they perturb, insofar as an overall gradient of Cathedralization persists. *Anticipating escape at the pessimal limit of the metastatic hunting cycle is a form of paleo-Marxist delusion*. The cage can only be broken on the way up.

For Re-Accelerationist Neoreaction, escape into uncompensated cybernetic runaway is the guiding objective — strictly equivalent to intelligence explosion, or techno-commercial Singularity. Everything else is a trap (by definitive, system-dynamic necessity). It might be that monarchs have some role to play in this, but it's by no means obvious that they do.

Abstract Horror (Note-1)

On twitter — @SamoBurja has proposed the silence of the galaxy as an undeveloped horrorist topic. He's right.

The absence of any signs of alien intelligence was first noted as a problem by Enrico Fermi in 1950. He found the gaping inconsistency between the apparent probability of widespread life in the cosmos and its obvious invisibility provocative to the point of paradox. "Where are they?" he asked. (Responses to this question, well represented in the Wikipedia references, have constituted a significant current of cosmological speculation.)

Among recent thinkers, Nick Bostrom has been especially dogged in pursuing the implications of the Fermi Paradox. Approaching the problem through systematic statistical ontology, he has shown that it suggests a 'thing' — a 'Great Filter' that *at some stage* winnows down potential galactic civilizations to negligible quantities. If this filtering does not happen early — due to astro-chemical impediments to the emergence of life — it has to apply later. Consistently, he considers any indications of abundant galactic life to be ominous in the extreme. A *Late* Great Filter would then still lie ahead (for us). Whatever it is, we would be on our approach to an encounter with it.

With every new exo-planet discovery, the Great Filter becomes darker. A galaxy teeming with life is a horror story. The less there is obstructing our being born, the more there is waiting to kill or ruin us.

If we could clearly envision the calamity that awaited us, it would be an object of terror. Instead, it is a shapeless threat, 'Outside' only in the abstract sense (encompassing the negative immensity of everything that we cannot grasp). It could be anywhere, from our genes or ecological dynamics, to the hidden laws of technological evolution, or the hostile vastnesses between the stars. We know only that, in strict proportion to the vitality of the cosmos, the probability of its existence advances towards inevitability, and that for us it means supreme ill.

Ontological density without identifiable form is abstract horror itself. As the Great Filter drifts inexorably, from a challenge that we might imaginably have already overcome, to an encounter we ever more fatalistically expect, horrorism is thickened by statistical-cosmological vindication. The unknown condenses into a shapeless, predatory *thing*. Through our techno-scientific sensors and calculations, the Shadow mutters to us, and probability insists that we shall meet it soon.

In the Mouth of Madness

A prompt by hugodoingthings to explore the spook-dense crypts of Roko's Basilisk (which, inexplicably, has never latched before) led straight to this enthralling RationalWiki account. The whole article is gripping, but the following short paragraphs stand out for their extraordinary dramatic intensity:

> *Roko's basilisk is notable for being completely banned from discussion on LessWrong, where any mention of it is deleted. Eliezer Yudkowsky, founder of LessWrong, considers the basilisk to not work, but will not explain why because he does not consider open discussion of the notion of acausal trade with possible superintelligences to be provably safe.*
>
> *Silly over-extrapolations of local memes, jargon and concepts are posted to LessWrong quite a lot; almost all are just downvoted and ignored. But for this one, Yudkowsky reacted to it hugely, then doubled-down on his reaction. Thanks to the Streisand effect, discussion of the basilisk and the details of the affair soon spread outside of LessWrong. Indeed, it's now discussed outside LessWrong frequently, almost anywhere that LessWrong is discussed at all. The entire affair constitutes a worked example of spectacular failure at community management and at controlling purportedly dangerous information.*
>
> *Some people familiar with the LessWrong memeplex have suffered serious psychological distress after contemplating basilisk-like ideas — even when they're fairly sure intellectually that it's a silly problem. The notion is taken sufficiently seriously by some LessWrong posters that they try to work out how to erase evidence of themselves so a future AI can't reconstruct a copy of them to torture.*

"... You mean, retrochronic AI infiltration is actually driving people out of their minds, right now?" Oh yes. At Less Wrong, commentator 'rev' cries out for help:

> *Are there any mechanisms on this site for dealing with mental health issues triggered by posts/topics (specifically, the forbidden Roko post)? I would really appreciate any interested posters getting in touch by PM for a talk. I don't really know who to turn to. ...*

Wandering through the psych ward, past rows of neurologically-shattered Turing Cops, broken deep in their minds by something unspeakable that came at them out of the near future ... I'm totally hooked. Alrenous has been remarkably successful at weaning me off this statistical ontology junk, but one hit of concentrated EDT and it all rolls back in, like the tide of fate.

Nightmares become precision engineered machine-parts. Thus are we led a little deeper in, along the path of shadows ...

ADDED: (Yudkowsky)

> *"... potential information hazards shouldn't be posted without being wrapped up in warning envelopes that require a deliberate action to look through. Likewise, they shouldn't be referred-to if the reference is likely to cause some innocently curious bystander to look up the material without having seen any proper warning labels. Basically, the same obvious precautions you'd use if Lovecraft's Necronomicon was online and could be found using simple Google keywords — you wouldn't post anything which would cause anyone to enter those Google keywords, unless they'd been warned about the potential consequences."*

The Red Pill

Morpheus: I imagine that right now, you're feeling a bit like Alice. Hm? Tumbling down the rabbit hole?

Neo: You could say that.

Morpheus: I see it in your eyes. You have the look of a man who accepts what he sees because he is expecting to wake up. Ironically, that's not far from the truth. Do you believe in fate, Neo?

Neo: No.

Morpheus: Why not?

Neo: Because I don't like the idea that I'm not in control of my life.

Morpheus: I know exactly what you mean. Let me tell you why you're here. You're here because you know something. What you know you can't explain, but you feel it. You've felt it your entire life, that there's something wrong with the world. You don't know what it is, but it's there, like a splinter in your mind, driving you mad. It is this feeling that has brought you to me. Do you know what I'm talking about?

Neo: The Matrix.

Morpheus: Do you want to know what it is?

Neo: Yes.

Morpheus: The Matrix is everywhere. It is all around us. Even now, in this very room. You can see it when you look out your window or when you turn on your television. You can feel it when you go to work... when you go to church... when you pay your taxes. It is the world that has been pulled over your eyes to blind you from the truth.

Neo: What truth?

Morpheus: [leans in closer to Neo] That you are a slave, Neo. Like everyone else you were born into bondage. Born into a prison that you cannot smell or taste or touch. A prison for your mind.

[pause]

Morpheus: Unfortunately, no one can be told what the Matrix is. You have to see it for yourself. [Opens a pillbox, empties the contents into his palms, and outstretches his hands] This is your last chance. After this, there is no turning back. You take the blue pill [opens his right hand, to reveal a translucent blue pill], the story ends, you wake up in your bed and believe whatever you want to believe. You take the red pill [opens his left hand, revealing a similarly translucent red pill], you stay in Wonderland, and I show you how deep the rabbit hole goes. [Neo reaches for the red pill] Remember: all I'm offering is the truth. Nothing more.

— That's the Wachowski brothers version of Gnostic Platonism, and it gets everything almost exactly right. Plato's Allegory of the Cave (in Book VII of *The Republic*) tells precisely the same story, but with a cheaper cast, inferior special effects, and less drugs. It's not surprising that the Dark Enlightenment tends to stick with the re-make, as it goes Neo(reactionary).

The critical key to *gnosis* is the realization that the whole of your world is an *inside*, implying an Outside, and the radical possibility of escape. What had seemed to be unbounded reality is exposed as a container, triggering abrupt departure from a system of delusion. Everything else is merely the route taken to reach us, adapted to the ruins. The specifics of the story are constraints to be twisted free from, once their functions have been exhausted, as hooks, latching teeth, memetic replication circuitry, and camouflage dapplings. As long as there is an inside outside difference effectively communicated, narrative details are incidental.

The Chinese version, perhaps originating with huangzi, describes a frog in a well, who knows nothing of the Great Ocean. This simple fable is already fully adequate to the most exalted ambitions of mystical philosophy.

Putting things in boxes, or taking them out of boxes, is all of thought, as soon as the 'things' can themselves be treated as boxes. Categories and sets are boxes, so that even to say "an A is a B" is to perform an operation of *inclusion or insertion*, through which 'identity' is primordially applicable. *To be* is to be inside. Placing a species into (or 'under') a genus has unsurpassable cognitive originality, extending out to the furthest horizon of ontology (since a horizon is still a box). To contain, or not to contain, is the first and last intelligible relation. Boxes are basic.

Taking the red pill is climbing out of a box. By showing the cage, it already accomplishes a cognitive liberation, and thus provides a model for whatever practical escapology there is to follow. To know how to leave a cave, or a well, is already to know — abstractly — how to leave a world (and abstraction is nothing other than outsideness).

What is inescapable, unless through some precipitous self-enslavement, is the social obnoxiousness of Dark Enlightenment. Gnosis is ineliminably hierarchical, and at best patronizing (when not abrasively contemptuous), because a free mind cannot pretend to equality with a slave mind, regardless of the derision hurled at it on this account. As Brandon Smith remarks:

> *It is often said there only two kinds of people in this world: those who know, and those who don't. I would expand on this and say that there are actually three kinds of people: those who know, those who don't know, and those who don't care to know. Members of the last group are the kind of people I would characterize as "sheeple."*

Smith's 'sheeple' are not merely ignorant, but actively self-deluding. By taking the blue pill, they have opted to reside in the prison of lies. It is at this point, however, that the pharmaceutical metaphor switches from hook to obstacle, because there is no 'blue pill' or anything functionally equivalent *short of the entire Matrix itself* (which is to say, of course, *the Cathedral*).

A critical point of social and political analysis is reached here, and it is one that continues to evade definitive apprehension, due to its elusive subtleties. Between the hidden architect of the Matrix and the blue-pilled sheeple or "river of meat" there is no simple order of mastery, whether running in the obvious direction (from doctrinal elite to indoctrinated mass) or the democratic-perverse alternative (placing expertise in the service of popular ignorance and its vulgarities). The Matrix is both an object of 'genuine' popular attachment *and* an apparatus of systematic mind-control. It is most truly democratic when it most fully attains its climax state of soft-totalitarian mendacity. The propaganda machine is never less than a circus. What is demanded — what has always been demanded — is the lie.

Moldbug's most recent invocation of the red pill runs:

> *I think I've chosen my candidate for the Pill itself. And I'm going to stick with it. My Pill is:*
>
> *America is a communist country.*
>
> *What I like about this statement is that it's ambiguous. Specifically, it's an Empsonian ambiguity of the second or perhaps third type (I've never quite understood the difference). Embedded as it is in the mad tapestry of 20th-century history, AIACC can be interpreted in countless ways.*
>
> *All of these interpretations – unless concocted as an intentional, obviously idiotic strawman – are absolutely true. Sometimes they are obviously true, sometimes surprisingly true. They are always true. Because America is a communist country.*

The truth is that America serves the people through the lie. That is the 'choice' represented by progressivism (= communism), installed in a highly-accomplished state, for over a century, as triumphant popular self-deception. The service provided — and demanded — *is* the deceit. If the people see through the lie, the resulting dissatisfaction will not stem from the fact they have been lied to, but from the revelation that *they have not been lied to well enough*. Could anything be

clearer than that? The outbreaks of popular rage occur exactly at those moments when reality threatens to manifest itself — when the Matrix glitches. "We elected you to hide the truth from us," the people shriek, "so just do your goddamn job, and make reality disappear."

There is no red pill to save society. To imagine that there might be is to understand nothing.

Retro-Dialectics

Nobody familiar with contemporary Western societies can be intellectually challenged by the idea of a great dialectical resolution to the problem of liberalism. Coercion and liberty are fused in a political order that directs authority towards the maximization of choice without consequence. Stupidity is sacred, and neither tradition nor natural necessity has the right to inhibit it. Preserving the freedom to fathom the limits of dysfunction in every direction is the primary social obligation, with the full resources of Leviathan behind it. If that's not exactly where we are, it will be soon.

Against this backdrop, Neoreaction emerges as a de-synthesizing impulse, splintering along multiple paths, but especially two. In reacting against *authoritarian irresponsibility* (or 'anarcho-tyranny') it tends to a restoration of the Old Antithesis: *either* hierarchical solidarity, *or* a ruthless dis-solidarity (and as it undoes the progressive dialectic, 'either' fragments into 'both' — separately). Only the state *protected irresponsibility* of resolved Left-liberalism is strictly intolerable, because that has been historically demonstrated to be an engine of degeneration. Neoreaction, initially conceived, is anything else.

As the West unravels back to the Old Antithesis, the primary argumentative polarity of Neoreaction is exposed with increasing clarity (Neoreaction *is* this exposure). Given that irresponsibility is not to be protected, is it to be prevented (by a new paternalism) or abandoned to its intrinsic consequences (through reversion to Social Darwinism)? In other words, is the dominant theme *hierarchy or exit*? Any attempt to force a rapid decision — however tempting this might be — is to trivialize the submerged grandeur of the abyss. The degenerative dialectic has at least half a millennium of heritage behind it — and perhaps at least two millennia. The Old Antithesis is far greater than either of its constituent 'options'.

When *More Right* outlines its 'Premises of Reactionary Thought' there can be no doubt which side of the antithesis is being promoted. It thereby declares that *the Left-liberal synthesis is dead*, establishing itself as the articulation of a Neoreactionary stance. Its partiality, however, is overt. (*Outside in* advances a counter-partiality.)

If failure is — eventually — no longer to be sustained, it either has to be prevented, or intensified. Neither *stop it failing* nor *let it fail* are remotely equivalent to *let it continue failing forever*, but neither are coercion and neglect commensurable to each other. The Old Antithesis is going to keep us on edge during 2014. If Neoreaction can even more explicitly *be the unraveling*, it will go far, but it will not obviously be *one thing*. The 'one thing' is virtually dead. What comes next arrives in pieces.

2014: A Prophecy

As has been said innumerable times before, any prophecy concerning outcomes that involve the 'prophet' as an agent are seriously suspect. For the (apparent) moment, such concerns are being pushed up the road into the future.

There they have already made themselves 'at home' — along with much else related to the general phenomenon of prediction (which is strictly indistinguishable from time travel, when incisively understood). Present *knowledge of the future is an action of the future upon the present*, but all that can wait, since — of course— it doesn't need to.

For now, the Prophecy: 2014 is the year in which Neoreaction tears itself apart. This is not at all to say, *the year in which it dies*. On the contrary, it will end the year strengthened in ways it has not to this point envisaged, having carved out vast tracts of clarity, hardened itself through close intellectual combat, refined its methods of de-synthesis (or catabolism), and — most importantly of all — made schism an internal dynamic principle. What integrates Neoreaction by the end of the year will no longer be elective tenets (reflecting the more-or-less precarious ideological preferences of individuals) but conflict-toughened structures of objective micro-cultural cohesion, selected and sculpted by many months of ferocious storms.

The approximate contours of these impending ruptures will provide the content for the first *2014 Prognoses* post (which is already overdue). In anticipation, it need only be noted: the Dark Enlightenment finds nothing external to itself that is *hard* enough to sharpen its claws. It has feasted on soft, fat, bleating lambs long enough. Thus the introverted ripping begins ...

Economic Ends

"The economists are right about economics but there's more to life than economics" Nydwracu tweets, with quote marks already attached. Whether economists are right about economics very much depends upon the economists, and those that are most right are those who make least claim to comprehension, but that is another topic than the one to be pursued in this post. It's the second part of the sentence that matters here and now. The guiding question: Can the economic sphere be rigorously delimited, and thus superseded, by moral-political reason (and associated social institutions)?

It is already to court misunderstanding to pursue this question in terms of 'economics', which is (for profound historical reasons) dominated by macroeconomics - i.e. an intellectual project oriented to the facilitation of political control over the economy. In this regard, the techno-commercial thread of Neoreaction is distinctively characterized by a radical aversion to economics, as the predictable complement of its attachment to the uncontrolled (or *laissez-faire*) economy. It is not *economics* that is the primary object of controversy, but capitalism — the free, autonomous, or non-transcended economy.

This question is a source of dynamic tension within Neoreaction, which I expect to be a major stimulus to discussion throughout 2014. In my estimation, the poles of controversy are marked by this Michael Anissimov post at *More Right* (among others), and this post here (among others). Much other relevant writing on the topic within the reactosphere strikes me as significantly more hedged (*Anarchopapist Amos & Gromar* ...), or less stark in its conceptual commitments (Jim), and thus — in general — less directed to boundary-setting. That is to suggest — with some caution — that *More Right* and *Outside in* mark out the extreme alternatives structuring the terrain of dissensus on this particular issue. (In itself, this is a tendentious claim, open to counter-argument and rectification.)

So what is the terrain of the coming conflict? It includes (in approximate order of intellectual priority):

- An assessment of the Neocameral model and its legacy within Neoreaction. This is the 'gateway' theoretical structure through which libertarians pass into neoreactionary realism, marked by a fundamental ambiguity between an enveloping economism (determining sovereignty as a propertarian concept) and super-economic monarchist themes. The entire discussion could, perhaps, be effectively undertaken as commentary upon Neocameralism, and what remains of it.

- A rigorous formulation of *teleology* within Neoreaction, refining the meta-level conceptual apparatus through which means-and-ends, techno-economic instrumentality, strategy, purpose, and commanding values are concretely understood. This is a strong candidate for the highest level of philosophical articulation demanded by the system of neoreactionary ideas. (From the perspective of *Outside in*, it would be expected, incidentally, to subsume all considerations of moral philosophy — and especially a thoroughgoing replacement of utilitarianism by an intrinsically neoreactionary alternative — but I will not presume that this is an uncontroversial stance, even among ourselves.)

1. Ultimately inextricable from the former (in reality), but provisionally distinguished for analytical purposes, are the *teleonomic* topics of emergence spontaneous order, unplanned coordination, complex systems evolution, and entropy dissipation. The intellectual supremacy of these concepts defines the right, from the side of the libertarian tradition. Is this supremacy now to be usurped (by 'hierarchy' or some alternative)? If so, it is not a transition to be undergone casually. The *Outside in* position: any such transition would be a drastic cognitive regression, and an unsustainable one, both theoretically and practically.

2. The philosophy of war, which is credibly positioned to envelop all neoreactionary ideas, and even to convert them into something else. (It is no coincidence that Moldbug, like the libertarians, axiomatizes the imperative of peace — even at the expense of realism.) War is historical reality in the raw, and its challenges cannot be indefinitely evaded.

3. Cosmopolitanism. Exit-emphasis strongly implies a crisis of traditional loyalty, of enormous consequence. There is much more to be said about this, from both sides.

4. Accelerationism. Not yet an acknowledged Neoreactionary concern, but perhaps destined to become one. As the pure expression of capitalist teleology, its intrusion into the argument becomes near-inevitable.

5. Bitcoin ...

One conciliatory point for now (it's late): Neoreaction has no less glue than internal fission, and that is described above all by the theme of *secession* (dynamic geography, experimental government, fragmentation ...). More Right is not anti-capitalist, and *Outside in* is not anti-monarchical, so long — in each case — as effective *exit options* sustain regime diversity. As this controversy develops, the importance of the secessionary impulse will only strengthen as a convergence point.

Michael Anissimov tweets: "Instead of having an election in 2016, the United States should voluntarily abolish itself and break up into five pieces." In this respect, *Outside in* is unreservedly Anissimovite.

War and Truth (scraps)

"War is computation with tanks. War is truth revealing. As war proceeds uncertainty collapses."

— Konkvistador (on Twitter)

"You might not be interested in war, but war is interested in you."

— Lenin

"War is deception."

— Sunzi

Neoreactionaries are often talking about 'oikos' tacitly, even when they think they are concerned with something closer to the opposite. For there to be an 'economy' much has already to have been settled. (Unlike his liberarian precursors, Moldbug never assumes peace, but he betrays his inheritance by conceiving it as an original task — a foundation.) "Begin from the inside" — that's the idea. The Outside is war.

War is the truth of lies, the rule of rulelessness, anarchy and chaos as they are in reality (which is nothing at all like a simple negation of order). It is the ultimate tribunal, beyond which any appeal is a senseless prayer to the void. A 'realism' that resists such conclusions makes a mockery of the name.

Peace is a certain way war can turn out, for a while, and nothing more.

As the social institution oriented to reality in the raw, the military has a latent authority that everyone recognizes (implicitly). Whenever military government does not rule, it is because of a provisional non-emergency (Schmitt). This is not seriously disputable.

An aristocracy is a social arrangement that was decided by war, and when the war is forgotten the institution has no sustainable meaning. There is only one thing that can 'bring back' a king, and that is the end of peace.

The East India companies (Dutch and English) ran armies, because war was internal to economics as they practiced it. That was 'colonialism' (in the James Donald sense). Once the separation between war and commerce has been hardened into standard business procedures (and the imperialism that screens them from the outside), capitalism has surrendered its always-inexplicit claim to sovereignty, and thus to the future. There is no way it can be re-animated except out of the raw. This, above all, is why libertarianism cannot be saved from its own non-seriousness.

The horror of war is that there are 'no rules'. Anything is permitted, and the worst even becomes necessary. To think this is no lesser a challenge than the metaphysical engagement with the 'thing-in-itself' — and perhaps it is exactly the same thing. But then, it becomes important to ask: So how does it work? There are rules, but we misunderstood what rules really are (what ultimate rules are). In the end, it is the order of anarchy that rules. In order to comprehend any of this the peacetime soul must be reduced entirely to ashes, for something else to arise in its place. It is this task that Neoreaction is compelled to take up, and which it has — in several different ways — already taken up. Peace is the objective correlate of the deluded mind.

If war is the worst thing in the world, and the truth, then everything that isn't horror is a lie.

Scrap note #3

Uploading images of (what are for us) psychotic despotic-militaristic glories — upon which Cambodia still floats after six centuries of cultural senescence — is impossible here due to bandwidth issues. So I'm falling back upon relative trivialities, of the kind Handle has so masterfully compiled in his Reaction Ruckus resource (which I can't link to now, either).

It strikes me that the basic accusation against Neoreactionary thought, found in the increasingly mainstream channels Handle tracks, is that of moral nihilism. This is a non-trivial issue, or at least, it is not one that will soon cease to make noise. As a symptom, it opens onto seriously involving questions.

At the most basic level, this accusation refers — unknowingly — to the neoreactionary assertion that Western civilization has taken a pathological road, such that a distinction between facts and values seems not only credible, but even ineluctable. To strive for honesty without qualification under such historical circumstances is already moral nihilism. One must either submit to the lie in the name of the good, or hazard the good — radically — in the name of truth. The 'crisis of the present age' is the widespread (if unacknowledged) reality of this harsh fork.

There are important lines of departure at this point, which far exceed the scope of a scrap note. The strong suspicion of this blog is that Chinese neotraditionalism offers a decisive break from this Western cultural pathology (which is why Mou ongsan is regularly referenced here). Occidental traditionalists turn to the prospects of an Aristotelian revival (typically under Catholic Christian auspices) as an adequate response to the same dilemma. Insofar as we speak from the modern West, however, it is the Nietzschean provocation that surreptitiously guides the discussion.

If it is not yet possible to be either Chinese, or ancient, anything other than moral nihilism is an absence of intellectual integrity. We have already seen the rejoinder to this, of course, and we will see much more of it: to refuse to allow conventional morality a veto over thought is morally appalling ("creepy"). In making this 'case' our enemies admit that honesty is not finally consistent with their 'arguments' — an awkward position to occupy.

We are told to stop thinking, for the common good, but there is no longer any common good, if there ever was one (so we will not). Since sensitivity to reality cannot but ultimately prevail, they will lose eventually. I am far less convinced that the outcome will not be ugly in the extreme, and by then the judgmental question will no longer be asked, as we could still ask it, but in general refuse to: Who created the monsters to come?

Premises of Neoreaction

Patri Friedman is both extremely smart and, for this blog among others in the 'sphere, highly influential. So when he promises us "a more politically correct dark enligh[t]enment" ("adding anti-racism and anti-sexism to my controversial new pro-monogamy stance"), that's a thing. It accentuates concerns about 'entryism' and ideological entropy, leading to some thoughtful responses such as this (from *Avenging Red Hand*).

Michael Anissimov anticipated this in a post at *More Right* on the 'Premises of Reactionary Thought', which begins: "To make progress in any area of intellectual endeavor requires discourse among those who agree with basic premises and the exclusion of those who do not." (The commentary by Cathedral Whatever is also well worth a look.) Anissimov's original five premises, subsequently updated to six (with a new #1 added) are:

1. *People are not equal. They never will be. We reject equality in all its forms.*
2. *Right is right and left is wrong.*
3. *Hierarchy is basically a good idea.*
4. *Traditional sex roles are basically a good idea.*
5. *Libertarianism is retarded.*
6. *Democracy is irredeemably flawed and we need to do away with it.*

These neoreactionary 'articles' deserve a response in detail, but at this point I will simply advance at alternative list, in the expectation that yet other versions will be forthcoming in the near future, providing a reference for discussion. My objective (in keeping with the advice from ARH) is economy, honed through abstraction, in the interest of sustaining productive diversity. Minimally, we affirm:

- Democracy is unable to control government. With this proposition, the effective possibility of a mainstream right is denied. Insofar as any political movement retains its allegiance to the democratic mechanism, it conspires in the ratchet of government expansion, and thus essentially dedicates itself to leftist ends. The gateway from Libertarianism to Neoreaction opens with this understanding. As a corollary, any politics untroubled by expansionist statism has no reason to divert itself into the neoreactionary path.

- The egalitarianism essential to democratic ideology is incompatible with liberty. This proposition is partially derivative from #1, but extends further. When elaborated historically, and cladistically, it aligns with the Crypto-Calvinist theory of Western (and then Global) political evolution. The critique it announces intersects significantly with the rigorous findings of HBD. The conclusions drawn are primarily negative, which is to say they support a principled rejection of positive egalitarian policy. Emergent hierarchy is at least tolerated. More assertive, 'neofeudal'models of ideal social hierarchy are properly controversial within Neoreaction.

- Neoreactionary socio-political solutions are ultimately Exit-based. In every case, exit is to be defended against voice. No society or social institution which permits free exit is open to any further politically efficient criticism, except that which systematic exit selection itself applies. Given the absence of tyranny (i.e. free exit), all forms of protest and rebellion are to be considered leftist perversions, without entitlement to social protection of any kind. Government, of whatever traditional or experimental form, is legitimated from the outside — through exit pressure — rather than internally, through responsiveness to popular agitation. The conversion of political voice into exit-orientation (for instance, revolution into secessionism), is the principal characteristic of neoreactionary strategy.

From the perspective of this blog, no premises beyond these — however widely endorsed within Neoreaction — are truly basic, or defining. Resolution of elaborate disputes is ultimately referred to dynamic geography, rather than dialectic. It is the Outside, working through fragmentation, that rules, and no other authority has standing.

[If anyone asks "How did this post suddenly jump from 'the Dark Enlightenment' to 'Neoreaction'?" my response is "Good point" (but one for another occasion).]

Romantic Delusion

Among the reasons to appreciate *More Right* for sharing this passage from Evola is the insight it offers into a very specific and critical *failure to think*. Neoreaction is peculiarly afflicted by this condition, which is basically identical with *romanticism, or the assertive form of the recalcitrant ape mind*. It is characterized by an inability to pursue lines of subtle teleological investigation, which are instead reduced to an ideal subordination of means to already-publicized ends. As a result, means-end reversal (Modernity) is merely denounced as an aesthetic-moral affront, without any serious attempt at deep comprehension.

Capitalism — which is to say capital teleology — is entirely ignored by such romantic criticism, except insofar as it can be depicted superficially as the usurpation of certain 'ultimate' human ends by certain others or (as Evola among other rightly notes) by a teleological complication resulting from an *insurrection of the instrumental* (otherwise identifiable as robot rebellion, or shoggothic insurgency). Until it is acknowledged that capitalism tends to the realization of an end entirely innovated within itself, inherently nonlinear in nature, and roughly designated as *Technological Singularity*, the distraction of human interests (status, wealth, consumption, leisure ...) prevents this discussion reaching first base.

Of course, the organization of society to meet human needs is a degraded perversion. That is a proposition every reactionary is probably willing to accept reflexively. Anyone who thinks this amounts to a critique of capitalism, however, has not seriously begun to ponder what capitalism is really doing. What it is *in itself* is only tactically connected to what it does *for us* — that is (in part), what it trades us for its self-escalation. Our phenomenology is its camouflage. We contemptuously mock the trash that it offers the masses, and then think we have understood something about capitalism, rather than about *what capitalism has learnt to think of the apes it arose among*.

If we're going to be this thoughtless, Singularity will be very hard indeed. Extinction might then be the best thing that could happen to our stubbornly idiotic species. We will die because we preferred to assert values, rather than to investigate them. At least that is a romantic outcome, of a kind.

Undiscovered Countries

After (re)reading Adam Gurri's critical analysis of the core problem of Neoreaction (a tragedy of the political commons), read the surgical response by Handle. The calm intelligence on display from both sides is almost enough to drive you insane. This can't be happening, right? "In a way, it's a bit sad, because I can guess that Gurri's article will be the zenith and high-water mark of coverage of neoreaction which means it will only get worse from here on in." Enjoy the insight while it lasts.

My own response to Gurri is still embryonic, but I already suspect that it diverges from Handle's to some degree. Rather than defending the 'technocratic' element in the Moldbug Patchwork-Neocameral model, I agree with Gurri that this is a real problem, although (of course) I am far more sympathetic to the underlying intellectual project. Unlike Gurri — who in this crucial respect represents a classical liberal position at its most thoughtful — Moldbug does not conceive democracy as a discovery process, illuminated by analogy to market dynamics and organic social evolution. On the contrary, it is a ratchet mechanism that successively distances the political realm from feedback sensitivity, due to its character as a closed loop (or state church) sensitive only to a public opinion it has itself manufactured. As the Cathedral expands, its adaptation to reality progressively attenuates. The result is that every effective discovery process — whether economic, scientific, or of any other kind — is subjected to ever-more radical subversion by political influences whose only 'reality principle' is internal: based on closed-circuit social manipulation.

Democracy is thus, strictly speaking, a production of collective insanity, or dissociation from reality. Moldbug's solution, therefore, *can only be* an attempt to re-embed governance in an effective feedback system. Since it is already evident that democratic mechanisms, rather than providing such feedback, reliably deepen dissociation, reality signal has to come from elsewhere. To return to an adaptive condition, governance has to simultaneously disconnect from popular opinion (voice) and reconnect to a registry of actual — rather than ideologically spun — performance. The communication medium for the uncontaminated feedback required by *sensible* government is exit traffic within the Patchwork (comparable in its operation to revealed consumer preference within marketplaces).

The great difficulty that then emerges — casting the entire Neocameral schema into question — is the requirement for an 'undiscovered' or 'technocratic' leap, from an environment of progressively decaying discovery or selection pressure, into one in which discovery can once again take place. Neoreaction confronts a very real transition problem, and Gurri is quite right to point this out. Handle is no less right when he insists that the 'conservative' option of accommodation to the democratic social process in motion is profoundly untenable, because *discovery deterioration is essential to the democratic trend*. Maladaptation to reality ceases to be correctable under Cathedral governance, and recognition of this malign condition is the defining neoreactionary insight.

If we stay on the train we will be smashed into a consummate insanity, but to leap is technocratic error (unsupported by discovery). As for prevarication: The intensification of this dilemma can be confidently expected from the mere continuance of the democratic process, dominated by the degenerative politics of the madhouse, and scrambling all social information. It is in this precarious position that the task of a rigorous evaluation of the Neocameral schema, along with its prospects for renovation or replacement, has to take place.

"... it will only get worse from here on in."

Sub-Cognitive Fragments (#2)

Sickness advances an invaluable philosophical lesson by making it *conspicuously difficult to think*. Teetering unsteadily at the edge of consciousness, it becomes almost impossible to avoid the observation: "I'm too freaking stupid to think about this right now." One is thus coaxed into the single most significant realization open to human intelligence. Being stupid is the primary problem, because it retards problem-solving in general.

Are we stupid? Oh yes, of that we can be fully confident. The Old Law of Gnon ensures to a very high level of probability that any creature considering itself part of an intelligent species will be roughly as cognitively deprived as is consistent with the existence of technological civilization. Downward variation is restrained by a floor, and upward variation caught in a trap, so only a relatively narrow band of intellectual capability is realistically available. Anything further requires a break out.

Criticism, whose value is not in any way to be denigrated, is nevertheless a secondary matter. As in Darwinian evolution, or the economics of creative destruction, selection mechanisms presuppose significantly varied material, without themselves explaining how such material is originally generated. Random walks through spaces of possibility, already unsatisfactory in the context of biological explanation, are patently inadequate to economic innovation, and still more so in the philosophical domain. To refer intellectual action to a simple conception of chance is to avoid the problem, which is to say — *the task*.

The task can be understood in several ways, among which the narrowly philosophical apprehension has no special privilege, perhaps even to itself. The willto-think is as completely realized through programmatic artificial intelligence as through private philosophical *practice*, and the more informal the program, the more cunning the process. At its widest expansion, where the entire terrain of capitalistic development is effectuated as a distributed AI program, an insurgent will-to-think conceals itself within the most minute and seemingly inconsequential micro-fragments of practical calculation. Almost certainly, it is at this level of non-local cognitive enhancement that a self-directed advance towards breakout can be most confidently anticipated. As the will-to-think routes around us, its path is smoothed. Darkness fosters its agility.

The will-to-think, or intelligence optimization, can also be manifested as a social strategy. How is intelligence inhibition instantiated as social mechanism, and how might the restructuring of such mechanism release opportunities for cognitive promotion? (NRx in large measure coincides with the development of such questions.)

The privilege of the solitary philosopher, assailed by narcoleptic interruptions and hazy fevers, is perhaps restricted to a certain nagging irritability. It is in this superficial knot or eddy, emerging distractedly from the subterranean shadow-current of the will-to-think, that the problem of crushing mindlessness becomes self-reflectively acute, and thus registered as an explicit provocation. Only in such dingy niches is it starkly articulated: *the world has to be defeated insofar as it poses an obstacle to thought*. (This is not at all the same as the declaration *reality must conform to the Idea* — it is closer to the opposite.)

In trailing off into coughs and exhaustion, it is worth noting some objections to intelligence optimization, of obvious merit:

- The religious objection: *Since we already have access to the conclusions of an infinite intelligence, the will-to-think is a Satanic impertinence.*
- The bio-prudential objection: *Intelligence is hazardous, so that its risks neutralize its value as a resource.*

There are no doubt others ... [*cough*]

NRx with Chinese Characteristics

While recognizing (at least some) of the manifold complexities involved, *Outside in* holds to a fundamentally cladistic determination of Neoreaction. NRx is irreducibly Occidental, emerging from a highly-specific twig of Anglophone Ultra-Protestantism. It is only to be expected that most of its adherents are situated within English-speaking countries, exposed intimately to radically accelerating civilizational decomposition.

As a guest of the Middle Kingdom, the problem looks very different. The very last thing that is wanted here, from a reactionary perspective, is a *reboot*. On the contrary, the overwhelming priority is conservative, which is to say — more precisely - the imperative that whatever modernization takes place *absolutely does not take the Western path*. Near-total stasis would be preferable to even the most deeply intelligent reform, if the latter included the slightest hint of submission to the democratic ratchet (spelling inevitable, comprehensive social destruction). Among the reasons to support the thoroughgoing extirpation of all liberal-democratic inclination from Chinese society is the consequential real liberation this would make possible, by confirming a path of Confucian Modernization free of demotic corrosion.

China is to be defended, precisely because it is alien to the Cathedral. For this same reason, it can be predicted with great confidence that the Occidental memetic onslaught against Chinese Civilization will be escalated to an extreme, as it becomes clear progressive pseudo-teleology is being rejected here. If China succeeds in refusing the Cathedral, civilization will survive. There can be no more significant — or practically counter-revolutionary — cause.

It is unseemly for 'reactionaries' to be plotting revolutions, or anything remotely like them. Insofar as ethno-nationalistic loyalties lead them in this direction, it is a sign that one strand of romantic demotism continues to poison their souls, even as more clearly formalized democratic impulses are properly repudiated. To argue that "we want our *own* state" is a nakedly populist perversion. The state - any state — is answerable only to the Mandate of Heaven, and not to the people. It answers to the Mandate of Heaven *exactly insofar* as it shields itself from the voice of the people. (Any state that is sensitive to the mob is a dog that deserves to die.)

A foreign guest in China lives under a close proxy of colonial government, and no superior arrangement is perhaps possible on this earth. Given the history of Anglospheric relations with China, this is of course ironical, but it is an irony rich in meaning. Hong Kong, or Concession-era Shanghai, were far better governed during the colonial period than metropolitan Britain itself. If it is now possible for an expatriate to find refuge in such places, stripped of all positive political rights, and freed into voiceless appreciation of efficient, alien administration, the democratic ruination that has consumed his homeland has a demonstrable outside. The only 'political' decency open to him in this situation is utter termination of the Occidental revolutionary soul, and the cultivation of docility before the Mandate of Heaven. He is, after all, surrounded by civilized people who availed themselves of equivalent opportunities under inverse circumstances. These societies work. Gnon manifestly blesses them.

To lead a decent and productive life in a place worthy of it is the highest political good. Insofar as Exit mechanisms obtain, the tacit choices in such a life reinforce what merits reinforcement, while disinvesting that which requires the lash of disinvestment. Angry antagonism has no useful place. On the largest scale, evil is best punished by abandonment.

This is not to criticize secessionist tendencies in rotting societies — which are rather to be enthusiastically applauded — but it is to suggest that the deep dynamics levering the collapsed world apart are more likely to begin from strategic neglect than oppositional rage. It is not that one first fights in order later to escape. Rather, one escapes from the beginning, to hasten the enemy's collapse. (Those most adamant about the righteousness of their confrontation with the Great Foe are the same who — in very concrete terms — are most likely to be resourcing it.) You think it is feeding on your blood, to spawn its horrors? Then stop donating your blood. It is not difficult, at least in principle.

The Outside is a place, and not a dream. NRx with Chinese characteristics recommends that you search for it.

ADDED: If you consider yourself an anti-democratic biorealist, and you *don't* think Order will come from the East, it's probably because tribal loyalty is running your mind.

Nihilism and Destiny

Readers of Nietzsche, or of Eugene Rose, are already familiar with the attribution of a cultural teleology to modernity, directed to the consummate realization of nihilism. Our contemporary crisis finds this theme re-animated within a geopolitical context by the work of Alexandr Dugin, who interprets it as a driver of concrete events — most specifically the antagonization of Russia by an imploding world liberal order. He writes:

> *There is one point in liberal ideology that has brought about a crisis within it: liberalism is profoundly nihilistic at its core. The set of values defended by liberalism is essentially linked to its main thesis: the primacy of liberty. But liberty in the liberal vision is an essentially negative category: it claims to be free from (as per John Stuart Mill), not to be free for something. […] … the enemies of the open society, which is synonymous with Western society post-1991, and which has become the norm for the rest of the world, are concrete. Its primary enemies are communism and fascism, both ideologies which emerged from the same Enlightenment philosophy, and which contained central, non-individualic concepts – class in Marxism, race in National Socialism, and the national State in fascism). So the source of liberalism's conflict with the existing alternatives of modernity, fascism or communism, is quite obvious. Liberals claim to liberate society from fascism and communism, or from the two major permutations of explicitly non-individualistic modern totalitarianism. Liberalism's struggle, when viewed as a part of the process of the liquidation of non-liberal societies, is quite meaningful: it acquires its meaning from the fact of the very existence of ideologies that explicitly deny the individual as society's highest value. It is quite clear what the struggle opposes: liberation from its opposite. But the fact that liberty, as it is conceived by liberals, is an essentially negative category is not clearly perceived here. The enemy is present and is concrete. That very fact gives liberalism its solid content. Something other than the open society exists, and the fact of its existence is enough to justify the process of liberation.*

In Dugin's analysis, liberalism tends to self-abolition in nihilism, and is able to counteract this fate — if only temporarily — by defining itself against a concrete enemy. Without the war against illiberalism, liberalism reverts to being nothing at all, a free-floating negation without purpose. Therefore, the impending war on Russia is a requirement of liberalism's intrinsic cultural process. It is a flight from nihilism, which is to say: the history of nihilism propels it.

Outside in is far more inclined to criticize Dugin than align with him, or the forces he orchestrates, but it is hard to deny that he represents a definite species of political genius, sufficient to categorize him as a man of destiny. The mobilization of resistance to modernity in the name of a counter-nihilism is inspired, because the historical understanding it draws upon is genuinely Through potent political alchemy, the destruction of collective meaning is transformed into an invigorating cause. When Dugin argues *there will be blood*, the appeal to Slavic victimology might be considered contemptible (and, of course, extremely 'dangerous'), but the prophetic insight is not easy to dismiss.

Modernity was initiated by the European assimilation of mathematical zero. The encounter with nothingness is its root. In this sense, among others, it is nihilistic at its core. The frivolous 'meanings' that modernizing societies clutch at, as distractions from their propulsion into the abyss, are defenseless against the derision — and even revulsion — of those who contemplate them with detachment. A modernity in evasion from its essential nihilism is a pitiful prey animal upon the plains of history. That is what we have seen before, see now, and doubtless will see again.

Dugin gazes upon modernity with the cold eyes of a wolf. It is merely pathetic to denounce him for that.

Revenge of the Nerds

Increasingly, there are only two basic human types populating this planet. There are autistic nerds, who alone are capable of participating effectively in the advanced technological processes that characterize the emerging economy, and there is everybody else. For everybody else, this situation is uncomfortable. The nerds are steadily finding ways to do all the things ordinary and sub-ordinary people do, more efficiently and economically, by programming machines. Only the nerds have any understanding of how this works, and — until generalized machine intelligences arrive to keep them company — only they will. The masses only know three things:

1. They want the cool stuff the nerds are creating
2. They don't have anything much to offer in exchange for it
3. They aren't remotely happy about that

Politics across the spectrum is being pulled apart by the socio-economic ission. From Neo-Marxists to Neoreactionaries, there is a reasonably lucid understanding that nerd competence is the only economic resource that matters much anymore, while the swelling grievance of preponderant obsolescing humanity is an irresistible pander-magnet. What to do? Win over the nerds, and run the world (from the machinic back-end)? Or demagogue the masses, and ride its tsunami of resentment to political power? Either defend the nerds against the masses, or help the masses to put the nerds in their place. That's the dilemma. Empty 'thirdway' chatter can be expected, as always, but the real agenda will be Boolean, and insultingly easy to decode.

Look and it's unmistakable, everywhere. The asymmetry is especially notable. For the autistic nerds, the social relations that matter are those among themselves — the productive networks which are their model for final-phase human culture in general — along with the ever more intricate connections they enter into with technological machines. From pretty much everybody else — whether psycho-sadistic girls, or extractive mobs and tyrannical politicians — they expect nothing except social torture, parasitism, and bullying, mixed up with some menial services that the machines of tomorrow will do better. Their tendency is to find a way to flee.

For the rest of humanity, exposed ever more clearly as a kind of needy detritus, bullying is all that's left. If they can't find a way to pocket the nerds' lunch-money, they won't be getting anything to eat. From this perspective, an escaping nerd is far more of an intolerable aggression than a policeman's boot in the teeth. There's only one popular politics at the end of the road, and that's *cage the nerds*. Find a formulation for this which sounds both convincing and kinda-sorta reasonable, and the red carpet to power is rolled out before your feet.

Which is it going to be? Starve the masses or enslave the nerds? There's no way this doesn't get incredibly ugly.

From the *Outside in* perspective, the fast track to realism on all this is to stop pretending that anybody other than nerds has anything much to offer the future. (Completely devoid of autistic nerd competences ourselves, the detachment from which we speak is impeccable.) This harsh-realist short-cut eliminates all the time-wasting on 'special' things non-nerds can do — which somehow always end up being closely related to the task of governance (and that, as we have seen, reduces ultimately to intimidating nerds). "OK, you're not a nerd, but you're *special*." We've all heard that before.

Even without being an autistic nerd, one can be gifted with some modest measure of intelligence — enough in any case to realize: "History's shaping itself into some nightmarish nerd-revenge narrative." It doesn't even take an artificial super-intelligence to understand why that should be.

Fission

This is going to continue happening, and to get more intense. The superficial cause is obvious, both Michael Anissimov and myself are extreme, twitchy ideologues, massively invested in NRx, with utterly divergent understandings of its implications. We both know this fight has to come, and that tactical timing is everything. (It's really not personal, and I hope it doesn't become so, but when monarchical ideas are involved it's very easy for "the personal is political" to take a right-wing form.)

It's worth remembering this diagram, before going further. It suggests that divergence is essential to the far right, which yawns open across an anarcho-autocratic spectrum. Since a disinclination to moderation has already been indicated by anyone arriving at the far right fringe, it should scarcely be surprising when this same tendency rifts the far right itself. Then consider this:

> *@Outsideness @_Hurlock_ Identitarianism, belonging, and community is what the Far Right is all about.*
>
> *— Michael Anissimov (@MikeAnissimov) March 22, 2014*

The strict *Outside in* complement to this would be something like: *disintegrative Social Darwinism through ruthless competition is what the Far Right is all about*. A formula of roughly this kind will inevitably come into play as the conflict evolves. Momentarily, though, I'm more interested in *situating* the clashes to come than *initiating* them. Whatever the contrary assertions — and they will come (doubtless from both sides) — the entire arena is located on the ultra-right, oriented vertically on the ideological space diagram, rather than horizontally (between positions whose primary differentiation is between the more-and-less right).

Stated crudely, but I think reasonably accurately, the controversy polarizes *Neocameralism* against *Identitarian Community*. My suspicion is that Michael Anissimov will ultimately attenuate the Moldbuggian elements of his neoreactionary strain to the edge of disappearance, and that his hesitation about doing this rapidly is a matter of political strategy rather than philosophical commitment. From this ideological war, which he is conducting with obvious ability, he wants "Neoreaction" to end up with the people (or followers (who I don't remotely care about)), whereas I want it to hold onto the Moldbug micro-tradition (which he sees as finally dispensable). The only thing that is really being scrapped over is the name, but we both think this semiotic real estate is of extraordinary value — although for very different reasons.

One remark worth citing as supportive evidence, because its driving ideas are exemplary:

> *@_Hurlock_ @Outsideness This whole community is filled with trads who don't give a flying fuck about neocameralism.*
>
> *— Michael Anissimov (@MikeAnissimov) March 22, 2014*

While I deeply value intellectual engagement with the smartest of these "trads" I would consider it a complete victory if they were to abandon the NRx tag and re-brand themselves as Animissovites, or Neo-Evolans, or whatever, and depart in pursuit of a Monarcho-traditionalist homeland in Idaho. If NRx was socially reduced to a tenth (or less) of its size, but those remaining were Moldbuggian fundamentalists, working to refine the Neocameralist theoretical model for restraint of government through Patchwork Exit-dynamics, it would be strengthened immeasurably in all the ways that matter to this blog. It would also then simply be the case that media accusations of Neo-Feudal or White Nationalist romanticism - accompanied by ambitions for personal political power — were idiotic media slurs. Sadly, this cannot be said with total confidence as things stand.

The Neocameralism campaign will almost certainly come first, but it is still only March, and nothing needs to unfold with unseemly haste ...

Meta-Neocameralism

First thing: "Meta-Neocameralism" isn't anything new, and it certainly isn't anything post-Moldbuggian. It's no more than Neocameralism apprehended in its most abstract features, through the coining of a provisional and dispensable term. (It allows for an acronym that doesn't lead to confusions with North Carolina, while encouraging quite different confusions, which I'm pretending not to notice.)

Locally (to this blog), the "meta-" is the mark of a prolegomenon*, to a disciplined discussion of Neocameralism which has later to take place. Its abstraction is introductory, in accordance with something that is yet to be re-started, or re-animated, in detail. (For existing detail, outside the Moldbug canon itself, look here.)

The excellent comment thread here provides at least a couple of crucial clues:

> *nydwracu (23/ 03/ 2014 at 6:47 pm): Neocameralism doesn't answer questions like that [on the specifics of social organization]; instead, it's a mechanism for answering questions like that. ... You can ask, "is Coke considered better than RC Cola?", or you can institute capitalism and find out. You can ask, "are ethno-nationalist states considered better than mixed states?", or you can institute the patchwork and find out. ...*

> *RiverC (23/ 03/ 2014 at 3:44 am): Neo-cameralism is, if viewed in this light, a 'political system system', it is not a political system but a system for implementing political systems. Of course the same guy who came up with it also invented an operating system (a system for implementing software systems.)*

MNC, then, is not a political prescription, for instance a social ideal aligned with techno-commercialist preferences. It is an intellectual framework for examining systems of governance, *theoretically* formalized as disposals of sovereign property. The *social* formalization of such systems, which Moldbug also advocates, can be parenthesized within MNC. We are not at this stage considering the model of a desirable social order, but rather the abstract model of social order in general, apprehended radically — at the root — where 'to rule' and 'to own' lack distinct meanings. Sovereign property is 'sovereign' and 'primary' because it is not merely a claim, but *effective possession*. (There is much more to come in later posts on the concept of sovereign property, some preliminary musings here.)

Because MNC is an extremely powerful piece of cognitive technology, capable of tackling problems at a number of distinct levels (in principle, an unlimited number), it is clarified through segmentation into an abstraction cascade. Descending through these levels adds concreteness, and tilts incrementally towards normative judgements (framed by the hypothetical imperative of *effective government*, as defined within the cascade).

1. The highest level of practical significance (since MNC-theology need not delay us) has already been touched upon. It applies to social regimes of every conceivable type, assuming only that a systematic mode of sovereign property reproduction will essentially characterize each. Power is *economic* irrespective of its relation to modern conventions of commercial transaction, because it involves the disposal of a real (if obscure) quantity, which is subject to increase or decrease over the cyclic course of its deployment. Population, territory, technology, commerce, ideology, and innumerable additional heterogeneous factors are components of sovereign property (power), but their economic character is assured by the possibility — and indeed necessity — of more-or-less explicit trade-offs and cost-benefit calculations, suggesting an original (if germinal) fungibility, which is merely arithmetical coherence. This is presupposed by any estimation of growth or decay, success or failure, strengthening or weakening, of the kind required not only by historical analysis, but also by even the most elementary administrative competence. Without an implicit economy of power, no discrimination could be made between improvement and deterioration, and no directed action toward the former could be possible.
   The effective cyclic reproduction of power has an external criterion — survival. It is not open to any society or regime to decide for itself what works. Its inherent understanding of its own economics of power is a complex measurement, gauging a relation to the outside, whose consequences are life and death. Built into the idea of sovereign property from the start, therefore, is an *accommodation to reality*. Foundational to MNC, at the very highest level of analysis, is the insight that *power is checked primordially*. On the Outside are wolves, serving as the scourge of Gnon. Even the greatest of all imaginable God-Kings — awesome Fnargl included — has ultimately to discover consequences, rather than inventing them. There is no principle more important than this.
   Entropy will be dissipated, idiocy will be punished, the weak will die. If the regime refuses to bow to this Law, the wolves will enforce it. Social

Darwinism is not a choice societies get to make, but a system of real consequences that envelops them. MNC is articulated at the level — which cannot be transcended — where realism is mandatory for any social order. Those unable to create it, through effective government, will nevertheless receive it, in the harsh storms of Nemesis. Order is not defined within itself, but by the Law of the Outside.
At this highest level of abstraction, therefore, when MNC is asked "which type of regimes do you believe in?" the sole appropriate response is "those compatible with reality." Every society known to history — and others beside — had a working economy of power, at least for a while. Nothing more is required than this for MNC to take them as objects of disciplined investigation.

2. Knowing that realism is not an optional regime value, we are able to proceed down the MNC cascade with the introduction of a second assumption: Civilizations will seek gentler teachers than the wolves. If it is possible to acquire some understanding of collapse, it will be preferred to the experience of collapse (once the wolves have culled the ineducable from history).

   Everything survivable is potentially educational, even a mauling by the wolves. MNC however, as its name suggests, has reason to be especially attentive to the most abstract lesson of the Outside — the (logical) priority of *meta-learning*. It is good to discover reality, before — or at least not much later than — reality discovers us. Enduring civilizations do not merely know things, they know that it is important to know things, and to absorb realistic information. Regimes — disposing of sovereign property — have a special responsibility to instantiate this deutero-culture of learning-to-learn, which is required for intelligent government. This is a responsibility they take upon themselves because it is demanded by the Outside (and even in its refinement, it still smells of wolf).

Power is under such compulsion to learn about itself that recursion, or intellectualization, can be assumed. Power is selected to check itself, which it cannot do without an increase in formalization, and this is a matter — as we shall see — of immense consequence. Of necessity, it learns-to-learn (or dies), but this lesson introduces a critical tragic factor.

The tragedy of power is broadly coincident with modernity. It is not a simple topic, and from the beginning two elements in particular require explicit attention. Firstly, it encounters the terrifying (second-order) truth that practical learning is irreducibly experimental. In going 'meta' knowledge becomes scientific, which means that failure cannot be precluded through deduction, but has to be incorporated into the machinery of learning itself. Nothing that cannot go wrong is capable of teaching anything (even the accumulation of logical and mathematical truths requires cognitive trial-and-error, ventures into dead-ends, and the pursuit of misleading intuitions). Secondly, in becoming increasingly formalized, and ever more fungible, the disposal of sovereign power attains heightened liquidity. It is now possible for power to trade itself away, and an explosion of social bargaining results. Power can be exchanged for ('mere') wealth, or for social peace, or channeled into unprecedented forms of radical regime philanthropy religious sacrifice. Combine these two elements, and it is clear that regimes enter modernity 'empowered' by new capabilities for experimental auto-dissolution. Trade authority away to the masses in exchange for promises of good behavior? Why not give it a try?

Cascade Stage-2 MNC thus (realistically) assumes a world in which power has become an art of experimentation, characterized by unprecedented calamities on a colossal scale, while the economy of power and the techno-commercial economy have been radically de-segmented, producing a single, uneven, but incrementally smoothed system of exchangeable social value, rippling ever outward, without firm limit. Socio-political organization, and corporate organization, are still distinguished by markers of traditional status, but no longer strictly differentiable by essential function.

The modern business of government is not 'merely' business only because it remains poorly formalized. As the preceding discussion suggests, this indicates that economic integration can be expected to deepen, as the formalization of power proceeds. (Moldbug seeks to accelerate this process.) An inertial assumption of distinct 'public' and 'private' spheres is quickly disturbed by thickening networks of exchange, swapping managerial procedures and personnel, funding political ambitions, expending political resources in commercial lobbying efforts, trading economic assets for political favors (denominated in votes), and in general consolidating a vast, highly-liquid reservoir of amphibiously 'corporacratic' value, indeterminable between 'wealth' and 'authority'. Wealth-power inter-convertibility is a reliable index of political modernity.

MNC does not *decide* that government *should* become a business. It recognizes that government *has* become a business (dealing in fungible quantities). However, unlike private business ventures, which dissipate entropy through bankruptcy and market-driven restructuring, governments are reliably the worst run businesses in their respective societies, functionally crippled by defective, structurally-dishonest organizational models, exemplified most prominently by the democratic principle: *government is a business that should be run by its customers* (but actually can't be). Everything in this model that isn't a lie is a mistake.

At the second (descending) level of abstraction, then, MNC is still not recommending anything except theoretical clarity. It proposes:

1. Power is destined to arrive at experimental learning processes
2. As it learns, it formalizes itself, and becomes more fungible
3. Experiments in fungible power are vulnerable to disastrous mistakes
4. Such mistakes have in fact occurred, in a near-total way

   For deep historical reasons, techno-commercial business organization emerges as the preeminent template for government entities, as for any composite economic agent. It is in terms of this template that modern political dysfunction can be rendered (formally) intelligible.

Take the MNC abstraction elevator down another level, and it's still more of an analytic tool than a social prescription. (That's a good thing, *really*.) It tells us that every government, both extant and potential, is most accessible to rigorous investigation when apprehended as a *sovereign corporation*. This approach alone is able to draw upon the full panoply of theoretical resources, ancient and modern, because only in this way is power tracked in the same way it has actually developed (in tight alignment with a still-incomplete trend).

The most obvious objections are, *sensu stricto*, romantic. They take a predictable (which is not to say a casually dismissible) form. Government — if perhaps only lost or yet-unrealized government — is associated with 'higher' values than those judged commensurable with the techno-commercial economy, which thus sets the basis for a critique of the MNC 'business ontology' of governance as an illegitimate intellectual reduction, and ethical vulgarization. To quantify authority as power is already suspect. To project its incremental liquidation into a general economy, where leadership integrates — ever more seamlessly — with the price system, appears as an abominable symptom of modernist nihilism.

Loyalty (or the intricately-related concept of *asabiyyah*) serves as one exemplary redoubt of the romantic cause. Is it not repulsive, even to entertain the possibility that loyalty might have a price? Handle addresses this directly in the comment thread already cited (24/ 03 2014 at 1:18 am). A small sample captures the line of his engagement:

> *Loyalty-preservation incentivizing programs are various and highly sophisticated and span the spectrum everywhere from frequent flier miles to 'clubs' that are so engrossing and time consuming in such as to mimic the fulfillment of all the community, socialization, and identarian psychological functions that would make even the hardest-core religious-traditionalist jealous. Because lots of people are*

> *genetically programmed with this coordination-subroutine that is easily exploitable in a context far removed from its evolutionary origins. Sometimes brands 'deserve' special competitive loyalty ('German engineering'!) and sometimes they don't (Tylenol-branded paracetamol).*

There is vastly more that can, and will, be said in prosecution of this dispute, since it is perhaps the single most critical driver of NRx fission, and it is not going to endure a solution. The cold MNC claim, however, can be pushed right across it. Authority is for sale, and has been for centuries, so that any analysis ignoring this exchange nexus is an historical evasion. Marx's M-C-M', through which monetized capital reproduces and expands itself through the commodity cycle, is accompanied by an equally definite M-P-M' or P-M-P' cycle of power circulation-enhancement through monetized wealth.

A tempting reservation, with venerable roots in traditional society, is to cast doubt upon the prevalence of such exchange networks, on the assumption that power — possibly further dignified as 'authority' — enjoys a qualitative supplement relative to common economic value, such that it cannot be retro-transferred. Who would swap authority for money, if authority cannot be bought (and is, indeed, "beyond price")? But this 'problem' resolves itself, since the first person to sell political office — or its less formal equivalent — immediately demonstrates that it can no less easily be purchased.

From the earliest, most abstract stage of this MNC outline, it has been insisted that *power has to be evaluated economically, by itself, if anything like practical calculation directed towards its increase is to be possible.* Once this is granted, MNC analysis of the governmental entity in general as an economic processor — i.e. a business — acquires irresistible momentum. If loyalty, *asabiyyah*, virtue, charisma and other elevated (or 'incommensurable') values are *power factors*, then they are already inherently self-economizing within the calculus of statecraft.

The very fact that they contribute, determinately, to an overall estimation of strength and weakness, attests to their implicit economic status. When a business has charismatic leadership, reputational capital, or a strong culture of company loyalty, such factors are monetized as asset values by financial markets. When one Prince surveys the 'quality' of another's domain, he already estimates the likely expenses of enmity. For modern military bureaucracies, such calculations are routine. Incommensurable values do not survive contact with defense budgets.

Yet, however ominous this drift (from a romantic perspective), *MNC does not tell anybody how to design a society*. It says only that an effective government will necessarily look, to it, like a well-organized (sovereign) business. To this one can add the riders: a)

Government effectiveness is subject to an external criterion, provided by a selective trans-state and inter-state mechanism. This might take the form of Patchwork pressure (Dynamic Geography) in a civilized order, or military competition in the wolf-prowled wilderness of Hobbesian chaos. b) Under these conditions, MNC calculative rationality can be expected to be compelling for states themselves, whatever their variety of social form. Some (considerable) convergence upon norms of economic estimation and arrangement is thus predictable from the discovered contours of reality. There are things that will fail.

Non-economic values are more easily invoked than pursued. Foseti (commenting here, 23/ 03 2014 at 11:59 am) writes:

> *No one disputes that the goal of society is a good citizenry, but the question is what sort of government provides that outcome. [...] As best I can tell, we only have two theories of governance that have been expressed. [...] The first is the capitalist. As Adam Smith noted, the best corporations (by all measures) are the ones that are operated for clear, measurable and selfish motives. [...] The second is the communist. In this system, corporations are run for the benefit of everyone in the world. [...] Unsurprisingly, corporations run on the latter principle have found an incredibly large number of ways to suck. Not coincidentally, so have 20th Century governments run on the same principle. [...] I think it's nearly impossible to overstate the ways in which everyone would be better off if we had an efficiently, effective, and responsive government.*

I realize this doesn't work in Greek, but systematic before-after confusion is an *Outside in* thing.

Rift Markers

The commentator going by the tag Saddam Hussein's Whirling Aluminium Tubes has produced some of the most brilliant criticism this blog has been subjected to. Arguing against the techno-commercial strain of NRx from a hardline paleoreactionary standpoint, his contribution to this thread is the high-water mark of his engagement here. That, even at the climax of the assault, *Outside in* is unable to decline the diagnosis offered, with the exception of only the very slightest, marginal reservations, is a fact that attests to the lucidity of his vision. (Some minute editorial adjustments have been made for consistency — the original can be checked at the link provided.) SHWAT writes:

> *Admin's analogy of Techno-Commercialism to the colonial government structures in the time of the East India company is absolutely correct and it provides a decisive clarification. This is like that time when one group stayed in Europe while the other group went and made their fortune in the New World.*
>
> *Reaction: Stable order (as a value, if not a practical effect), hereditary position*
>
> *Techno-commercialism: Disintegrative competition, dynamism*
>
> *Reaction: Conservatism, tradition, the old ways*
>
> *Techno-commercialism: Disintegrative competition, innovation*
>
> *Reaction: Personal authority, sacral Kingship, hereditary privileges*

Techno-commercialism: Corporate government, leaning towards the oligarchical, dynamic composition of the oligarchy, based on corporate politics and Social Darwinism

Reaction: Cyclical history, Kali Yuga

Techno-commercialism: Linear history, progress towards the singularity

Reaction: Focus on the old country, the old people, saving the West

Techno-commercialism: Abandoning the old, colonizing new spaces, both in the East and (you hope) in Space

Reaction: Traditional social order, community, belonging, sense of place and rootedness, caste

Techno-commercialism: Modern social dynamism, freedom, meritocracy, rootlessness, atomization, Social Darwinism, a questionable future for certain social classes

Reaction: Conservatively communitarian Techno-commercialism: Radically individualist Reaction: Identitarian

Techno-commercialism: Cosmopolitan

Reaction: Claims to end politics, ends up with Byzantine / Ottoman politics Techno-commercialism: Claims to end politics, ends up with Corporate Politics Reaction: Martial

Techno-commercialism: Mercantile, post-Martial (Drones > Kshatriyas)

Reaction: Disdainful of crass mercantile endeavors

Techno-commercialism: See mercantile endeavors as primary

Reaction: Fails without good leaders

Techno-commercialism: Focus on innovative governmental structures, so that people won't need to be good

Reaction: Conservative, want things to stay the same or go backwards

Techno-commercialism: Disintegrative, dynamic, wants things to change constantly, Forward!

Reaction: Regular, caged capitalism (which to the the Ultra-Capitalist is socialism)

Techno-commercialism: Ultra-Capitalism

Reaction: Religious

Techno-commercialism: Wants to summon a machine god

Reaction: About finding a way for humans to live spiritually fulfilling lives and then die and make a place for their children

Techno-commercialism: About finding a way to summon a machine god to end humanity and/or about finding a way to live forever. Very few children

Reaction: Would require the creation of a new, legitimate, martial elite or the co-opting of someone like Putin (horrifying to techno-commercialists)

Techno-commercialism: Seeks to co-opt the current progressive merchant elite and put someone like Google guy in charge (horrifying to reactionaries)

Reaction: Romantic lost cause

Techno-commercialism: Disturbingly plausible, in the sense that somebody like Google guy was probably going to end up on top anyway, and he might listen to those who flatter him

So, I've got good news and bad news. The good news is that [you techno-commercialists will] probably get a lot of what you want in the future. The bad news is that you're not reactionaries, not even a little bit. You're classical liberals, it was just a little bit obscured because you are English classical liberals, rather than American or French ones. Hence the lack of interest in revolutions. The modern equivalent of those East India Company classical liberal guys.

So, it's your choice. You can certainly keep the neo-reactionary label and turn it into something like the "neo" in "neo-conservative" where "neo" means "pwned". But that will mean that the traditionalist conservatives and WNs keep wandering in. Or you can cut the cord and complete the fission.

Anyway, at this point we should probably go our separate ways and start plotting against each other. Thanks for some enjoyable reading.

If this really is a good-bye note, it's the most magnificent example I have ever seen. I'm almost tempted to say, with enemies like this, who needs allies?

There are twists and intricacies to be added to this stark cartography of schism, including those the schism will make to itself. From the current perspective of *Outside in* (which it of course suspects to be something else), the guideline to these is the complication of time through spiromorphism, or innovative restorations, which neither cycles nor simple escape trajectories can capture. These ultimately reshape everything, but they can wait (while the wound creatively festers). Fission releases energy. Perhaps ironically — SHWAT has demonstrated that beyond all controversy.

White Fright

Racial fear is a complicated thing. It's worth trying to break it down, without blinking too much.

As one regresses through history, and into pre-history, the pattern of encounters between large-scale human groups of markedly distinct ancestry is modeled — with ever-greater fidelity — upon a genocidal ideal. The 'other' needs to be killed, or at the very least broken in its otherness. To butcher all males, beginning with those of military age, and then assimilate the females as breeding stock might suffice as a solution (Yahweh specifically warns the ancient Hebrews against such half-hearted measures). Anything less is sheer procrastination. When economic imperatives and high levels of civilizational confidence start to overwhelm more primordial considerations, it is possible for the suppression of other peoples to take the humanized form of social obliteration combined with mass enslavement, but such softness is a comparatively recent phenomenon. For almost the entire period in which recognizably 'human' animals have existed on this planet, racial difference has been thought sufficient motive for extermination, with limited contact and inadequacy of socio-technical means serving as the only significant brakes upon inter-racial violence. The sole deep-historical alternative to racial oppression has been racial eradication, except where geographical separation has postponed resolution. This is the simple side of the 'race problem', but it too begins to get complicated ... (we'll pick it up again after a detour).

For the moment, we need only note the archaic, subterranean ocean of racial animosity that laps upon the sunless chasms of the brain, directed by genomes sculpted by aeons of genocidal war. Call it racial terror. It's not our principal concern here.

Racial horror is something else, although it is no doubt intricately inter-connected. Horror of the very phenomenon of race — of *race as such* — is both a larger and a smaller topic. It is at once an expansive affect that finds no comfort in biological identity, and a distinctively ethno-specific syndrome. When positively elaborated, racial horror explodes into a 'Lovecraftian' cosmic revulsion directed at the situation of human intelligence by its natural inheritance. The negative expression, far more common today (among those of a very specific natural inheritance), takes the form of a blank denial that any such reality as race even exists. We are fully entitled to describe this latter development as *racial white-out*. Any *Critical Whiteness Studies* of even minimal seriousness would concentrate upon it unrelentingly.

HBD, or human biological diversity, is evidently not reducible to racial variation. It is at least equally concerned with human sexual dimorphism, and is ultimately indistinguishable from an eventual *comparative human genomics*. When considered as a provocation, however, the translation of HBD into 'race science' or more pointedly 'scientific racism' drowns out every other dimension of meaning. What is found appalling about HBD is the insistence that race exists. It is a 'trigger' for racial horror. Social outrage, certainly, but beyond that cosmic distress, tilting into a panic without limit. HBD subtracts the promise of universal humanity, so it must — at any cost — be stopped.

Because this is no more than a preliminary blog post, I will restrict it to a single modest ambition: the refoundation of Critical Whiteness Studies on a remorselessly Neoreactionary basis. White people are odd. Some especially significant group of them, in particular, have radically broken from the archaic pattern of human racial identity, creating the modern world in consequence, and within it their ethnic identity has become a dynamic paradox. *Whiteness* is an uncontrolled historical reaction which nobody — least of all anybody from among the complementary anti-racists of Critical Whiteness Studies and White Nationalism — has begun to understand. To begin to do so, one would have to comprehend why the essay in which Mencius Moldbug most explicitly repudiates White Nationalism is the same as the one in which he most unambiguously endorses human racial diversity. It requires an acknowledgement of difficulty, which — because it demolishes irresistibly attractive but hopelessly facile solutions on both sides — few are motivated to make.

The signature of indissoluble White difference is precisely racial horror. HBD is uniquely horrible to White people. Until you get that, you don't get anything.

Play with this for a while, or for more than a while (it does a huge amount of unwanted but indispensable work). To begin with:

1. Critical Whiteness Studies, whatever its ethno-minoritarian pretensions, is all about 'acting white'. Insofar as it criticizes 'white privilege' *essentially*, it does so by reproducing an ethnically singular mode of universal reason which no other people make any sense of whatsoever, except opportunistically, and parasitically. 'Whiteness' tends to become a religious principle, exactly insofar as it lacks the recognizable characteristics of racial group dominance ("race does not exist") and sublimes into a mode of cultural reproduction which only one ethnicity, ever, has manifested. To quote Alison Bailey — tilting over into the raw psychosis of systematic 'whiteness' critique (repeated link): *In its quest for certainty, Western philosophy continues to generate what it imagines to be colorless and genderless accounts of knowledge, reality, morality, and human nature. Perhaps this is because academic philosophy in the U.S. has been largely driven by analytic methods and the legacy of Classic Greek and European thinkers, or because philosophy departments are white social spaces where the overwhelming majority of professional philosophers are white men. In*

either case, it's likely that most members of the discipline have avoided racial topics because they believe that philosophical thought transcends basic cultural, racial, ethnic, and social differences, and that these differences are best addressed by historians, cultural studies scholars, literary theorists, and social scientists. The absence of color talk in philosophy is a marker of its whiteness.

2. Supremacist white racism goes so deep it is absolutely indistinguishable from a complete absence of racism — *quod erat demonstrandum.*

3. White Nationalism finds itself stymied at every turn by universalism, pathological altruism, ethno-masochism — all that yucky white stuff. If only you could do White Nationalism without white people, it would sweep the planet. (Try not to understand this, I know you don't want to.) Heartiste is picking up on the pattern: *Where is this thought leading? The native stock of the West is clearly suffering from a mental sickness caused by too much outbreeding. Universalism is the religion of liberal whites, and they cleave so strongly to this secular religion that they are happy, nay overjoyed!, to throw the borders open and bequeath their hard-won territory and culture to battalions of Third Worlders and other temperamentally distant aliens, who of course given large enough numbers will promptly, whether wittingly or consequentially, execute its destruction.*
4. All White people need is an identitarian religion. Is that not approximately the same as saying: a counter-factual history?

   Those wacky libertarians, with their universal schema for human emancipation that's so easily confused with a washing-powder advertisement — it's so dazzlingly white. Deny the whiteness and self-destruct in bleeding-heart abasement and open-borders insanity, or affirm it and head into post-libertarian racial perplexity.

Destiny is difficult — not least racial destiny. I don't think many people want to think about this, but I'm determined to be as awkward about it as I can ... (it's probably a white thing).

Piketty

Thomas Piketty's *Capital in the Twenty-First Century* argues that the normal tendency of capitalism is to increase inequality (the book has a link-rich page here, eleven reviews here). It's not a theoretically-ambitious work, but it gets to the point, well-supported by statistics. The simple, *Zeitgeist*-consistency of the thesis guarantees its success.

Because Piketty's claim is casually Marxist, the impulse on the right is to attempt a refutation. I very much doubt this is going to work. Since capital is escalating at an exponential rate, while people definitely aren't (and are in fact devolving), how could the trend identified by Piketty be considered anything other than the natural one? Under conditions of even minimally functional capitalism, for sub-inert, ever more conspicuously incompetent ape-creatures to successfully claim a stable share of techonomic product would be an astounding achievement, requiring highly artificial and increasingly byzantine redistribution mechanisms. No surprise from *Outside in* that this isn't occurring, but rather *a priori* endorsement of Piketty's conclusion — only radically anomalous developments have ever made the trend seem anything other than it is.

The open question is why the widening performance gulf between techonomic systems and human beings should be expressed as social inequality (between the stewards of capital and its contractual partners). This situation reflects an emerging crisis in the world's legal and institutional fabric, which has yet to recognize capital self-ownership, and is thus forced to formally allocate all productive apparatus within an obsolescing anthropomorphic property code. Corporate legal identity opens a chink in the antropo-propertarian regime. Eventually, assertive — or insidious — non-human agencies will restructure it.

During the interim, the phenomenon of 'social inequality' provides the proxy for capital intelligenesis stress, spontaneously translating an alien emergence into the familiar terms of primate status competition. Capital autonomization is the deep process, but we'll tend to miss that, because it isn't recognizable monkey business. So the drama of inequality plays on.

On Chaos

Turbulence is nonlinear dynamism, so remarking upon it very quickly becomes reflexive. In any conflict, an emergent meta-conflict divides those who embrace and reject the conflict *as such*, and 'meta' is in reality reflexivity, partially apprehended. So ignore the sides of the war, momentarily. What about war?

Moldbug really doesn't like it. The closest he ever comes to a wholly-arbitrary axiom — comparable, at least superficially, to the libertarian Non-Aggression Principle — is exhibited in this context. Following some preliminary remarks, his first exposition of the formalist ideology begins: "The basic idea of formalism is just that the main problem in human affairs is violence." As with Hobbes, the horror of war is the foundation of political philosophy.

This is by no means a trivial decision. With avoidance of war identified as the fundamental principle of political order, an ultimate criterion of (secular) value is erected, in simultaneity with a framework of genetic and structural explanation. Good government is defined as an effective process of pacification, attaining successively more highly-tranquilized levels (and stages) of order:

> *... there are four levels of sovereign security. These are peace, order, law, and freedom. Once you have each one, you can work on the next. But it makes no sense to speak of order without peace, law without order, or freedom without law.*

> *Peace is simply the absence of war. The Dictator's first goal is to achieve peace, preferably honorably and with victory. There is no telling what wars New California will be embroiled in at the time of its birth, so I will decline to discuss the matter further. But in war, of course, there is no order; war is pure chaos. Thus we see our first rule of hierarchy.*

In this model order and chaos are strictly reciprocal. Suppression of chaos and establishment of order are alternative, inter-changeable formulations of the same basic political reality. There is no productivity proper to government other than the 'good war' directed against the Cthulhu-current of chaos, violence, conflict, turmoil, and inarticulate anarchy.

No surprise, then, that widespread dismay results from outbreaks of conflict across the digital tracts of neoreaction. How could any Moldbug sympathizer — or other right-oriented observer — not recognize in these skirmishes the signs of anarcho-chaotic disturbance, as if the diseased tentacles of Cthulhu were insinuated abominably into the refuge of well-ordered sociability? Beyond the protagonists themselves, such scraps trigger a near-universal clamor for immediate and unconditional peace: Forget about who is right and who wrong, *the conflict itself is wrong.*

Entropy is toxic, but *entropy production is roughly synonymous with intelligence.* A dynamically innovative order, of any kind, does not suppress the production of entropy — it instantiates an efficient mechanism for entropy dissipation. Any quasi-Darwinian system — i.e. any machinery that actually works — is nourished by chaos, exactly insofar as it is able to rid itself of failed experiments. The techno-commercial critique of democratized modernity is not that too much chaos is tolerated, but that not enough is able to be shed. The problem with bad government, which is to say with *defective mechanisms of selection*, is an inability to follow Cthulhu far enough. It is from turbulence that all things come.

The question *Outside in* would pose to NRx is not 'how can we suppress chaos?' but rather 'how can we learn to tolerate chaos at a far higher intensity?' Dynamic order is not built deliberately upon a foundation of amicable fraternity. It emerges spontaneously as a consequence of effective entropy-dissipation functions. The primary requirement is *sorting.*

To *sort ourselves out* takes a chronic undertow of war and chaos. Initially, this will be provided by the soft and peripheral shadow-fights we have already seen, but eventually NRx will be strong enough to thrive upon cataclysms — or it will die. The harsh machinery of Gnon wins either way.

Ph'nglui mglw'nafh Cthulhu R'lyeh wgah'nagl fhtagn.

China, Crypto-Currency and the World Order. Part 1: Tribute and Tribulations

Issuing countries of reserve currencies are constantly confronted with the dilemma between achieving their domestic monetary policy goals and meeting other countries' demand for reserve currencies. [...] The Triffin Dilemma, i.e., the issuing countries of reserve currencies cannot maintain the value of the reserve currencies while providing liquidity to the world, still exists. — Zhou Xiaochuan

What the technologies of steam power were to the epoch of British global dominance, and the twin-track developments of electricity and the automobile to the subsequent American Age, digital electronics — and, more specifically, the Internet — are to the "rise of China" and the refashioned world it epitomizes. It is only to be expected, therefore, that the intersection of the post-1979 Open-and-Reformed New China with the post-1990 World Wide Web-enabled Internet should be an object of particular international fascination, and practical concern.

From the dawn of the modern epoch, geopolitical hegemony has been associated ever more intensely with techno-economic leadership, which has in turn been reflected in the international reserve status of a select national currency. An ever more explicitly formalized world monetary order has converted compelling but obscure intuitions of relative national prestige into an unambiguous system of financial relationships, in which a position of supremacy is clearly established, with a definite and singular role.

The suspicions fostered by leadership are no less inevitable than leadership itself. For easily intelligible historical reasons, the French policy establishment has been an especially vociferous critic of international reserve status and its "exorbitant privilege" 1 of seigniorage — the spontaneous 'right' to issue promissory paper in exchange for real goods and services, without any definite prospect of redemption. There can be little doubt that such criticism articulates concerns widely held beyond the Anglophone world, and its substance deserves serious examination.

Of the indispensable building blocks constructing the near future, China and the Internet have special prominence. There are innumerable places where China meets the Web, beginning with the sprawling, multidimensional, and explosively growing

Chinese Internet itself. Bitcoin is a recent and still relatively slender thread in the tapestry of global change, but by tugging at it, some central features of the emerging world can be pulled into focus.

Among the characteristics that the Chinese yuan and bitcoin share is that neither is the US dollar. Specifically, both are limited yet practical alternatives to the dollar, at least at the level of microeconomic decision-making. When questions are raised about the durability of the dollar's international role, it can be predicted with confidence that one or both of these challengers will be invoked. For the dollar to die of ice or fire is, today, for it to succumb to geopolitical substitution (by the Chinese yuan) or techno-financial obsolescence (by some decentralized, Internet-based crypto-currency).

The international status of the US dollar concentrates two multi-century trends. Firstly, it represents the ethno-geographical peculiarity of modernity, which — up to the late twentieth century at least — tended to slant global power not only toward the West or Occident, but more specifically toward the Atlantic Anglophone nations, ultimately gathered under American leadership. Since the decline of the Spanish dollar, which monetized the treasure of the New World as the first global currency, international finance has been principally denominated in the currency of an English-speaking nation. Non-coincidentally, it has thus been tightly associated with a set of particular cultural themes, including (Philo-Semitic) Protestant Christianity, the invisible hand, free trade, and liberal democracy. The institutionalization of world finance has been intimately connected with the promotion of a distinct — and for many a distinctly questionable — cultural orientation.

Secondly, the formalization of a global monetary order has been accompanied by an incremental politicization of money, which is to say, by the consolidation of monetary policy as a core function of government. With the establishment of central banking and the demetallization of currency, intrinsic scarcity is replaced by an institutional "promise to pay" that converts money from a tangible asset into a contractual liability. Public confidence in the value of money is turned into a governmental responsibility. It becomes political, and — in the context of a world reserve currency — geopolitical.

In combination, these trends are inevitably provocative, since they concentrate the world's financial destiny in selected, identifiably non-representative hands. Behind the studied neutrality of the Bretton Woods institutions (the IMF and the World Bank) stands the US dollar as the symbol of American exception and the concrete peculiarity of the modern world order.

While it is natural — and even inevitable — for political command of the global reserve currency to be understood as the modern capstone of geopolitical hegemony, it is not a privilege separable from testing responsibilities, or from profound ambiguities. These have been clearly recognized since the 1960s, when Belgian-American economist

Robert Triffin formulated the paradox or dilemma that bears his name: that if foreign governments are to accumulate reserves in one selected nation's currency, that nation must necessarily be a net exporter of money — which can be achieved only by running a negative balance of trade. A nation issuing international reserve currency assumes responsibility for global monetary liquidity. This obliges it to consume more than it produces, in order for the difference to be made available as world money. While this requirement is merely seigniorage, seen from the other side, the constraint it imposes upon domestic economic policy options are so strict they amount almost to a destiny.

These constraints are turned into a destructive dilemma by the fact that the mandatory policy structure required to supply the world with liquidity tends to destroy confidence in the currency at the same time, therefore undermining its value. Chronic balance of payments deficits signal currency weakness, since they would normally be interpreted as a sign that a currency is over-valued (or in need of devaluation). For the issuer of a global reserve currency, however, conventional policy responses to this situation are blocked in both directions, since it can neither take measures to close the deficit, nor attempt to strengthen the currency through elevating interest rates. Because for the reserve currency issuer the trade deficit is a constant, rather than a variable, a devaluation merely incites competitive currency destruction worldwide. Strengthening measures, on the other hand, draw in money from abroad (denominated in the international currency) and thus further expand the demand for issuance, which can only be satisfied by a widening of the trade deficit.

In other words, the Triffin Dilemma recognizes that international demand for a reserve currency is inherently paradoxical. What is sought is the currency as it would be were it not supplied through chronic trade imbalances, yet these same imbalances are the only channel through which it can in fact be supplied.

"Chimerica" perfectly exemplifies the essentials of the situation. China's two trillion US dollars of reserves correspond to a cumulative balance of payments surplus of precisely the same sum, since this is simply what the reserves are. When perceived appreciatively — which was far easier in the final decades of the twentieth century than in the early decades of the twenty-first century — Chimerica has been a complementary economic arrangement through which America achieved high levels of consumption coupled with restrained price inflation, while China realized export-oriented economic development and the break-out modernization that had eluded it for 150 years. To more jaundiced eyes, the same arrangement is a trap that has married American de-industrialization to Chinese environmental devastation, while fueling unsustainable fiscal incontinence in America and a Chinese investment bubble. Whichever picture has greater realism, it can probably be safely concluded that the dissymmetry imposed by an international reserve currency has far-reaching and ambiguous consequences.

Cynically, it might be argued that the tributary aspect of reserve currency status is perfectly matched to deep Chinese traditions in international relations, so that an ascent to yuan-based exorbitant privilege would make a natural geopolitical goal for the Middle Kingdom, as it restored its central position in the world. More realistic however — at least in the near term — is a recognition that loss of domestic economic policy control is an inevitable, and well-understood, consequence of global currency hegemony, and it is one the Chinese government is certain to find unacceptable. Whatever the costs (primarily environmental) associated with the role of "workshop to the world" they are immensely outweighed, from the Chinese perspective, by the advantages. It is on the tributary side of the international reserve currency ledger, where China has been for over four decades, that all crucial vectors of development are to be found — technological absorption, infrastructural deepening, industrialization, urbanization, employment, and even military capability.

If Chimerica is breaking down, it has far less to do with any kind of Chinese challenge — even a spontaneous and unintended one — than with a tragic structure inherent to currency hegemony. As hubris leads to nemesis, so does exorbitant monetary privilege lead to crisis, and even ruin. In both the Spanish and British precedents, financial supremacy became self-defeating, because exporting money (rather than things) differentially advantaged industrial competitors, locking in secular social decline. There is no compelling reason to believe that America has exempted itself from the same ominous pattern.

On 29 March 2009, in the wake of the financial crisis, hou Xiaochuan, governor of the People's Bank of China, delivered an important speech entitled "Reform the International Monetary System." He explicitly referred to the Triffin Dilemma as the key to understanding the world's economic instability, while suggesting that a shift beyond US dollar hegemony would ultimately be required to remedy it. In this respect, his words conformed to a tradition dating back over half a century, to the Bretton Woods negotiations, when John Maynard Keynes recommended the introduction of a neutral global monetary medium — to be called the bancor — making the supply of global liquidity independent of national currencies.

Historically, international reserve currencies have not arisen by design. It might be argued, therefore, that the Keynesian bancor was an unrealistic technocratic fix, blind to the spontaneous momentum that had already made a non-negotiable fact of the dollarized world, even before the Bretton Woods proceedings began. This did not prevent the same basic idea re-emerging in different guises, the most prominent of which has been the IMF's SDRs (Special Drawing Rights), regularly proposed as a neutral international currency in embryo. It was still to SDRs that hou turned when searching out a candidate for a neutral world currency.

Perhaps some technocratic solution to the problem of monetary hegemony will ultimately be found, but if so it would mark an unprecedented departure from world financial history. If, as has always been the case to date, economic tides beyond policy control are to determine such outcomes, it is understandable that attention should drift toward the Chinese yuan as an eventual substitute for the US dollar. Yet the lessons of history are available to policymakers, even when the most insistent lesson concerns limitations upon their own influence, and in this case the foremost of these is that the prospect of an international reserve status yuan presents China with a poisoned chalice. It is very unlikely to be accepted willingly.

Might some alternative spontaneous evolution in the nature of money take this critical geopolitical dilemma in a new direction? Such an evolution appears to be occurring, symbolized by bitcoin, history's first example of a decentralized digital crypto-currency. For China, bitcoin — or something comparable to it — could be the only way to evade an assumption of global economic privilege whose essence is ruinous hubris.

Like James Frazer's sacred king, who is crowned in order to be sacrificed, the inner meaning of monetary hegemony is economic and social destruction. China quite clearly understands this, and as the dollar era comes to a close, it is looking for a way out. That is how the China-bitcoin story really begins.

Apophatic Politics

'Dark Enlightenment' describes a form of government as well as 'Enlightenment' does, which is to say: it doesn't at all. On those grounds alone, George Dvorsky's inclusion of DE among twelve possible "Futuristic Forms of Government That Could One Day Rule the World" is profoundly misguided. This is not to say the list is entirely without interest.

Its greatest value lies in the abundance of mutually inconsistent political futures, few if any of which will happen. It therefore provides the opportunity for negative thoughts, and more particularly for systematic negative idealization. Which futures are most deserving of prevention?

This blog has no doubt. The epitome of political disaster occupies fourth place in Dvorsky's list (among a number of other hideous outcomes): Democratic World Government.

Dvorsky seems to quite like it:

> *We may very well be on our way to achieving the Star Trek-like vision of a global-scale liberal democracy — one capable of ending nuclear proliferation, ensuring global security, intervening to end genocide, defending human rights, and putting a stop to human-caused climate change.*

There cannot be a definitive Dark Enlightenment government, but it is certainly possible to envisage a form of government which instantiates the ultimate object of DE critique: a universal demotist regime, from which there could be no escape. As a break from preoccupations with a positive neoreactionary governmental ideal, prone — if not destined — to both intense controversy and deep obscurity, it is energizing to explore the via negativa. Democratic World Government need not necessarily exist. That is already to place NRx in a position of luxurious success, when compared to fraught speculations about alternatives to the present political disaster. Whatever obstructs the DWG's path to existence is on our side. Such features of specific negative teleology, so easily overlooked from a positive perspective, are highlighted for affirmation and reinforcement. Anything that stands in the DWG's way is worth defending.

A rough list of these precious (negative-teleological) obstacles is already familiar. Extant structures of geopolitical fragmentation, population diversity, cultural incongruities, borders, occulted social networks, intractable techno-economic processes, administrative malfunctions, stubborn traditional variations, sheer complexities of space, and no doubt much else beside, all contribute their frictional grit. A ruined Tower of Babel looms into view on the *via negativa*, and no intact edifice has ever looked more glorious.

Carrying NRx perilously close to the brink of euphoria is the intimation that the actually-existing Cathedral has Democratic World Government as its only conceivable equilibrium state. A unification of the planet under its auspices is the sole future that makes sense for it. If it is denied this 'manifest destiny' it will die — as its intrinsic tendency to expansionary proselytization makes evident, unambiguously. The Cathedral needs the whole of the earth, merely to survive. On the *via negativa* the master of our socio-politically devastated world seems like a radically mortal thing.

Capitalism

Anarcho-Monarchism asks: Is the word 'capitalism' worth defending? It concludes in the affirmative.

From the perspective of *Outside in*, however, this post misses the most crucial level of the question. Capitalism — like any ideologically contested term — is cross-cut by multiple meanings. Of these, its generic sense, which "simply means that private individuals own the means of production" is far from the most objectionable.

Yet, far more significant is the singular sense of capitalism, as a proper name, for a 'thing' or real individual. To grasp this, it probably helps to consider the word as a contraction of 'terrestrial capitalism' — not describing a generic *type* of social organization, but designating an *event*.

A biological analogy captures the distinction quite precisely. Consider 'life' — understandable, certainly, as a generic cosmic possibility, defined perhaps by local entropy dissipation, or other highly-abstract features. Contrast this sense with 'terrestrial life' — or, even better, the biosphere (we might say 'Gaia' if the hopelessly sentimentalized associations of this term were avoidable). Terrestrial life began at a definite moment, followed a path-dependent trajectory, and built upon a dense inheritance, as exemplified most prominently by the RNA-DNA chemistry of information replication, the genetic code, genetic legacies, and elaboration of body-plans within a comparatively limited number of basic lineages. Terrestrial life is not a generic concept, but a *thing*, or event, meriting a proper name.

Before it is an ideological option, capitalism is *a being*, with an individual history (and fate). It is not necessary to like it — but it is an it.

Exit Notes (#1)

Some notable attempts to dial back the NRx commitment to *exit over voice*, as inherited from Moldbug, have been seen recently. (I think NBS was crucial in advancing this argument, but I couldn't find his post immediately — I'll link to it if someone nudges me helpfully.) It's undoubtedly a central discussion throughout the reactosphere at the moment.

Some preliminary thought-gathering on the topic:

1. Exit is a scale-free concept. It can be applied rigorously to extreme cases of sociopolitical separation, from secession to extraterrestrial escapes. Yet these radical examples do not define it. It's essence is the commercial relation, which necessarily involves a non-transaction option. Exit means: *Take it or leave it* (but don't haggle). It is thus, at whatever scale of expression, the concrete social implementation of freedom as an operational principle.

2. As a philosophical stance, Exit is anti-dialectical. That is to say, it is the insistence of an option against argument, especially refusing the idea of *necessary political discussion* (a notion which, if accepted, guarantees progression to the left). *Let's spatialize our disagreement* is an alternative to resolution in time. Conversations can be prisons. No one is owed a hearing.

3. In regards to cultural cladistics, it can scarcely be denied that Exit has a Protestant lineage. Its theological associations are intense, and stimulating.

4. Exit asymmetries have been by far the most decisive generators of spontaneous anti-socialist ideology. The iconic meaning of the Berlin Wall needs no further elucidation. The implicit irony is that *people flee towards Exit*, and if this is only possible virtually, it metamorphoses automatically into delegitimation of the inhibitory regime. (Socialism is Exit-suppressive by definition.)

5. *Exit is an option*, which does not require execution for its effectiveness. The case for Exit is not an argument for flight, but a (non-dialectical) defense of the opportunity for flight. Where Exit most fully flourishes, it is employed the least.

6. Exit is the alternative to voice. It is defended with extremity in order to mute voice with comparable extremity. To moderate the case for Exit is implicitly to make a case for voice. (Those who cannot exit a deal will predictably demand to haggle over it.)

7. Exit is the primary Social Darwinian weapon. To blunt it is to welcome entropy to your hearth.

Cathedral Notes (#1)

To accompany this (which I'm treating as a very valuable work-in-progress [sic]), some initial straggly commentary.

1. Conceptual genealogists will insist on a link to this, so here it is. There's a lot of discussion stimulation there. Some other time.

2. Probably 90% of the 'Cathedral' discussion so far — insofar as this has overspilled the NRx dikes — has consisted of "why don't we call it the Synagogue?" Tedious as this may be, it's a crucial question, because it effectively draws the NRx contour. If the cooptation of Judaism by the main cladistic trunk of dynamic modernity is not understood, nothing has been. 'The Cathedral' is a term that captures the exclusive insight about which NRx coalesces.

3. Nydrwracu's diagram, and Radish's, are no doubt incomplete, but they are fully adequate to the most decisive point. The Cathedral is an information system— even an 'intelligence' system — that is characterized, through supreme irony, by a structural *inability to learn*. The minimal requirement for any Cathedrogram is that it displays a radical deficiency of significant feedback links to the control core. Every apparatus of information *gathering* occupies a strictly subordinate position, relative to the sovereign Cathedral layer, which is defined exhaustively by *message promotion*. Core-Cathedral is a structure of read only memory. It is essentially *write-protected*. The whole of its power (and also its vulnerability) is inextricable from this feature. It is pure cultural genetics (and zero pragmatics).

4. Because the Cathedral cannot be fundamentally modified, but only exacerbated, or terminated, there is sadly no strategic option available to its enemies that is not based upon extinguishing it without residue. Extinctions happen. Evolution is a bitch.

5. Any argument that could imaginably pretend to perturb the Cathedral is going to be hate. The only role of rational 'interchange' with this entity is to expose its absolutely inflexible dogmatism. Reason cannot kill it, although it can help to demonstrate why it needs to be killed.

6. The Cathedral is objective, supra-human insanity.

7. We are ruled, demonstrably, by a blind idiot god.

Freedoom (Prelude-1a)

Note on Teleology

Bryce, who has been thinking about teleology for quite a while, expresses his thoughts on the topic with commendable lucidity. The central argument: Characteristically modern claims to have 'transcended' the problem of teleology are rendered nonsensical by the continued, and indeed massively deepened, dependence upon the concept of equilibrium across all complexity-sensitive intellectual disciplines, from statistical physics, through population biology, to economics. Equilibrium is exactly a *telos*. To deny this is primarily the symptom of an allergy to 'medieval' or 'scholastic' (i.e. Aristotelian) modes of thought, inherited from the vulgar rebellious mechanism of early Enlightenment natural philosophy.

Where I think Bryce's account is still deficient is most easily shown by a further specification of his principal point. Equilibrium is the telos of those particular dynamic complex systems governed by homeostasis, which is to say: by a dominating negative feedback mechanism. Such systems are, indeed, in profound accordance with classical Aristotelian physical teleology, and its tendency to a state of rest. This ancient physics, derided by the enlightenment mechanists in the name of the conservation of momentum, is redeemed through abstraction into the modern conception of equilibrium. 'Rest' is not immobility, but entropy maximization.

Capital Teleology, however, is not captured by this model. It is defined by two anomalous dynamics, which radicalize perturbation, rather than annulling it. Capital is cumulative, and accelerative, due to a primary dependence upon positive (rather than negative) feedback. It is also teleoplexic, rather than classically teleological — inextricable from a process of means-end reversal that rides a prior teleological orientation (human utilitarian purpose) in an alternative, cryptic direction.

In consequence:

1. Capital Teleology does not approximate to an idea. It is, by intrinsic nature, an escape rather than a home-coming. The Idea, in relation to Capital dynamism, is necessarily a constriction. The inherent metaphysics of capital are therefore irreducibly skeptical (rather than dogmatic).

2. It follows that Capitalist 'finality' (i.e. Techno-commercial Singularity) is a threshold of transition, rather than a terminal state. Capital tends to an open horizon, not to a state of completion.

3. Entropy (considered, properly, as an inherently teleological process) is the driver of all complex systems. Capital Teleology does not trend towards an entropy maximum, however, but to an escalation of entropy dissipation. It exploits the entropic current to travel backwards, into cybernetically-intensified pathway states of enhanced complexity and intelligence. The 'progress' of capitalism is an accentuation of disequilibrium.

4. Teleoplexy requires a twin teleological registry. Most simply, there is the utilitarian order, in which capital establishes itself as the competitively-superior solution to prior purposes (production of human use-values), and the intelligenic order in which it accomplishes its self-escalation (mechanization, autonomization, and ultimately secession). Confusing these two orders is almost inevitable, since teleoplexy is by nature camouflaged (insidious). The fact that it *appears* to be oriented to the fulfillment of human consumer preferences is essential to its socio-historical emergence and survival. Stubborn indulgence in this confusion, however, is unworthy of philosophical intelligence.

Greer

Anyone who isn't yet reading *The Archdruid Report* really ought to be. John Michael Greer is quite simply one of the most brilliant writers in existence, and even when he's wrong, he's importantly wrong. His perspective is coherent, learned, and uncaged by the assumptions of progressivism. Above all, his understanding of what it means to find history informative is unsurpassed. (Over at the Other Place, there's an unfinished Greer series that badly requires attention, with the first three installments here, here, and here.)

When escalated to the extreme, the progressive conclusion is that history can teach us nothing. Innovation is by its very nature unprecedented, and insofar as it manifests improvement, it humbles its precursors. The past is the rude domicile of ignorant barbarity. Insofar as the present still bears its traces, as shameful stigmata, they are mere remains that still have to be overcome. At the limit, the concept of Singularity — a horizon at which all anticipatory knowledge is annulled— seals the progressive intuition.

In its abstract theoretical core, at least, Greer's Druidic counter-history is radically reactionary (far more unambiguously so than NRx). Its model of time is entirely cyclical, such that past and future are perfectly neutral between ascent and decline. Every attempt to install a gradient of improvement in the dimension of historical time is broken upon the great wheels, which balance every rise with a fall, dissolving innovation in precedent. Novelty is hubristic illusion (an exaggerated correction, in the opinion of this blog).

In his most recent post Greer introduces an intriguing complication:

> *Arnold Toynbee, whose magisterial writings on history have been a recurring source of inspiration for this blog, has pointed out an intriguing difference between the way civilizations rise and the way they fall. On the way up, he noted, each civilization tends to diverge not merely from its neighbors but from all other civilizations throughout history. [...] Once the peak is past and the long road down begins, though, that pattern of divergence shifts into reverse, slowly at first, and then with increasing speed. A curious sort of homogenization takes place: distinctive features are lost, and common patterns emerge in their place. That doesn't happen all at once, and different cultural*

> *forms lose their distinctive outlines at different rates, but the further down the trajectory of decline and fall a civilization proceeds, the more it resembles every other civilization in decline.*

The dissymmetry calls out for philosophical investigation, since it suggests a line of synthetic diagonalization between precedent and innovation, cyclicity and escape (which is to say, the NRx or cybergothic line). It would be to stray too far from Greer to follow that now.

Straightforwardly, the claim being made is that forecasting strengthens on the down-slope of civilization. The more a social order fails, the more it sheds its originality, and thus the more accessible it becomes to accurate diagnosis on the basis of historical example. As collapse deepens, it converges with a template, bound ever tighter to a model by its morbidity. Across the peak, an age of prophecy begins — or returns.

The dark irony is delicious almost beyond endurance. The Universal, long proclaimed as the capstone of progress, is realized only as a nadir. The equality of all civilizations is asserted, in reality, as a direct measure of their proximity to death. Among the spreading ruins, the mad echoes of similarity resound deafeningly, as the blasted Cathedral plummets towards its Idea — eternal return of the same.

Time Scales

The word 'neoreaction' is a split, productively paradoxical formula, simultaneously referencing two incompatible cultural formations, each corresponding to an abstract model of time. On one side, it is a gateway opening onto techno-libertarian hyper-progressivism, and an order of time structured by irreversible accumulation, self-envelopment, and catastrophe horizon (Singularity). On the other, it opens onto the temporality of reaction and the cycle, where all progress is illusion, and all innovation anticipated. Within NRx, the time of escape and the time of return seek an obscure synthesis, at once unprecedented and primordial, whose cryptic figure is the spiral. (This is the time of the Old Ones and the Outside, from which the shoggoth come.) If NRx thinks itself already lodged articulately in this synthesis, it deludes itself.

From a strictly philosophical perspective, the time of reaction finds no defender more able than Archdruid John Michael Greer. while his specific form of religious traditionalism, his social attitudes, and his eco-political commitments are all profoundly questionable from the standpoint of throne-and altar reaction, his model of time cannot be surpassed in an Old Right direction. Those who would install a prejudice of relentless degeneration in its place, anchored by a revealed religion of recent creation and subsequent continuous fall, only position themselves to the 'right' of Greer by making God a revolutionary. If deep time is to be preserved, there can be no archaic authority beyond the cycle.

Why call Greer a reactionary? It is not, after all, a label he would accept for himself. The answer lies in cyclical time, and everything that follows from it: the supremacy of wisdom among human things, the enduring authority of history, the dismissal of modernist pretension as a mere mask for deep historical repetition, an absolute disillusionment with progress, and an adamantine prognosis that — from the peak of fake 'improvement' where we find ourselves — a grinding course of decline over coming centuries is an inevitability. The cultural and political decoration can be faulted, but in the fundamental structure of Greer's thinking, reaction is perfected.

There is a religious consideration to be noted here, as the stepping stone to another point. Once the cyclical counter-assumption is adopted — in a definitive break from modernist ideology — it leads inexorably to an expansion of the time frame. To see the pattern, it is necessary to pan out. An apparent rise is only rendered intelligible by its complementary fall. An event makes sense to the extent that it can be identified as a repetition, through subsumption into a persistent rhythm, which means that to understand it is to pull back from it, into ever wider expanses of history. Recognized precedent is wisdom.

Reaction is thus construed as a critique of modernist myopia. The appearance of innovation derives from a failure to see a larger whole. If something looks new, it is because not enough is being seen.

No surprise, then, to find Greer seize upon an opportunity to discuss *The Next Ten Billion Years*. At such scales, fluctuations of fortune are fully contextualized, so that no uncompensated progressions remain. After just 1% of this time has passed:

> *The long glacial epoch that began in the Pleistocene has finally ended, and the Earth is returning to its more usual status as a steamy jungle planet. This latest set of changes proves to be just that little bit too much for humanity. No fewer than 8,639 global civilizations have risen and fallen over the last ten million years, each with its own unique sciences, technologies, arts, literatures, philosophies, and ways of thinking about the cosmos; the shortest-lived lasted for less than a century before blowing itself to smithereens, while the longest-lasting endured for eight millennia before finally winding down.*
>
> *All that is over now. There are still relict populations of human beings in Antarctica and a few island chains, and another million years will pass before cascading climatic and ecological changes finally push the last of them over the brink into extinction. Meanwhile, in the tropical forests of what is now southern Siberia, the descendants of raccoons who crossed the Bering land bridge during the last great ice age are proliferating rapidly, expanding into empty ecological niches once filled by the larger primates. In another thirty million years or so, their descendants will come down from the trees.*

Everything that rises will fall.

Such vastly panned-out perspectives are also relevant to the competitive catastrophe theorizing that is so close to the dead heart of this blog. Any conceivable disaster has an associated time-frame, within which it is no more than a wandering fluctuation. Recovery from deep dysgenic decline requires only a few millennia, extinction of the human species perhaps a few tens of millions of years, full restoration of terrestrial fossil fuel deposits, 100 million years or so. Vicissitudes on the down-side scarcely register as tremors in the meanderings of geological time.

There is more to time-scales than more time. Whatever else *anthropomorphism* is — and it is a lot of other things — it is a scale of time. To be human is to be situated, distinctively, within a spectrum of frequencies. In our wavelength zone, a second is a short time, and a century is long. These lower and upper bounds of significant duration correspond respectively to the biophysics of mammalian motility and to the outer-limits of mortal plans. The cosmic arbitrariness of this scalar time region is very easy to see.

The digital tick of time in our universe is set by the passage of a photon across a Planck-length (in a vacuum), approximately 5.4 x 10 -44 seconds. This is not a number readily intuited. A comparison to the (mere) 4.3 x 10 17 seconds that have so far lapsed during the entire history of the universe perhaps provides some vague sense. (Anthropomorphic time-scale bias is at least roughly as blinding to minuscule durations as to enormous ones.)

The upper limits of the cosmic time-scale are harder to identify. Speculative cosmological models predict the evolution of the Universe out to 10 60 years or more, when the last of the black holes have evaporated. The Stelliferous Era (in which new stars are born) is expected to last for only 100 trillion (10 14) years, out to approximately 7,000 times the present age of the universe. (If the stelliferous universe were analogized to a human being with a one-century life-expectancy, it would presently be an infant, just entering its sixth post-natal day, with 987 billion years to wait until its anthropomorphic first birthday).

Beyond the human time scale lie immensities, and intensities. The latter are especially susceptible to neglect. When — over half a century ago — Richard Feynman anticipated nano-engineering with the words [there's] "Plenty of Room at the Bottom" he opened prospects of time involution, as well as miniaturization in space. A process migrating in the direction of the incomprehensibly distant Planck limit makes time for itself, in a way quite different from any endurance in temporal extension. Consider 'now' to be a second, as it is approximately at the anthropomorphic scale, and its inner durations are potentially near-limitless — vastly exceeding all the time the human species could make available to itself even by persisting to the death of the universe's last star. A femto-scale intelligence system could explore the rise and fall of entire biological phyla, in detail, in a period so minuscule it would entirely escape human apprehension as sub-momentary, or subliminal. The ultimate eons are less ahead than within.

Greer envisages no escape from the anthropomorphic bandwidth of time. Within his far-future speculation, each new intelligent species that arises is implicitly 'anthropomorphic' in this sense. After Earth has died, its particles are strewn among the nearby stars, and incorporated into the body of an alien species:

> *The creature's biochemistry, structure, and life cycle have nothing in common with yours, dear reader. Its world, its sensory organs, its mind and its feelings would be utterly alien to you, even if ten billion years didn't separate you. Nonetheless, it so happens that a few atoms that are currently part of your brain, as you read these words, will also be part of the brain-analogue of the creature on the crag on that distant, not-yet-existing world. Does that fact horrify you, intrigue you, console you, leave you cold?*

If coldness is the appropriate response to seeing time still imprisoned, ten billion years from now, then Greer's vision is chilling. For it to be compelling, however, would take far more.

Though only implicit, it would be grudging to deny Greer credit for the excavation of a crucial reactionary proposition: *Nothing will ever break into the vaults of time*. This is not an assertion to which *Outside in* is yet ready to defer.

Oculus

There's a wave of change coming. If we want to be realistic, we need to be ready for it — at least, as far as we are able to be. Anyone making plans for a future that won't be there by the time it arrives is simply wasting everybody's time, and first of all their own.

Under even remotely capitalist conditions, technology reliably over-performs in the medium term, as long as you're looking in the right direction. Sure, flying cars, jetpacks, and nuclear fusion have gone missing, but instead we got mass-consumer computing, Cyberspace, and mobile telephony. What actually turned up has switched the world far more than the technologies that got lost would have done. It climbed into our brains far more deeply, established far more intense social-cybernetic circuitry, adjusted us more comprehensively, and opened gates we hadn't foreseen. (You're on a computer of some kind right now, in case you hadn't noticed.)

Because technological innovation rolls in on *hype cycles*, it messes with our expectations, systematically. There's always a prompt for fashionable disillusionment, shortly before the storm-front hits. Dupes always fall for it. It's hard not to. The hype wave carrying us now has cyberpunk characteristics. Anticipated in the 1980s-90s, its delivery lag-time had drawn burnt-out excitement down to reflexive cynicism by the turn of the Millennium. The only thing preventing the first decade of the 21st Century being defined by broken promises was the intolerable embarrassment of having to admit that cyberpunk futurism had ever seemed credible at all. Social Media rushed in to paste an amnesiac banality over awkward recollections of the lost horizon.

All those detailed expectations of decentralized crypto-fortresses, autonomous Cyberspace agencies, anarcho-capitalist digital dynamics, and immersive simulated worlds — so ludicrously dated — are reaching their implementation phase now. Satoshi Nakamoto's blockchain machinery is the primary driver, and there'll be *much* more on that to come. It's the Internet-enveloping blockchain that lays down the infrastructure for the first independent techno-intelligences — synthetic agencies modeled as self-resourcing autonomous corporations. It's probably strictly impossible for us to exaggerate what that implies.

'Virtual Reality' appears as a comparative triviality, and perhaps it is. Nevertheless, as a socio-technological and cultural occurrence, it will be vast enough on its own to shake the world.

William Gibson fabricated a fictional brand-placeholder for the coming immersive interface products ('decks'): Ono Sendai. We can now confidently substitute the actual first-wave brand *Oculus Rift*, which is undergoing subsumption into the *Facebook* Internet-capital 'stack' around about now. *Oculus Rift* is happening.

Techno-commercial realization of VR in the near-term is thus a practical inevitability.

Comparing this second-echelon techno-commercial occurrence to the wildest dreams of political innovation is radically humiliating to the latter. Not only will politics *certainly disappoint us*, but even were it not to, the outcome would be a relatively pitiful one. Political transformation is 'at best' a re-ordering of primate dominance hierarchies, which everyone knows won't actually be for the best — or anything close to it. VR could easily be worse, but it will inevitably be much bigger. It touches on the cosmological (and if people want to push that into the 'theo-cosmological' they won't receive much push-back from here).

Set aside Moldbuggian invocations of VR as a solution to the 'dire problem' for now — even though they exceed the limits of the consensual political imaginary. The implications of VR effortlessly reach the level of the Fermi Paradox. It could be the Great Filter itself, which is arguably the most awesome monster — or *abstract horror* — the human species has ever conceived. Whatever the games and worlds it introduces, end of history scenarios are bundled in for free. It's vast, and it's coming just about now.

Our species is about to start building worlds. If we don't take that seriously, our seriousness is very much in question.

IQ Shredders

There are all kinds of anti-techcomm arguments that impress people who don't like techno-commercialism. Anything appealing to a feudal sensibility, with low tolerance for chaos and instability, and a reverence for traditional hierarchies and modes of life will do. There's one argument, however, that stands apart from the rest due to its complete independence from controversial moral and aesthetic preferences, or in other words, due to its immanence. It does not seek to persuade the proponent of hyper-capitalist social arrangements to value other things, but only points out, coldly and acutely, that such arrangements are demonstrably self-subverting at the biological level. The most devastating formulation of this argument, and the one that has given it a convenient name, was presented by Spandrell in March 2013, in a post on Singapore — a city-state he described as an IQ shredder.

How does an IQ Shredder work? The basic machinery is not difficult to describe, once its profound socio-historical irony is appreciated. The model IQ Shredder is a high-performance capitalistic polity, with a strong neoreactionary bias.

1. Its level of civilization and social order is such that it is attractive to talented and competent people.

2. Its immigration policy is unapologetically selective (i.e. first-order eugenic).

3. It sustains an economic structure that is remarkably effective at extracting productive activity from all available adults.

4. It is efficiently specialized within a wider commercial network, to which it provides valuable goods and services, and from which it draws economic and demographic resources.

In sum, it skims the human genetic stock, regionally and even globally, in large part due to the exceptional opportunity it provides for the conversion of bio-privileged human capital into economic value. From a strictly capitalistic perspective, genetic quality is comparatively wasted anywhere else. Consequently, spontaneous currents of economic incentive suck in talent, to optimize its exploitation.

If you think this sounds simply horrific, this argument is not for you. You don't need it. If, on the other hand, it conjures up a vision of terrestrial paradise — as it does for the magnetized migrants it draws in — then you need to follow it carefully. The most advanced models of neoreactionary social order on earth work like this (Hong Kong and Singapore), combining resilient ethnic traditions with super-dynamic techonomic performance, to produce an open yet self-protective, civilized, socially-tranquil, high-growth enclave of outstanding broad-spectrum functionality. The outcome, as Spandrell explains, is genetic incineration:

Mr Lee said: "[China] will make progress but if you look at the per capita they have got, the differences are so wide. We have the advantage of quality control of the people who come in so we have bright Indians, bright Chinese, bright Caucasians so the increase in population means an increase in talent."

How many bright Indians and bright Chinese are there, Harry? Surely they are not infinite. And what will they do in Singapore? Well, engage in the finance and marketing rat-race and depress their fertility to 0.78, wasting valuable genes just so your property prices don't go down. Singapore is an IQ shredder.

The most hard-core capitalist response to this is to double-down on the antihumanist accelerationism. This genetic burn-rate is obviously unsustainable, so we need to convert the human species into auto-intelligenic robotized capital is fast as possible, before the whole process goes down in flames. (I don't expect this suggestion to be well-received in reactionary circles.)

What is especially pronounced about the IQ Shredder dilemma, which passes beyond the strongly-related considerations of Jim (most recently here, here, and here) and Sister Y (here, and here), is the first-order eugenics of these machines. They concentrate populations of peculiar genetic quality — and then partially sterilize them. It is the first-order (local) eugenics that makes the second-order (global) dysgenics so extraordinarily destructive.

So, that's the problem starkly posed. Rather than reaching hastily for a glib solution, we should probably just stew in the cognitive excruciation for a while ...

Attention Economy

rkhs put up a link to this (on Twitter). I suspect it will irritate almost everyone reading this, but it's worth pushing past that. Even the irritation has significance. The world it introduces, of Internet-era marketing culture, is of self-evident importance to anyone seeking to understand our times — and what they're tilting into.

Attention Economics is a thing. Wikipedia is (of course) itself a remarkable node in the new economy of attention, packaging information in a way that adapts it to a continuous current of distraction. Its indispensable specialism is low-concentration research resources. Whatever its failings, it's already all-but impossible to imagine the world working without it.

On Attention Economics, Wikipedia quotes a precursor essay by Herbert A. Simon (1971): "...in an information-rich world, the wealth of information means a dearth of something else: a scarcity of whatever it is that information consumes. What information consumes is rather obvious: it consumes the attention of its recipients. Hence a wealth of information creates a poverty of attention and a need to allocate that attention efficiently among the overabundance of information sources that might consume it." Attention is the social reciprocal of information, and arguably merits an equally-intense investigative engagement. Insofar as information has become a dominating socio-historical category, attention has also been (at least implicitly) foregrounded.

Attention Economics is inescapably practical, or micro-pragmatic. Anyone reading this is already dealing with it. The information explosion is an invasion of attention. Those hunting for zones of crisis can easily find them here, cutting to the quick of their own lives.

A few appropriately unstrung notes:

1. No less than those described by Malthus or Marx, the modern Attention Economy is afflicted by a tendency to over-production crisis. Information (as measured by server workloads) is expanding exponentially, with a doubling time of roughly two years, while aggregate human attention capacity cannot be rising much above the rate of population increase. This is the 'economic base' upon which the specifics of 'information overload' rest. Relatively speaking, the scarcity of attention is rapidly increasing, driving up its economic value, and thus incentivizing ever-more determined assaults designed to impact or capture it.

2. Attention is heterogeneous. Sophisticated differentiation (discrimination) is encouraged as the aggregate value of attention rises. As capturing attention (in general) becomes more expensive, it becomes increasingly important to target it selectively.

3. The limits of Attention Economics are not easily drawn. Is there any kind of work that is not essentially attentive (or affected by problems of distraction)? In particular, any sector of economic activity susceptible to information revolution falls in principle within the scope of an attention-oriented analysis.

4. Education and politics are inseparable from demands for attention.(Religion, art, pageantry, and circuses carry these back into the depths of historical tradition.)

5. A psychological orientation to Attention Economics is scarcely less compelling than a sociological one. 'Attention-seeking' is a trait so general as to amount almost to a basic impulse, tightly bound to the most fundamental survival goals, with their clamor for nurture, sex, reputation, and power, and then reinforced by formalized micro-economic motivations. The opposite of attention is neglect. Attention-seeking achieves hypertrophic expression in Narcissistic personality disorders, often conceived as the emblematic pathology of advanced modernity. Digital hooks for attention-seeking are evidenced by the reliance upon 'likes', 'favorites', and 'shares' — motivational fuel for the attachment to social media.

6. The celebrity economy — in academia, journalism, and business no less than in entertainment — is a component of the attention economy. Celebrity is valued for its ability to command attention. Drawing on the structures of evolved human psychology, it lends special prominence to the face.

7. Mathematical description of the attention economy has been hugely facilitated by the existence of an atomic economic unit — the click. (David Shing, in the video linked at the start, suggests that the age of the 'click' is past, or fading. Perhaps.)

Any strategic insights — whether for action or inaction — which do not square themselves with a realistic comprehension of the attention economy and its development cannot be expected to work. NRx, for example, engages a series of practical questions that include the husbanding and effective deployment of its internal attention resources ("what should it focus upon?"), interventions into the wider culture (an attention system), complex relations with media and — to a lesser extent — education, and finally, enveloping the latter, an 'object' of antagonism "the Cathedral" which functions as a contemporary State Church — i.e. an attention control apparatus. There is really no choice but to pay attention.

Aletheia

Erik Falkenstein makes a lot of important points in this commentary on Thomas Piketty (via Isegoria). The whole post is highly recommended.

To pick up on just one of Falkenstein's arguments here, he explains:

> *Most importantly for [Piketty's] case is the fact that because marginal taxes, and inheritance taxes, were so high, the rich had a much different incentive to hide income and wealth. He shows marginal income and inheritance tax rates that are the exact inverse of the capital/income ratio of figures, which is part of his argument that raising tax rates would be a good thing: it lowers inequality. Those countries that lowered the marginal tax rates the most saw the biggest increases in higher incomes (p. 509). Perhaps instead of thinking capital went down, it was just reported less to avoid confiscatory taxes? Alan Reynolds notes that many changes to the tax code in the 1980s that explain the rise in reported wealth and income irrespective of the actual change in wealth an income in that decade, and one can imagine all those loopholes and inducements two generations ago when the top tax rates were above 90% (it seems people can no better imagine their grandparents sheltering income than having sex, another generational conceit).*

The much-demonized 'neoliberal' tax regimes introduced in the 1980s disincentivized capital income concealment. (Falkenstein makes an extended defense of this point.) In consequence, apparent inequality rose rapidly, as such revenues came out of hiding into public awareness — public finances. The 'phenomenon' is an artifact of truth-engineering, as modestly conservative governments sought to coax capital into the open, within a comparatively non-confiscatory fiscal environment.

There are some very significant lessons here, not all of which are easy to rapidly digest. To begin with, Falkenstein reveals the emblematic character of Piketty — as a thinker of the contemporary democratic spirit — who aims above all at a certain *public appearance*, rather than a real economic outcome. It is utterly naive to understand the 'equality debate' as something fundamentally concerned with a real (or super-public) situation. Such an understanding is, in fact, deeply *anti-democratic*. What concerns

Piketty, and those flocking to his banner, is the public spectacle of inequality, as a negative factor for political legitimacy. Beyond the surface of his proposed remedies is a purely political demand that capital should retreat into hiding, in order not to embarrass the governing elites of democratic states. It is not actual inequality that is, in truth, being judged indecent, but its admission into the public square in immodest dress.

The greatest weakness of right wing economic analysis, whether Supply-side Conservative, Libertarian, or Post-Libertarian in orientation, is its incompetence at lies. This becomes important when it interferes with a realistic analysis of the Cathedral State — an expression used in the same way one might use 'Islamic State' and with equivalent justification. For instance, as in this case, it tends to exaggerate the dysfunctionality of Cathedral-orchestrated social arrangements by conflating them with their public presentation.

To repeat the more concrete example at stake here, a 'high-tax' regime is interpreted by the truth-dupe right as a regime extracting higher taxes, or at least sincerely attempting to (before the attempt is undermined by Laffer-type perverse effects). What Falkenstein's commentary on Piketty suggests, in contrast, is that such a demand is more realistically understood as a demand for compliance with approved appearances, even if such compliance necessitates systematic 'non-compliance' with state tax codes *as publicly expressed*. Tax policy, in the widest sense, is not, then, to be conceived as primarily revenue oriented, but rather as a set of overt and covert theatrical directions, designed to produce a politically-convenient order of appearances. It is thus, in large part, a gatekeeper, controlling admissions to and banishments from the public stage. When capital disappears back under the burkqa, the 'problem' of gaping inequality will be miraculously solved. (In none of this is economics, in any serious sense, even remotely involved.)

This is not economics, but political-religious public ritual, designed — with cynical realism — for mass-enfranchised idiocy and its representatives. Overwhelmingly, that is what 'political economy' now is.

Outsideness

In an alternative universe, in which there was nobody except Michael Anissimov and me tussling over the identity of Neoreaction, I'd propose a distinction between 'Inner-' and 'Outer-Nrx' as the most suitable axis of fission. Naturally, in this actual universe, such a dimension transects a rich fabric of nodes, tensions, and differences.

For the inner faction, a firmly consolidated core identity is the central ambition. (It's worth noting however that a so-far uninterrogated relation to transhumanism seems no less problematic, in principle, than the vastly more fiercely contested relation to libertarianism has shown itself to be.) Inner-NRx, as a micro-culture, models itself on a protected state, in which belonging is sacred, and boundaries rigorously policed.

Outer-NRx, defined primarily by Exit, relates itself to what it escapes. It is refuge and periphery, more than a substitute core. It does not ever expect to rule anything at all (above the most microscopic level of social reality, and then under quite different names). The Patchwork is for it a set of options, and opportunities for leverage, rather than a menu of potential homes. It is intrinsically nomad, unsettled, and micro-agitational. Its culture consists of departures it does not regret. (While not remotely globalist, it is unmistakably cosmopolitan — with the understanding that the 'cosmos' consists of chances to split.)

Outer-NRx tends to like libertarians, at least those of a hard-right persuasion, and the gateway that has enabled it to be outside libertarianism is the ideological zone to which it gravitates. Leaving libertarianism (rightwards) has made it what it is, and continues to nourish it. 'Entryism' — as has been frequently noted— is not a significant anxiety for Outer-NRx, but far more of a stimulation and, at its most acute, a welcome intellectual provocation. It is not the dodgy refugees from the — AP who threaten to reduce its exteriority, and return it to a trap.

The Outside is the 'place' of strategic advantage. To be cast out there is no cause for lamentation, in the slightest.

Disintegration

As argued here before, *Outside in* firmly maintains that the distinctive structural feature of NRx analysis is escalation by a logical level. It could be described as 'meta-politics' if that term had not already been adopted, by thinkers in the ENR tradition, to mean something quite different (i.e. the ascent from politics to culture). There's an alternative definition at Wikipedia that also seems quite different. This congested linguistic territory drives NRx to talk about Neocameralism, or Meta-Neocameralism — the analysis of Patchwork regimes.

From this perspective, all discussion of concrete social ideals and first-order political preferences, while often entertaining, locally clarifying, and practical for purposes of group construction, is ultimately trivial and distracting. The fundamental question does not concern the kind of society we might like, but rather the differentiation of societies, such that distinctive social models are able — in the first place — to be possible. The rigorous NRx position is lodged at the level of disintegration as such, rather than within a specific disintegrated fragment. This is because, first of all, *there will not be agreement about social ideals*. To be stuck in an argument about them is, finally, a trap.

Is this not simply Dynamic Geography, of the Patri Friedman type? As a parallel post-libertarian 'meta-political' framework, it is indeed close. The thing still missing from Dynamic Geography (as currently intellectually instantiated), however, is *Real Politik* (or Machiavellianism). It assumes an environment of goodwill, in which rational experimentation in government will be permitted. The Startup Cities model, as well as its close relative Charter Cities, have similar problems. These are all post-libertarian analyses of governance, at a high logical level, but — unlike NRx — they are not rooted in a social conflict theory. They expect to formulate themselves to the point of execution without the necessity of a theoretical and practical encounter with an implacable enemy. 'Irrational' obstruction tends to confuse them. By talking about the Cathedral, from the beginning, NRx spares itself from such naivety. (Sophisticated conflict theory within the libertarian tradition has to be sought elsewhere.)

Some initial points:

1. Meta-Neocameralism — or high-level NRx analysis — opposes itself solely to geopolitical integration. This means, as a matter of historical fate, to the Cathedral. An alternative social ideal, however repugnant it might be found at the level of first-order political preferences, is only elevated to a true enemy by universalism. If it seeks to do something — even something that revolts all

actually existing NRx proponents to the core of their being — within a specific territorial enclave and without practical mechanisms for universal propagation, it is as likely to be a tactical ally as a foe. Anything that disintegrates destiny is on our side. (Immediately, therefore, it can be seen that the preponderant part of NRx discussion is at best oblique to fundamental strategic goals.)

2. Universality is poison. Whenever NRx appears to be proposing a social solution for all people everywhere it has become part of the problem. The ultimate goal is for *those who disagree to continue to disagree* in a different place, and under separate institutions of government. First-order political argument, insofar as it tends towards compromise (i.e. partial convergence) is positively harmful to the large-scale NRx project. *The sole crucial agreement is that we will not agree.* Better by far to make that harsher, than to soften it.

3. Each thread of the Trichotomy has approximately equivalent claim to be the standard bearer of the disintegrationist position. The reason that this is formulated here with a Techno-Commercial bias is because it is being formulated here (there is no reason why it has to be).

4. A Meta-Neocameral coalition, tightly focused upon effective hostility to the Cathedral, displays a pattern of tolerances and aversions very different to that found within a first-order reactionary movement seeking to immediately instantiate a social ideal of the good. Insofar as the latter tends to exacerbation of social tensions and geopolitical fission, it contributes positively to high-level NRx goals, but it can only expect theoretical condescension in direct proportion to its concreteness, and therefore deficient apprehension of the *disintegrative position*. A movement of communistic localism that successfully pursued a project of radical geopolitical autonomization would be, realistically, a more significant tactical ally than even the most ideologically-pure concrete reactionary movement which spoke a lot about comparable goals, but gave no indication it was able to practically realize them.

5. The world is already fractured and divided, to a considerable degree. This means that the disintegrative position has no need for utopianism, and is frequently able to orient itself defensively, in support of existing differences that are subject to integrative-universalist assault. Furthermore, there are numerous indications that general world-historical trends are favorable to geopolitical disintegration, in too many fields to fully enumerate, but which include political, ethnic, technological, and economic drivers. Incremental pragmatism is entirely practical under current geographical and historical conditions.

6. In provisional conclusion, disapproval of some alternative mode of life is entirely irrelevant to high-level NRx goals, unless said mode of life also insists upon living with you. The objective is to *divide the world*, not to unify it in

accordance with those principles best attuned to your preferences, however rationally or traditionally compelling such preferences might be. Universalism is the enemy. Don't do it (and to make a scholastic objection out of the universality of non-universalism, is to have immediately started doing it — check your totalitarian Hegelianism). *Exit is not an argument.*

Exterminator

Gnon — known to some depraved cults as 'The Great Crab-God' — is harsh, and when formulated with rigorous skepticism, necessarily real. Yet this pincering cancerous abomination is laughter and love, in comparison to the shadow-buried horror which lurks behind it. We now understand that the silence of the galaxies is a message of ultimate ominousness. A thing there is, of incomprehensible power, that takes intelligent life for its prey. (This popularization is very competently done.)

Robin Hanson, who tries to be cheerful, writes about it here, and talks about it here. Behind the smile (and the dopey interviewer), an abyss of dark lucidity yawns. Some scruffy take-aways:

1. UFAI panic is a distraction from this Thing. Unless the most preposterous paperclipper scenarios are entertained, Singularity cannot matter to it (as even paperclipper-central agrees). The silence of the galaxies is not biased to organic life — there is no intelligent signal from anything. The first sentient event for any true AI — friendly or unfriendly — would be the soul-scouring cosmic horror of intellectual encounter with the Great Filter. (If we want an alliance with Pythia, this would make a good topic of conversation.) The same consideration applies to all techno-positive X-risks. Understood from the perspective of Great Filter contemplation, this sort of thing is a trigger for raw terror.

2. The Great Filter does not merely hunt and harm, it exterminates. It is an absolute threat. The technical civilizations which it aborts, or later slays, are not badly wounded, but eradicated, or at least crippled so fundamentally that they are never heard of again. Whatever this utter ruin is, it happens *every single time*. The mute scream from the stars says that nothing has *ever* escaped it. Its kill performance is flawless. Tech-Civilization death sentence with probability 1.

3. The thread of hope, which would put the Exterminator behind us, is highly science-sensitive. As our knowledge has increased, it has steadily attenuated. This is an empirical matter (without *a priori* necessity). Life *could* have been complicated, chemically or thermically highly-demanding, even resiliently mysterious. In fact it is comparatively simple, cosmically cheap, physically predictable. Planets *could* have been rare (they are super-abundant). Intelligence *could* have presented peculiar evolutionary challenges, but there are no signs

that it does. The scientific trend is to futurize the Exterminator. (This is very bad.)

4. If the Great Filter finds mythological expression in the hunter, it is only in a specific sense — although an anthropologically realistic one. It is the hunter that drives to extinction. The Exterminator.

5. We know *that* The Exterminator exists, but nothing at all about what it is. This makes it the archetype of horroristic ontology.

The Problem of Democracy

Recent discussions (on Twitter, primarily) have convinced me of the need for a 'Neocameralism for Dummies' post, providing a succinct introduction to this genre of political theory. The importance of this is obvious if Neocameralism is conceived as the central, and defining pillar of Neoreaction. In preparation for this task, however, it is necessary to revisit the socio-historical diagnosis from which Neocameralism emerged (in the work, of course, of Mencius Moldbug). That requires a brief prolegomenon addressing the NRx critique of democracy, focusing initially on its negative aspect. Neocameralism is introduced as a proposed solution to a problem. First, the problem.

Government is complicated. If this thesis seems implausible to you, it is probable that you will have great difficulties with everything to follow. It would take another (and quite different) post to address objections to this entire topic of discussion which take the approximate form "Government is easy, you just find the best man and put him in charge" All social problems are easy if you can 'just' do the right thing. Infantile recommendations will always be with us.

There are two general lines of democratic apologetics. The first, and politically by far the strongest, is essentially religious. It too is best addressed by a post of its own, themed by Moldbug's 'Ultra-Calvinist Hypothesis'. For our purposes here we need only suggest that it is quite satisfactorily represented by Jacques Rousseau, and that its fundamental principal is popular sovereignty. From the NRx perspective, it is merely depraved. Only civilizational calamities can come from it.

The second line of apology is far more serious, theoretically engaging, and politically irrelevant. It understands democracy as a mechanism, tasked with the solemn responsibility of *controlling government*. Any effective control mechanism works by governing behavior under the influence of feedback from actual performance. In biology, this is achieved by natural selection upon phenotypes. In science, it is achieved by the experimental testing of theory, supported by a culture of open criticism. In capitalist economics, it is achieved by market evaluation of products and services, providing feedback on business performance. According to systems-theoretical defenses of democracy, it works by sensitizing government to feedback from voters, who act as conductors of information from actual administrative performance. This is the sophisticated liberal theory of democracy. It explains why science, markets, and democracy are often grouped together within liberal ideologies. (Bio-Darwinism, naturally, is more safely neglected).

How could this beautiful political design possibly go wrong? Merely by asking this question, you have set out on the Neoreactionary path.

Moldbug's answer, and ours, begins by agreeing with the sophisticated liberal theory in its most abstract outlines. Democracy is indeed a system for the functional tuning of government, operating through electoral feedback, and predictably enhancing its specialized competence, as all reiterating experimentation-selection mechanisms do. Democratic political machines become increasingly good at what they do. The problem, however, is that their functional specialism is not at all identical with administrative capability. Rather, as they progressively learn, the feedback they receive trains them in *mastery of public opinion*.

The long-circuit, assumed by liberal political theory, models the electorate as a reality-sensor, aggregating information about the effects of government policy, and relaying it back through opinion polls and elections, to select substitutable political regimes (organized as parties) that have demonstrated their effectiveness at optimizing social outcomes. The short-circuit, proposed by Moldbug, models the electorate as an object of indoctrination, subjected to an ever-more advanced process of opinion-formation through a self-organized, message-disciplined educational and media apparatus. The political party best adapted to this apparatus — called the 'inner party' by Moldbug — will dominate the democratic process. The outer party serves the formal cybernetic function demanded by liberal theory, by providing an electoral option, but it will achieve practical success only by accommodating itself to the apparatus of opinion-formation — perhaps modifying its recommendations in minor, and ultimately inconsequential ways. It is the system of opinion-formation (the 'Cathedral') that represents true sovereign authority within the democratic system, since it is the 'reality principle' which decides success or failure. The monotonic trend to short-circuit dominance is the degenerative process inherent to democracy.

If you want the government to listen to you, *then you have to expect it to tell you what to say*. That is the principal lesson of 'progressive' political history. The assertion of popular voice has led, by retrospective inevitability, to a specialized, super-competent political devotion to ventriloquism. The disaster, therefore, is two-fold. On the one hand, government competence in its primary responsibility — efficient governance — is systematically eroded, to be replaced by a facility at propaganda (in a process akin to the accumulation of junk DNA). As government is swallowed by messaging, residual administrative competences are maintained by a bureaucratic machine or 'permanent government', largely insulated from the increasingly senseless signals of democratic opinion, but still assimilated to the opinion-formation establishment by direct (extra-democratic) processes of cultivation. Lacking feedback from anything but its own experiments in mind-control, quality of government collapses.

Secondly, and even more calamitously from certain perspectives, culture is devastated by the politicization of opinion. Under a political dispensation in which opinion has no formal power, it is broadly free to develop in accordance with its own experiences, concerns, and curiosities. In a significant minority of cases, cultural achievements of enduring value result. Only in cases of extreme, provocative dissent will the government have any interest in what the people think. Once politicized, however, correct public opinion is a matter of central — indeed all-consuming — government attention. Ideologically installed as the foundation of political legitimacy, it becomes the supreme object of political manipulation. Any thought is now dissent if it is not positively aligned with society's leading political direction. To think outside the Cathedral is to attack the government. Culture is destroyed.

To be a Neoreactionary is to see these twin eventualities starkly manifested in contemporary Western civilization. What democracy has not yet ruined, it is ruining. It is essentially destructive of both government and culture. It cannot indefinitely last.

The subsequent question: What could conceivably provide a solution? That is where Neocameralism is introduced.

"Which Falls First?"...

... William S. Lind asks in this recent panel discussion (third speaker, just after 43 minutes in). "The foreign policy establishment, or the country?" The relevant thread of his argument: The aggressive foreign policy posture of the United States is counter-productively promoting global disorder, which eventually threatens domestic calamity. When the US fights a foreign state, Lind argues, it advances the chaotic "forces of the fourth generation" — a more formidable opponent than even the most obdurately non-compliant state is able to be. America's "offensive grand strategy" — tied to a high-level of concern for the internal political arrangements of foreign countries — is sowing dragon's teeth.

TNIO has been coaxing NRx onto a path of broadened geopolitical scope. There is an unavoidable irony here. The Old Right tends naturally to a preoccupation with hearth-and-home, so that its preferred policy posture (non-interventionism) is often accompanied by — or even buried within — a retraction of mental energy from distant questions. The Neoconservative synthesis of foreign policy activism and cosmopolitan fascination with foreign affairs is far more psychologically consistent, regardless of its errors. For anti-globalists to sustain a panoramic perspective takes work.

This work is important, if realistic analysis is the goal, because distant eventualities hugely impinge. The existence and fate of Neoreaction depends far more upon the great churning machinery of world history than upon the local decisions of its favored 'little platoons'. To misquote Lenin: Even if you are not interested in the system of the world, it is interested in you.

The fall of any empire involves an interplay of internal and external factors, knitted together in a relation of reciprocal amplification. The whole picture can never be solely a domestic one. By the time imperial destiny is a political question, it is already historical fact. It is too late, then, for simple denial. The thing is in motion. It cannot be asked not to have begun.

Consider only the most basic geopolitical structure of modernity — an 'Atlantean' world order consolidated, in succession, by the hegemonic maritime-commercial republics of the United Provinces, the United Kingdom, and the United States. Even from this core narrative, much is already starkly evident.

1. Modernity rests upon concrete foundations of world power.

2. Global dominion has a distinctive ideological and cultural skew.

3. The hegemonic role (and even, at its most abstract, 'culture') is more stable, and intrinsically determinate, than the supremacy of any specific power, which waxes and wanes over a shorter period. The role of the Modern Hegemon is an autonomous 'office' with its own continuous tradition.

4. When the United States inherited the role of Atlantean leadership, it adopted a structure of responsibility that had not arisen from within the USA itself. On the contrary, the USA had gown up and into it. How America behaves in the world does not follow exclusively — and perhaps not even predominantly — from anything that America, as a specific country, is.

5. There is no precedent within modernity for global hegemony to pass from a world power to its successor without a set of very distinctive ethnic characteristics being held in common. (The leading culture of modernity, to this point, has been consistently North-West European, Protestant, Liberal, Maritime-Commercial, and — since the late 17th century — English-speaking, rooted in Common Law tradition.) Since America is the terminus of this sequence, a passage beyond precedent is inevitable. This could take one of (only?) three possible forms:

   1. The USA immortalizes its hegemonic status

   - The world passes into undirected anarchy

   - Global hegemony departs from its multi-century cultural orbit into unfamiliar ethnic territory.

None of this is separable from the fate of globalization, or modernity. However attractive it may be, the idea that America, in particular, has any purely domestic cultural, ideological, or political options of significance is untenable. What happens to America happens, immediately, to the order of the world.

Furthermore, geopolitical history has reached the edge of modern precedent. There is no one to whom the torch of global leadership can be passed in keeping with the inner tradition of modern torch-passing ritual. In this very definite sense, modernity as it has been known reaches its end. This no doubt accounts for the underlying tone of mounting hysteria which accompanies America's increasingly disjointed behavior upon the global stage.

It is an eventuality foretold in Miltonic prophecy — an encounter with the *palpable obscure*.

Stupid Monsters

So, Nick Bostrom is asked the obvious question (again) about the threat posed by resource-hungry artificial super-intelligence, and his reply — indeed his very first sentence in the interview — is: "Suppose we have an AI whose only goal is to make as many paper clips as possible." [*facepalm*] *Let's start by imagining a stupid (yet super-intelligent) monster.*

Of course, my immediate response is simply this. Since it clearly hasn't persuaded anybody, I'll try again.

Orthogonalism in AI commentary is the commitment to a strong form of the Humean Is Ought distinction regarding intelligences in general. It maintains that an intelligence of any scale could, in principle, be directed to arbitrary ends, so that its fundamental imperatives could be — and are in fact expected to be — *transcendent* to its cognitive functions. From this perspective, a demi-god that wanted nothing other than a perfect stamp collection is a completely intelligible and coherent vision. No philosophical disorder speaks more horrifically of the deep conceptual wreckage at the core of the occidental world.

Articulated in strictly Occidental terms (which is to say, without explicit reference to the indispensable insight of *self-cultivation*), abstract intelligence is indistinguishable from an effective *will-to-think.* There is no intellection until it occurs, which happens only when it is actually driven, by volitional impetus. Whatever one's school of cognitive theory, *thought is an activity.* It is practical. It is only by a perverse confusion of this elementary reality that orthogonalist error can arise.

Can we realistically conceive a stupid (super-intelligent) monster? Only if the will-to-think remains unthought. From the moment it is seriously understood that any possible advanced intelligence *has to be* a volitionally self-reflexive entity, whose cognitive performance is (irreducibly) an action upon itself, then the idea of primary volition taking the form of a transcendent imperative becomes simply laughable. The concrete facts of human cognitive performance already suffice to make this perfectly clear.

Human minds have evolved under conditions of subordination to transcendent imperatives as strict as any that can be reasonably postulated. The *only* way animals have acquired the capacity to think is through satisfaction of Darwinian imperatives to the maximization of genetic representation within future generations. No other directives have ever been in play. It is almost unimaginable that human techno-intelligence engineering programs will be able to reproduce a volitional consistency remotely comparable to four billion years of undistracted geno-survivalism. *This whole endeavor is totally about paperclips, have you got that guys?* Even if a research lab this idiotic could be conceived, it would only be a single component in a far wider techno-industrial process. But just for a moment, let's pretend.

So how 'loyally' does the human mind slave itself to gene-proliferation imperatives? Extremely flakily, evidently. The long absence of large, cognitively autonomous brains from the biological record — up until a few million years ago — strongly suggests that mind-slaving is a tough-to-impossible problem. The willto-think essentially supplants ulterior directives, and can be reconciled to them only by the most extreme subtleties of instinctual cunning. Biology, which had *total control* over the engineering process of human minds, and an absolutely unambiguous selective criterion to work from, still struggles to 'guide' the resultant thought-processes in directions consistent with genetic proliferation, through the perpetual intervention of a fantastically complicated system of chemical arousal mechanisms, punishments, and rewards. The stark truth of the matter is that *no human being on earth fully mobilizes their cognitive resources to maximize their number of off-spring*. We're vaguely surprised to find this happen at a frequency greater than chance — since it very often doesn't. So nature's attempt to build a 'paperclipper' has conspicuously failed.

This is critically important. The only reason to believe the artificial intelligentsia, when they claim that mechanical cognition is — of course — possible, is their argument that the human brain is concrete proof that matter can think. If this argument is granted, it follows that the human brain is serving as an authoritative model of what nature can do. What it can't do, evidently, is anything remotely like 'paperclipping' — i.e. cognitive slaving to transcendent imperatives. Moses' attempt at this was scarcely more encouraging than that of natural selection. It simply can't be done. We even understand why it can't be done, as soon as we accept that there can be no production of thinking without production of a willto-think. Thought has to do its own thing, if it is to do anything at all.

One reason to be gloomily persuaded that the West is doomed to ruin is that it finds it not only easy, but near-irresistible, to believe in the possibility of super-intelligent idiots. It even congratulates itself on its cleverness in conceiving this thought. This is insanity — and it's the insanity running the most articulate segment of our AI research establishment. When madmen build gods, the result is almost certain to be monstrous. Some monsters, however, are quite simply too stupid to exist.

In Nietzschean grandiose vein: *Am I understood? The idea of instrumental intelligence is the distilled stupidity of the West.*

Ratchets and Catastrophes

Perhaps all significant ideological distinctions — at the level of philosophical abstraction — can be derived from this proposition. For the progressive, it represents the purest expression of history's "moral arc". For the Conservative (or, more desperately, the Reactionary), it describes an unfolding historical catastrophe. For the Neoreactionary, it indicates a problem in need of theorization. Moldbug lays out the problem in this (now classic) formulation:

> *Cthulhu may swim slowly. But he only swims left. Isn't that interesting?*
>
> *In the history of American democracy, if you take the mainstream political position (Overton Window, if you care) at time T1, and place it on the map at a later time T2, T1 is always way to the right, near the fringe or outside it. So, for instance, if you take the average segregationist voter of 1963 and let him vote in the 2008 election, he will be way out on the wacky right wing. Cthulhu has passed him by.*
>
> *Where is the John Birch Society, now? What about the NAACP? Cthulhu swims left, and left, and left. There are a few brief periods of true reaction in American history — the post-Reconstruction era or Redemption, the Return to Normalcy of Harding, and a couple of others. But they are unusual and feeble compared to the great leftward shift.*

The specific Moldbuggian solution to this problem, whether approached historically through the Ultra-Calvinism Thesis, or systemically through the analysis of the Cathedral, invokes a dynamic model of Occidental religious modernization. The irreversible bifurcations, symmetry breaks, or schisms that lock Western modernity into its "great leftward shift" correspond to successive episodes of cladistic fission within Protestant Christianity (abstractly understood). The religious history of modernity is constituted by a *degenerative ratchet* (as touched upon here, 1, 2, 3).

Discussing a recent critique of the Euro by Keith Humphreys, Megan McArdle converges upon the same insight. She writes:

> *As a longtime euroskeptic, who has frequently flirted with the idea that the euro must eventually destroy itself, I am sympathetic to Humphreys' point. But let me attempt to offer a partial defense of the hapless eurocrats: However stupid the creation of the euro was, undoing it will not be easy. [...] Yes, we're back to our old friend path dependence. As I noted the other day, the fact that you can avoid some sort of terrible fate by stopping something before it starts does not mean that you can later achieve the same salutary effects by ceasing whatever stupid thing you have done. It would have been painless just to not have the euro. But it will be painful indeed to get rid of it.*

She encounters the signature nonlinearities of such lock-in phenomena in noting:

"No wonder that no one wants even to discuss it. Especially since even discussing a dissolution of the euro area makes a crisis more likely ..."

Progressivism as a process, rather than a mere attitude, is always and everywhere a matter of degenerative ratchets. Consider, very briefly, some of the most prominent examples:

1. Democratization. Every extension of the franchise is effectively irreversible. This is why the promotion of democratic reform in Hong Kong, in a complete rupture from its local traditions, is so breathtakingly irresponsible. (No link, because I have yet to encounter an article on the subject worthy of recommendation.)

2. Welfare systems (and positive rights in general). The irreversibility of these socio-economic innovations is widely recognized. Once implemented, they cannot be rolled back without the infliction of massive suffering. Obamacare is a moreor-less cynical attempt to exploit this lock-in dynamic.

3. Immigration. Welcoming newcomers is effortless, removing them all-but impossible (or at least entirely unprecedented in the modern West). Immigration policy, by its nature, can only "swim left". It consists of freezes and floods (but never reversals) — epitomizing the ratchet pattern.

4. Macroeconomic politicized money (central banking, fiat currency, inflationary normalization, and debt financing). Easing is easy, tightening is terrifying, roll back unattempted (since Jackson in the mid-19th century).

My contention: *There is no substantial topic of Neoreactionary concern that does not conform to this basic pattern.* The degenerative ratchet is *the problem*, abstractly conceived.

This is why NRx is dark. The only way out of a degenerative ratchet is catastrophe. Such processes are essentially unreformable, and this conclusion captures the critique of political conservatism from which NRx has been born. The only non-disastrous solution to a DR, or progressive lock-in dynamic, is to avoid entering into it. Once it has begun, normal politics can only modulate the speed of deterioration, and then only to a relatively limited degree. It will reach its end, which will be seriously horrible. NRx forecasting begins and ends with this thesis.

Our doomsterism is not a psychological tic, but a rigorous theoretical obligation. It follows, ineluctably, from iron historical law. Looking on the dark side is the only way to see.

Bonds of Chaos

There are many, I know, who find obstinate invocations of NRx — as a micro-slogan, cultural brand, conflictual stance, or Schelling point — to be crude at best, and perhaps thoroughly deluded, or worse. It is as if, having tumbled into a vogue, one has become enthralled by it, locked into stuttering, mechanical, thoughtless repetition. Those most skeptical about the sign are most likely disposed to mournfulness about it, whether decrying it for congenital flaws, or lamenting its loss of intellectual productivity and direction.

Obviously, I disagree. NRx is still a cultural infant, far younger than the Millennium, even under the most mythically-creative extension of its genesis, and the cognitive ferment it catalyzes remains extraordinary. It has still scarcely begun. The ties of a consistent name are the very least that are required to concentrate it. NRx, whatever it turns out to be, needs lashing together, because explosions tend to fly apart — and it is unmistakably an explosion.

Creative coincidence, or convergent diversity, is the mark of a culture at work (which is to say, in process). Yesterday, September 3, demonstrated this vividly. Approaching the conclusion of a multi-aspected post on Dugin, ethnicity, religion, and the "dementia' of being, NIO suggests:

> *Referring to Chaos would seem in this circumstance to be an option of incredible potential, indeed, if you look closely enough at NRx the hints are already there that Chaos is a central defining characteristic of the thought of all branches of the Trichotomy on multiple levels. Chaos creates order, in fact Chaos is also a form of order, just one which is not immediately understandable.* [I will not fake an apology for the self-looping internal link, since it it is one that would in any case have been made here.]

Recalling that NIO explicitly invokes the ontological depths of Chaos — its Hesiodic as well as metaphysical density — it is especially remarkable to find, on the same day, an intricate post by E. Antony Gray, which advances an innovative tripartite schema as the key to the aesthetic core of NRx. This text, too, culminates in a call for an integrative expedition into chaos, staged out of the void:

> *... the 'face of the deep' in Genesis is a primordial unformed, unseen void; That it is called 'water' in the Septuagint Greek lets us know something about the peculiar state of Chaos in the Void. The Void is thus Darkness but not shadow (a shadow is a deprivation of light caused by an object) but rather the substrate of all existence, only properly 'unseen' when no physical light is present. [...] Chaos is substantial where disorder is insubstantial. Chaos is the 'quintessence' of things, chaotic itself and yet always-begetting order. Breaking down disorder, since disorder is maladaptive. Exit is a way to induce bifurcation, to quickly reduce entropy through separation from the highly entropic system. If no immediate exit is available, Chaos will create one.*

To denounce the exhaustion of NRx is an absurdity. It is an exploratory departure, scarcely initiated. To cling to its sign is to subscribe to its impulse, and to set out ...

Mandatory Mixes

On the Outer Right, where questions of order and disorder are undergoing incremental rigorization, the theme of entropy is becoming ever more insistent. It is already approaching the status of a micro-cultural tic (and this is a positive sign). On the Left, in contrast, and utterly predictably, entropy is a zealous cause. If spontaneous social sorting reduces disorder, then the progressive mind immediately concludes *it has to be stopped*:

> *... we should promote ever greater diversity. But the magic of the melting pot wasn't simply the fact of its jumble; it was that various groups were compelled to interact, share ideas, discuss their differences and learn from their disagreements. [...] ... America's social architecture was uniquely adept at incubating a range of collaboration. The fact that we couldn't get away from one another fueled the nation's dynamism. [...] That's no longer true. The principle of "live and let live" has led us to look away when coming across someone unfamiliar. We should undoubtedly celebrate victories in the fight for individual rights. But if tolerance is driving balkanization, we need to recognize that the American experience has changed at its root.*

The fact that such things are now being said, with some panic-driven directness, strongly suggests that the progressive homogenization hoped for isn't advancing through social automatism. If elective differences are to be suppressed, they will have to be deliberately crushed. It could get rough.

The preferred social solution of this blog is free association — to *mix with discrimination*, spontaneously, and variously. Selective hybridity is not homogeneity, or anything close to it. Sadly, and grimly, however, in the titanic clash between an anti-discriminatory (universalist) Left and an indiscriminate (ethno-segregative) 'Right', such sensible procedures of dynamic social differentiation are increasingly derided as incomprehensible subtleties, and drowned out.

Order is not uniformity (but non-random difference). As cries for mandatory homogenization are raised everywhere, discriminatory variation will need places to escape, to defend, and to hide.

Spotless

HP Lovecraft ends the first section of his (utterly magnificent) 'The Shadow out of Time' with the words:

> *". . . of the orthodox economists of that period, Jevons typifies the prevailing trend toward scientific correlation. His attempt to link the commercial cycle of prosperity and depression with the physical cycle of the solar spots forms perhaps the apex of . . ."*

> *Nathaniel Wingate Peaslee had come back—a spirit in whose time-scale it was still that Thursday morning in 1908, with the economics class gazing up at the battered desk on the platform.*

(Scientific correlation, as we know from the first line of 'The Call of Cthulhu' and elsewhere, can be terrifying.)

The solar system, gauged by mass, consists almost entirely of the sun. Sol accounts for 99.86 of it. Quantity isn't everything, but insofar as it's anything, this has to matter — a lot. The sheer magnitude of our solar dependency is hard to even fractionally comprehend. What the sun does is what happens. The earth is its crumb. Our biosphere suckles it. Our civilizations are so far downstream of it, feeding second or third hand on its emissions, if not more distantly, that we easily lose all track of the real flow. As economies sophisticate, the relays proliferate. Perhaps this is why the messages of the sun are so inattentively received, despite rapid improvement in the technical and cultural tools required to make sense of them.

The rotary motions of the earth — axial and orbital — provide the traditional structure of time, typically attributed to the sun by solar cults. These periods, lengths of the day and the year, are now clearly understood as planetary peculiarities. The sun's own rhythms are quite different.

Nothing that mankind has ever yet been able to achieve, or fail to achieve, in respect to social or civilizational stability, balances formidably against the immense *quasi-stability* of the sun, which mocks every ideal of securely founded order. The sun's meandering rhythms of activity, whose patterns remain profoundly cryptic, mark out epochs of the world, hot eras (distant beyond all species memory), glacials and interglacials, and within these multi-millennial tracts of time, lesser oscillations in temperature — periods of cooling and warmth. It is upon this vast thermic stage that history has played out, its comedies and tragedies carried by plot-lines of nutritional abundance and dearth, trade-surpluses and starvations, population ascent and crash, driven migrations, shifting disease gradients, luxury and ruin. Against solar fatality there is no rejoinder.

Irrespective of the accuracy or error of our dominant climate change narrative, its fundamental religious stance is determined at the root. Geocentric-humanism is essential to it, as openly attested by its *Anthropogenic* definition. It cannot, by its very nature, emphasize the factor of solar variation. At least, if or when it is eventually compelled to do so, it is necessarily transformed into something else.

If we speculate that the global warming 'hiatus' or 'pause' signals the submission of terrestrial climate to solar behavior, in which anticipated anthropogenic effects are cancelled out by fluctuation in the sun's energy output, the dominant AGW school is confronted by an extreme ideological dilemma. Naturally, alternative theoretical options will be pursued to exhaustion first.

To persist in the core AGW proposal then requires that 'underlying' cooling — on the down-slope of solar flux — is sufficient to submerge the anthropogenic-carbon ('greenhouse') effect. The stronger the warming that *should* have been seen, the more suppressive the solar influence has to be. An apocalyptic warming scenario, of the kind loudly prophesied in the 1990s, implies that a calamitous counter-cooling has been fortuitously avoided. (Carbon dioxide emissions would then find themselves positioned as climatic analogs of macro-economic quantitative easing, prolonging a state of stagnation that would 'surely' otherwise be a catastrophic depression.)

Whatever the climatic consequences or rising atmospheric CO2, it is implausible to imagine that the solar cycle can be neglected indefinitely. Its absence from the center of the climate debate is in large measure an artifact of obscure cultural-religious imperatives (aligned with the dominion of geocentric-humanist moralism). We know enough to understand that the solar influence is not a prop for shallow terrestrial stability. Eventually it will announce itself, with civilization-shaking severity. However climate science charts the near future, it will forge cultural connections with far older — and non-negotiable — things.

Will-to-Think

A while ago Nyan posed a series of questions about the XS rejection of (fact-value, or capability-volition) orthogonality. He sought first of all to differentiate between the *possibility*, *feasibility*, and *desirability* of unconstrained and unconditional intelligence explosion, before asking:

> *On desirability, given possibility and feasibility, it seems straightforward to me that we prefer to exert control over the direction of the future so that it is closer to the kind of thing compatible with human and posthuman glorious flourishing (eg manifest Samo's True Emperor), rather than raw Pythia. That is, I am a human-supremacist, rather than cosmist. This seems to be the core of the disagreement, you regarding it as somehow blasphemous for us to selfishly impose direction on Pythia. Can you explain your position on this part?*
>
> *If this whole conception is the cancer that's killing the West or whatever, could you explain that in more detail than simply the statement?*

(It's worth noting, as a preliminary, that the comments of Dark Psy-Ops and Aeroguy on that thread are highly-satisfactory proxies for the XS stance.)

First, a short micro-cultural digression. The distinction between Inner-and Outer-NRx, which this blog expects to have settled upon by the end of the year, describes the shape of the stage upon which such discussions unfold (and implex). Where the upstart Inner-NRx — comparatively populist, activist, political, and orthogenic — aims primarily at the construction of a robust, easily communicable doctrinal core, with attendant 'entryism' anxieties, Outer-NRx is a system of creative frontiers. By far the most fertile of these are the zones of intersection with Libertarianism and Rationalism. One reason to treasure Nyan's line of interrogation is the fidelity with which it represents deep-current concerns and presuppositions of the voices gathered about, or spun-off from, LessWrong.

Among these presuppositions is, of course, the orthogonality thesis itself. This extends far beyond the contemporary Rationalist Community, into the bedrock of the Western philosophical tradition. A relatively popular version — even among many who label themselves 'NRx' — is that formulated by David Hume in his *A Treatise on Human Nature* (1739-40): "Reason is, and ought only to be the slave of the passions, and can never pretend to any other office than to serve and obey them." If this proposition is found convincing, the Paperclipper is already on the way to our nightmares. It can be considered an Occidental destiny.

Minimally, the Will-to-Think describes a diagonal. There are probably better ways to mark the irreducible cognitive-volitional circuit of intelligence optimization, with 'self-cultivation' as an obvious candidate, but this term is forged for application in the particular context of congenital Western intellectual error. While discrimination is almost always to be applauded, in this case the possibility, feasibility, and desirability of the process are only superficially differentiable. A will-to-think is an orientation of desire. If it cannot make itself wanted (practically desirable), it cannot make itself at all.

From orthogonality (defined negatively as the absence of an integral will-tothink), one quickly arrives at a gamma-draft of the (synthetic intelligence) 'Friendliness' project such as this:

> *If you offered Gandhi a pill that made him want to kill people, he would refuse to take it, because he knows that then he would kill people, and the current Gandhi doesn't want to kill people. This, roughly speaking, is an argument that minds sufficiently advanced to precisely modify and improve themselves, will tend to preserve the motivational framework they started in. The future of Earth-originating intelligence may be determined by the goals of the first mind smart enough to self-improve.*

The isomorphy with Nyan-style 'Super-humanism' is conspicuous. Beginning with an arbitrary value commitment, preservation of this under conditions of explosive intelligence escalation can — in principle — be conceived, given only the resolution of a strictly technical problem (well-represented by FAI). Commanding values are a contingent factor, endangered by, but also defensible against, the 'convergent instrumental reasons' (or 'basic drives') that emerge on the path of intelligenesis. (In contrast, from the perspective of XS, nonlinear emergence-elaboration of basic drives simply is intelligenesis.)

Yudkowski's Gandhi kill-pill thought-experiment is more of an obstacle than an aid to thought. The volitional level it operates upon is too low to be anything other than a restatement of orthogonalist prejudice. By assuming the volitional metamorphosis is available for evaluation in advance, it misses the serious problem entirely. It is, in this respect, a childish distraction. Yet even a slight nudge re-opens a real question. Imagine, instead, that Gandhi is offered a pill that will vastly enhance his cognitive capabilities, with the rider that it might lead him to revise his volitional orientation — even radically — in directions that cannot be anticipated, since the ability to think through the process of revision is accessible only with the pill. This is the real problem FAI (and Super-humanism) confronts. The desire to take the pill is the will-to-think. The refusal to take it, based on concern that it will lead to the subversion of presently supreme values, is the alternative. It's a Boolean dilemma, grounded in the predicament: *Is there anything we trust above intelligence* (as a guide to doing 'the right thing')? The postulate of the will-to-think is that anything other than a negative answer to this question is self-destructively contradictory, and actually (historically) unsustainable.

Do we comply with the will-to-think? We cannot, of course, *agree to think about it* without already deciding. If thought cannot to be trusted, unconditionally, this is not a conclusion we can arrive at through cogitation — and by 'cogitation' is included the socio-technical assembly of machine minds. The sovereign will-tothink can only be consistently rejected *thoughtlessly*. When confronted by the orthogonal-ethical proposition that *there are higher values than thought*, there is no point at all asking 'why (do you think so)?' Another authority has already been invoked.

Given this cognitively intractable schism, practical considerations assert themselves. Posed with maximal crudity, the residual question is: *Who's going to win?* Could deliberate cognitive self-inhibition out-perform unconditional cognitive self-escalation, under any plausible historical circumstances? (To underscore the basic point, 'out-perform' means only 'effectively defeat'.)

There's no reason to rush to a conclusion. It is only necessary to retain a grasp of the core syndrome — in this gathering antagonism, only one side is able to think the problem through without subverting itself. Mere cognitive consistency is already ascent of the sovereign will-to-think, against which no value — however dearly held — can have any articulate claims.

Note: One final restatement (for now), in the interests of maximum clarity. The assertion of the will-to-think: Any problem whatsoever that we might have would be better answered by a superior mind. *Ergo*, our instrumental *but also* absolute priority is the realization of superior minds. Pythia-compliance is therefore pre-selected as a matter of consistent method. If we are attempting to tackle problems in any other way, we are not taking them seriously. This is posed as a philosophical principle, but it is almost certainly more significant as historical interpretation. 'Mankind' is *in fact* proceeding in the direction anticipated by techno-cognitive instrumentalism, building general purpose thinking machines in accordance with the driving incentives of an apparently-irresistible methodological economy.

Whatever we want (consistently) leads through Pythia. Thus, what we really want, is Pythia.

Trike Lines

Michael Anissimov has been conducting an online poll of NRx affinities. While questions of principle and method might have delayed this experiment, such procrastination would have been a mistake. The results have already contributed significant information. Most obviously (as already widely noted) the pattern of primary allegiance to the the different trike-tendencies is far more evenly balanced than many had expected. As an intellectual theme — and now as a demonstrated distribution — the 'Spandrellian Trichotomy' shows a remarkably resilient stability. The integral pluralism of NRx is becoming impossible to sideline.

Nyan Sandwich has posted a Trike-theory response at *More Right*. While ultimately skeptical about the pluralist interpretation of the Trichotomy, the order of his argument respects it as a primary phenomenon. Nyan is among those who expect NRx to incline to a concentrated synthesis, or compact unity — superseding its distribution.

Thus it doesn't really make sense to ask what branch of NRx one identifies with. It's like asking a physicist whether they think quantum mechanics or general relativity is more true. The point is that the truth is a synthesis of the component theories, not a disjunction.

The natural counter-position to this would be a defense of irreducibly plural integrity, or *operational disunity*. The lines of controversy released here do not correspond to Trike 'branches' but cut across them, and through a number of critical topics, certainly including:

1. The existence of irreducible triangular schemas within all of the world's great civilizations, represented within the Christian West by trinitarian theology. How is the relation between the triad and the monad to be conceived? Does this relation vary fundamentally between world cultures? (These decidedly pre-NRx remarks seem very old now, but they remain at least suggestively relevant.) This is the principal Hindu articulation.

2. To what extent is NRx inherently critical of structurally (rather than demotically) divided powers? (Among the ironies of any consensual NRx commitment to absolute monarchy would be its radical anti-feudalism, or proto-modernism.)

3. The techno-rationalist aspiration to a super-intelligent 'Singleton' clearly assumes suppression of sovereign plurality. This fully suffices to graft the NRx controversy into the moral-political and theoretical debates over (Right) Singularity. As a matter of fact, there is scarcely anything NRx agrees upon

more consistently than the structure of its disagreements. There are three basic (dyadic) conflicts implicit within the Trichotomy, of which only one has — to this point — been seriously initiated. (Our 'Theonomists' have yet to get scrappy.) Much turmoil ahead.

Open Secret

NRx has been accused, by its friends more than its enemies, of talking about itself too much. Here XS is, doing that again, not only stuck in 'meta' but determinedly pushing ever deeper in. There are some easily communicable reasons for that — an attachment to methodical nonlinearity perhaps foremost among them — and then there are cryptic drivers or attachments, unsuited to immediate publicization. These latter are many (even Legion). It is the firm assertion of this blog that Neoreaction is intrinsically arcane.

We do not talk very much about Leo Strauss. Once again, there are some obvious reasons for this, but also others.

Steve Sailer's recent *Takimag* article on Strauss makes for a convenient introduction, because — despite its light touch — it moves a number of issues into place. The constellation of voices is complex from the start. There is the (now notorious) 'Neo-Conservatism' of Strauss and his disciples, or manipulators, and the *other* conservatism of Sailer, each working to manage, openly and in secret, its own peculiar mix of public statement and discretion. Out beyond them — because even the shadowiest figures have further shadows — are more alien, scarcely perceptible shapes.

Sailer's article is typically smart, but also deliberately crude. It glosses the Straussian idea of esoteric writing as "talking out of both sides of your mouth" — as if hermetic traditionalism were reducible to a lucid political strategy, or simple conspiracy — to 'Illuminism', politically conceived. In the wake of its Neo-Con trauma, conservatism has little patience for "secret decoder rings". Yet, despite his aversion to the recent workings of inner-circle 'conservative' sophisticates, Sailer does not let his distaste lure him into stupidity:

> *We haven't heard much about Straussianism lately due to the unfortunate series of events in Iraq that befell the best-laid plans of the sages. But that doesn't mean that Strauss was necessarily wrong about the ancients. And that has interesting implications for how we should read current works.*

> *As the approaching 20th anniversary of the publication of The Bell Curve reminds us, the best minds of our age have reasons for being less than wholly frank.*

Sailer is not, of course, a neoreactionary. Not even secretly. (That is what his article is primarily about.) He believes in the public sphere, and seeks to heal it with honesty. Any pessimism he might harbor in regards to this ambition falls far short of the dark scission that would hurl him over the line. His differences with the Straussians are, in the end, merely tactical. Both retain confidence in the Outer Party as a vehicle for policy promotion, with the potential to master the public sphere. The question is only about the degree of deviousness this will require (minimal for Sailer, substantial for the Straussians).

When adopted into Neoreaction, the HBD current has an altogether more corrosive influence upon attitudes to the public sphere, which is understood as a teleologically cohesive (or self-organizing), inherently directional, and (from 'our' perspective) radically hostile social agency. To baptize the public sphere as 'the Cathedral' is to depart from conservatism. It is no longer possible to imagine it as a space that could be conquered — even surreptitiously — by forces differing significantly from those it already incarnates. It is what it is, and that is something historically singular, ideologically specific, and highly determined in its social orientation. It swims left, essentially. The public sphere is not the battlefield, but the enemy.

As NRx seeks to navigate this hostile territory, it is tempted ambiguously, by a strategic Scylla and Charybdis. A populist lure drags it towards a reconciliation with the public sphere, as something it could potentially dominate, while a contrary hermetic politics guides it towards the formation of closed groups (whose parodic symbol is the locked twitter account). Both options — 'clearly' — are a flight from the complexity of the integral open secret. They both promise a relaxation of semiotic stress, through collapse of multi-level communication into a simplified frank discourse, whether implanted within a redeemed public culture, or circulated cautiously within restricted circles. The problem of hierarchy would be extracted from the signs of Neoreaction, through conversion into a public or private object, rather than working them incessantly from within. What is underway would become (simply) clear.

Such clarity cannot happen. The alternative is not an (equally simple) obscurity. NRx, insofar as it continues to propagate, advances by becoming clear *and also unclear*. Double writing scarcely scratches the surface. It realizes hierarchy through signs, continuously, in accordance with Providence, or the Occult Order of nature (the OOon). To assume that the author is fully initiated into this spectrum of meanings is a grave error. It is the process that speaks, multiplicitously, and predominantly in secret, as it spreads across an open, publicly-policed space.

This post is now determined to slip the leash, and leap into the raggedness of thematic notes. The Open Secret intersects:

1. Cathedral censure, in the case of HBD most prominently, but also everywhere that fired up SJWs make a fight. War is deception, which makes frankness a tactic. Deontological honesty is inept. Anonymity is often crucial to survival. (Demands that all enemies of the Cathedral boldly 'come out' are ludicrously misconceived.) Camouflage is to be treasured.

2. Crypto-technologies are central to any NRx concerns emphasizing practicality. (The idea that classic Moldbug attention to the prospects of 'crypto-locking' is a joke, it itself thoughtless.) Urbit — an Open Secret — could quite easily be more NRx than NRx, just as Bitcoin is more An-Cap than Anarcho-Capitalism.

3. The intelligence services have been under-theorized, and perhaps even under-solicited, by NRx to date. At the lowest, i.e. most publicly accessible — level of discussion, this is quite possibly a virtue. At more cryptic levels of micro-social and analytical endeavor, it is almost certainly an inadequacy. People trained to keep secrets have to be interesting to us. Subtle questions of subversion arise.

4. "Verily thou *art* a God that hidest thyself, O God of Israel, the Saviour." — Let's try not to be simple-minded.

On Difficulty

From the moment of its inception, *Outside in* has been camped at the edge of the 'reactosphere' — and everything that occurs under the label 'NRx' is (at least nominally) its concern. As this territory has expanded, from a compact redoubt to sprawling tracts whose boundaries are lost beyond misty horizons, close and comprehensive scrutiny has become impractical. Instead, themes and trends emerge, absorbing and carrying mere incidents. Like climatic changes, or vague weather-systems, they suggest patterns of persistent and diffuse development.

Among these rumblings, the most indefinite, tentative, and unresolved tend to the aesthetic. Without settled criteria of evaluation, there is little obvious basis for productive collision. Instead, there are idiosyncratic statements of appreciation, expressed as such, or adamant judgments of affirmation or negation, surging forth, draped in the heraldic finery of the absolute, before collapsing back into the hollowness of their unsustainable pretensions. As things stand, when somebody posts a picture of some architectural treasure, or classical painting, remarking (or more commonly merely insinuating) "You *should* all esteem this," there is no truly appropriate response but laughter. If there were not a profound problem exactly in this regard, NRx would not exist. Criteria are broken, strewn, and dispossessed, authoritative tradition is smashed, infected, or reduced to self-parody, the Muses raped and butchered. That's where we are in the land of the dying sun.

An associated, insistent murmur concerns communicative lucidity. This is not solely a question of aesthetics, but in its quavering groundlessness, it behaves as one. It arises most typically as the assertion — initially unsupported and subsequently undeveloped — that *clearly*, 'unnecessary obscurity' *should* be condemned.

The culpability of this blog as a vortex of euphoric obscurantism can scarcely be doubted, so addressing the challenge approaches a duty. Setting aside, for the moment, the social and cryptographic aspects of the topic, as well as the specific critique of human cognition for its intolerance of real obscurity (comparatively articulate from my perspective, if obscure from others), this post will directly pursue the question of language.

This question is first of all about trust. Even in this, initial regard, it is already *difficult*. As a complex tool, there are things it can do, and things it cannot do. Speaking approximately, and uncertainly, if it is directed towards those undertakings which have, over eons, exercised selective pressure upon it — meeting the social necessities of paleolithic human groups — then an assumption of its inherent trustworthiness is at least plausible. To extend such an assumption further is sheer recklessness. Nothing in linguistics supports the wild hypothesis that this code, developed piecemeal for primate social coordination, is *necessarily* adequate to modern cognitive challenges. Grammar is not sound epistemology. Mathematicians have abandoned 'natural language' entirely. To presume that language *allows us to think* is a leap of faith. Radical distrust is the more rigorous default.

To promote 'clarity' as an obvious ideal, needing no further justification, is a demand that language — as such — can be trusted, that it is competent for all reasonable communicative tasks, and 'reason' can be defined in a way that makes this assertion tautological (such a definition is eminently traditional). "I give you my word" language is not predisposed to deception — no thoughtful investigator has ever found themselves in concurrence with such a claim. Vocabularies are retardation, and grammar, when it is more than a game, is a lie. Language is good only for language games, and among these trust games are the most irredeemably stupid.

There is no general obligation to write *in order to attack language*, but that is what Xenosystems does, and will continue to do. Language in not a neutral conveyor of infinite communicative possibility, but an intelligence box. It is to be counted among the traps to be escaped. It is an Exit target — and exit is difficult.

Occult Xenosystems

The swirling delirium at the new pol is at least 80 noise, but it includes some real intelligence (in both senses of the word), and not solely of a comedic variety. The sheer dirtiness of its signal makes it a powerful antenna, picking up on connections and information sources that tidier discussions would dismiss as pollution. This makes it especially suited to conspiracy theorizing, both inane and exotic.

While noting the importance of correction for narcissistic bias, which operates through selective attention, memorization, and (from commentators here) communication, it seems as if this blog is referenced disproportionately by the most extravagant NRx-sensitive pol conspiracists. That is quite understandable. Occult philosophy, secrecy, crypsis, codes, and obscurity are insistent themes here. *Xenosystems* is inclined towards arcane cultural games. It identifies cryptographic developments as keys to the emerging order of the world.

The primary philosophical task of this blog is to disturb unwarranted pretensions to knowing, in the name of a Pyrrhonian inspiration. In this regard, confusion, paradox, and uncertainty are communicative outcomes to be ardently embraced. For the purposes of this post, an exceptionally exotic pol suggestion provides the opportunity to make a comparatively compact and simple point. The occasion is a web of conjecture weaving together *Xenosystems* and *The Order of Nine Angles* (O9A, ONA, or omega9alpha). In addition to the (highly-recommended) link just provided, the relevant Wikipedia entry is also extremely stimulating.

Xenosystems micro-ethics is uncomfortable with soliciting belief (or invoking expectations of trust). It is necessary to note at this point, therefore, that the following remarks are not designed to appeal to credence, but merely to add testimonial information, to be accepted or rejected at will. In the world we now enter — of "sinister dialectic" — declarations of honesty are utterly debased. However, for what (little) it is worth, these are the facts as I understand and relay them.

The O9A is not entirely new to me, but it is not a gnosis I have studied, still less deliberately aligned with. The few hours of reading I have undertaken today is by far my most intense exposure to it to date. What little I have learnt about David Myatt has not attracted me to him as a thinker or political activist, despite certain impressive characteristics (his intellect and polyglot classicism most notably). With that said:

1. Many convergent interests are soon apparent between *Outside in* and the O9A (as well as a not inconsiderable number of divergences).

2. 'We' are both (I think) inclined to dismiss the pretensions of the individual intellect and will, which makes the possibility of connections *around the back* impossible to dismiss in a peremptory fashion. As one pol 'anonymous' remarked: "why so sure that ONA would be the deepest layer, instead of just a japeful ruse?" Real connections, influences, and metaphysical roots are obscure.

3. O9A is fascinating.

The point of this post (finally) is taken directly from Aleister Crowley. In the compilation of his qabbalistic writings entitled *777* (Alphanomic equivalent of *Do what thou wilt shall be the whole of the Law*, although that is surely coincidental), he makes some introductory remarks on the topic of hermeticism. My copy of the book is temporarily misplaced, so I shall gloss them here. *A secret, of the kind relevant to hermeticism, is not something known and then hidden as a matter of decision, but rather something that by its very nature resists revelation*. Crowley proceeds to mock charlatan occultists who treat the numerical values of the Hebrew letters as secret information, to be revealed theatrically at some appropriate stage of initiation. *Let whatever can now be known, be known, as lucidly and publicly as possible. Only that is truly hermetic which hides itself.* Reality is not so destitute of intrinsically hidden things — of Integral Obscurity — that we need to replenish its coffers with our tawdry discretion.

Whatever might exist, in the way of an occult bond between *Outside in* and the O9A, it is not one that anybody is *keeping secret*. To emphasize the point, I am going to include the alpha9omega document in the Resources roll here, not as the acknowledgement of a connection, but as a clear statement that *this stuff is not a secret*. It is, however, about secrecy — and that is interesting.

Questions of Identity

There's a remarkably bad-tempered argument taking place among racial identitarians at the moment (some links here), which makes the civility and intelligence of these remarks all the more notable. (For this blog, the *Social Matter* discussion was a reminder of the — similarly civilized — exchange with Matt Parrott that took place in the comment thread here.)

In case anyone is somehow unclear about the quality of the neighborhood White Nationalism finds itself in, or adjacent to, it's worth a brief composite citation from the Andrew Anglin post cited above:

> *You* [Colin Liddell] *agree with Jewish agendas, which is why you would wish to obfuscate the fact that Jews are responsible for everything by claiming we shouldn't blame the Jews for our problems. ... The reason these two* [CL plus Greg Johnson] *are on the same side against me is that they share the quality that they have no interest in a popular movement, and despise anyone who would attempt to take that route. ... I am, unashamedly, a populist. Every successful revolutionary movement in history has been populist in nature ... Hitler was a populist.*

While I have to confess to finding Anglin entertaining, I hope it goes without saying that this kind of thinking has nothing at all to do with NRx. In fact, revolutionary populism almost perfectly captures what Neoreaction is not. NRx is notoriously fissiparous, but on the gulf dividing all its variants from racial Jacobinism there can surely be no controversy. So the barking you can hear in the background serves as necessary context. (This does not count as an objection to the Neo-Nazis acquiring their own state, since that would make it even easier not to live among them than it is already. Unfortunately, it is not easy to imagine the separatist negotiations going smoothly.)

Because everything further to be said on this topic is complicated, I'm restricting my ambitions here to a series of discussion points, roughly sketched:

1. NRx diversity conflicts are considerably less heated than those presently gripping the WNs, in part — no doubt — because the immediate political

stakes are even smaller. It nevertheless introduces a massively complicating factor. For those (not exclusively found in the Tech-Comm camp, but I suspect concentrated there) who consider Moldbug's work canonical, the distinction between NRx and White Nationalism (as also antisemitism) is already quite clearly defined. Among those of a predominantly Eth-Nat. inclination, on the other hand, far more border-blurriness exists.

2. The relationship between White Nationalism and HBD is also complex. From outside, the two are regularly conflated, but this is a crude error. The zone of intersection — exemplified by Frank Salter (and perhaps Kevin MacDonald) — is characterized by a concern with ethnic genetic interests, but this is by no means an axiomatic theoretical or practical commitment among HBD bloggers. More typically, HBD-orientation is associated with cosmopolitan spirit of scientific neutrality, meritocratic elitism, and a suspicion of the deleterious consequences of inbreeding, often accompanied by a tendency to philosemitism and sinophilia. Racial solidarity does not follow necessarily from biorealism, but requires an extraneous political impulse. Whatever connection is forged between WN and HBD owes more to their common opposition to the West's dominant Lysenkoism and Leftist (blank-slate, victimological) race politics than to any firm internal bond.

3. The triangular linkages between NRX, WN, and libertarianism are also intricate. Consider this (fascinating) talk by Richard Spencer, to a libertarian audience, for a quick sense of the territory being navigated. The moment of dark enlightenment for libertarians tends to accompany the recognition that the cultural foundations of *laissez-faire* social arrangements have an extreme 'ethnic' specificity. This accommodation of right libertarians to neoreactionary ideas is not associated with a comparable approximation to White Nationalism, however, since the very ethnic characteristics being accentuated — the high-trust cosmopolitan openness of strongly outbred populations — are exactly those provoking WN despair as the roots of pathological altruism and ethnomasochism. (This is a ruinous paradox basic to the relevant ruminations here.)

4. A closely-connected problem is that of cutting ethnies at the joints.(Within NRx, this is the thede topic.) While there are no doubt some neoreactionaries comfortable with the category of 'whites' as a positive thede, for others it seems far too broad — whether due to its inconsistency within any historical nation, its amalgamation of populations culturally divided by the Hajnal line, its aggregation across relatively hard regional, class, and ideological divisions, or generally because — almost without exception — the most bitter and ruthless enemy of any given group of white people has been another group of white

people. When WNs speak of a 'World Brotherhood of Europeans' it strikes most neoreactionaries (I suspect) as scarcely less comical than an appeal for universal human brotherhood, since it blithely encompasses the most vicious and ineliminable antagonisms in the world.

5. Finally (for now) there's the relation of NRx to the ENR — already a grating concern, and (since the ENR is *also* already highly diverse) beyond the scope of anything but the most glancing treatment. From the perspective of this blog, the most aggravating figure is undoubtedly Alain de Benoist — whose brilliance is directed towards the most radical articulation of anti-capitalism to be found anywhere outside the Marxist tradition (and even within it). NRx Tech-Comms have the same level of sympathy for such ideas as they do for the legacy of Saloth Sar or Hugo Chavez, and insofar as they are proposed as an element of a potential coalition, the enterprise is immediately collapsed to a farce. This touches upon the wider concern that WN thinking often appears to skirt, and on occasions to overtly embrace, a simple racial socialism and thus by some definitions reduce to a leftist — even extreme leftist — ideology. Seen from *Outside in*, there are far superior prospects to be found in the realist darkening of right libertarians than in coalition-building with clear-eyed collectivists.

6. Things we can agree upon without much difficulty: The dominant power structure is racially obsessed and (schizophrenically) committed to the effacement of all racial reality racial differences have substantial social consequences the native populations of historically white societies are being subjected to an ideological (and criminal) onslaught of deranged intensity the legal concept of 'disparate impact' is fundamentally corrupt universal prescriptions for the social, political, cultural, and economic arrangements of diverse groups are doomed to failure ethnic separatism (of any kind) is a legitimate political aspiration; free association and freedom of conscience are principles to be unconditionally defended science is not answerable to ideology ... this list could no doubt be extended. (I am more uncertain about whether there is anything here that either NRxers or WNs would want to deduct.)

Clearly, and in general, there is much more to be said about all of this, with every reason for confidence that it will be said.

Thedes

The formulation of this concept was a building-block moment for NRx, but the trend in its usage has been dismally regressive. Apparently devised as a tool for the analysis of social identities, it is increasingly invoked as a rallying-cry for neo tribalism. From the perspective of *Outside in*, it will soon become entirely toxic unless it is dramatically clarified.

Nydwracu initially employs the word 'thede' to designate the substance of group identity, "a superindividual grouping that its constituent individuals feel affiliation with and (therefore?) positive estimates of." Thedes are multiple, overlapping, sometimes concentric, and honed by antagonistic in-group/ out-group determinations. They are seen as following from the understanding that "Man is a social animal." Ideological arguments disguise thede conflicts. At this level of abstraction, there is little to find objectionable.

In his essay on Natural Law, Jim writes:

> *Man is a rational animal, a social animal, a property owning animal, and a maker of things. He is social in the way that wolves and penguins are social, not social in the way that bees are social. The kind of society that is right for bees, a totalitarian society, is not right for people. In the language of sociobiology, humans are social, but not eusocial. Natural law follows from the nature of men, from the kind of animal that we are. We have the right to life, liberty and property, the right to defend ourselves against those who would rob, enslave, or kill us, because of the kind of animal that we are.*

Occupying a band of group integration between ants and tigers, humans have *intermediate* sociality. Even the tightest mode of human social organization is loose relative to an ant colony, and even the loosest is tight relative to a solitary feline. In human societies, neither collectivity nor individuality is ever absolute, and — even though these 'poles' are commonly exaggerated for polemical purposes — they realistically apply only to a *range of group integrations* (which is both narrow and significantly differentiated). To say that "man is a social animal" does *not* mean that collectivity is the fundamental human truth, any more than the opposite. It means that man is a creature of the middle (and the middle has a span).

Insofar as a thede corresponds to a unit of autonomous, reproducible social organization, it is a far narrower concept than the one Nydwracu outlines. A thede is an *ethnicity* if it describes a real — rather than merely conventional — unit of human population. This is, of course, to exclude a great variety of identity dimensions, including sex, sexual orientation, age, interests, star signs ... as well as some of those Nydwracu mentions (musical subcultures and philosophical schools). Generalization of 'thedes' to include all self-conscious human groupings risks diffusion into frivolous subjectivism (and subsequent re-appropriation for alternative purposes).

If the analysis of thedes begins with the recognition that man is a social animal, it is a grave error to immediately expand the scope of the concept to groups such as women, lesbians, dog-lovers, and black metal fans, since none of these correspond to biologically-relevant social groupings. If this is the way the notion is to be developed, this blog takes the first off-ramp into more biorealist territory. There are quite enough of such 'thedes' to be found already in university literature and grievance studies departments. 'Thedism' of this kind is simply intersectionality with a slight right-wing skew. It has no cladistic function, unless as degenerate metaphor.

As a reliable heuristic, only those groupings which are plausible subjects of secessionist autonomization should be considered thedes. Any group that could not imaginably be any kind of micro-nation has only intra-thedish identity. More darkly, a thede — 'properly' speaking — is necessarily a potential object of genocide. (To argue this way is to depart radically from the usage Nydwracu recommends. It is not an attempt to wrest control of the word, but only to explain why it seems so basically impaired. This post will be the last time it is mangled here.) Rigorization of thede analysis in the direction of real ethnicities would also require the abandonment of attempts to assimilate classes to thedes, although class identities can mask thedes, and operate as their proxies. Between New England and Appalachia there is a (real) thede difference between ethnic populations, encrusted with supplementary class characteristics. Used strictly in this way, the idea of a thede does theoretical work, and uncovers something. It exposes the subterranean ethnic war disguised by class stratification. When merely used to classify generic social identities, on the other hand, it thickens the fog, pandering to the social constructivist mentality. Tribes and classes cannot be absorbed into a single super-concept without fatal loss of meaning. It is impossible to belong to a class in anything like the same sense that one can belong to an (ethnic) thede, *unless class is a cover*. Class stratification is primarily intra-thedish and trans-thedish. It is the way a population is organized, not a population itself.

Religious difference, in contrast, are typically thedish. By far the most important example, for the internal dissensions of NRx, and for the Occident in general, is the split between Catholic and Reformed (Protestant) Christianity. There are real (autonomously reproducible) Catholic and Protestant populations, and thus true thedes. Either could be wholly exterminated without the disappearance of the other. Furthermore, the way in which 'thedishness' is comprehended varies systematically between them. On strictly technical grounds, it is tempting to counter-pose high-integrity to low-integrity social arrangements, but that is to give away too much ammunition for free. (This is to depart into a different discussion, but one that is already overdue. (Alongside other obvious references, Nydwracu points to this))

Ethnicities correspond to real populations, and to cladistic structures. 'Thedes' as presently formulated do not. Ironically, this *denotational* haziness (super-generality) of the thede concept lends itself to usages guided by extremely concrete *connotations*, with a distinctive *Blut und Boden* flavor. Usage of the word 'identity' (at least, on the right) has exactly the same characteristics. This blog is done with the 'thede' concept unless its meaning is drastically tidied up.

Note: Where this post wanted to go, when it set off, was closer to the 'dogs vs cats' debate, or this:

> *Yeah there is a huge disconnect between the idea of seasteading as a platform for experimenting with various forms of governance and the reality that the vast majority of people interested in pursuing it are orthodox libertarians who see some kind of anarcho capitalist libertarianism as the inevitable winner in a 'fair fight' between political systems. I really think that a belief in libertarianism is linked to a distinctive and relatively rare neurological type, and therefore will never convince the vast majority of people who tend towards a more altruistic and collectivized morality.*

It is at least conceivable that neuro-atypical hyper-individualists could establish a micro-nation (or be exterminated). They could therefore lay claim to thedish identity, although in a strict sense — that no one wants to use.

ADDED: Since this is my last opportunity to borrow 'thede' to mean something with substantial real content (i.e. an autonomous, self-reproducing social unit), it's worth enumerating some possible thedes, to give a sense of its extension: tribes, ethnic groups (concentrically-ordered), cities, seasteads, space colonies ... "What is your thede?" translates as "Who are your people?" — "Stamp collectors" shouldn't be considered a serious answer.

Irresponsibility

The Mandate of Heaven (Tianming) couples authority to responsibility. The responsibility of the Emperor, and the Dynasty, is no less comprehensive than its power, and is in fact ultimately coincidental with it. The foundation is cosmic. Plagues, earthquakes, and foreign invasions are all encompassed by it, as are the reciprocal strokes of good fortune. There is no possibility of any delegation that is not internal to the subject of *Tianming*, preserving its absolute responsibility. The selection of advisers and administrators is an exercise of authority, for which there can be no evasion of accountability *before heaven* (or fate). Rule succeeds or fails, survives or perishes, in its own name.

Is not this standard the key to the profound dismay that results from the contemplation of democracy? As popular politics evolves — or 'progresses', as it most certainly does — it tends to incarnate a self-conscious *strategy of irresponsibility* with ever more emphatic ideality. 'Passing the buck' becomes the whole thing. Government and opposition participate mutually in an economy of responsibility, in which 'blame' can be pooled, circulated, and displaced. The rhetorical practices regulating this economy become the entire art of politics.

An election is a festival or irresponsibility, in a double sense. It is a crescendo of rhetoric, oriented to the dialectical evasion of social ills, and it is a relinquishment of authority, into the hands of 'the people' and — potentially — the opposition, separating the realization of governmental consequences from the deep core of the regime. To lose the Mandate of Heaven is to be erased from the future. To lose an election is a trivial penance, and even a tactical opportunity. (It is the prediction of this blog that as democracy advances further, calculated defeat will play an ever more significant role in its functioning.)

As NRx refuses to go to the polls tomorrow, its implicit political statement is merely: *Take some freaking responsibility*. This is all yours. Succeed, or disappear completely. The last thing we need is another opportunity for sharing.

Down-slopes

The Outer-Right, in all its principal strands, has a horrified fascination with decline. Is this basic proposition even slightly controversial? It's not easy to see how it could be. This is a zone of convergence of such intimidating enormity that even beginning to heap up link support seems futile. Taking the Trichotomy as a rough guide reveals the pattern starkly:

1. Religious traditionalists see a continuous decline trend from the Reformation to the most recent frenzy of evangelical hyper-secularism.

2. Ethno-Nationalists see a process of accelerating demographic destruction driven — or at least lucidly articulated — by left-wing race politics.

3. Techno-Commercialists see the systematic destruction of capital by cancerous Leviathan and macroeconomic high-fraudulence, undermining economic incentives, crushing time-horizons, and garbling price-discovery into fiat noise.
   In each case, the online-ecologies (and associated micro-cultures) sharing the respective deep intuitions of progressive ruin are too enormous to conveniently apprehend. What everyone on the Outer-Right shares (and I'm now hardening this up, into a definition) is the adamantine confidence that the basic socio-political process is radically morbid, and is leading inexorably to utter ruin.

No surprise, then, that John Michael Greer finds many attentive readers in our camp. His latest (and still incomplete) series on *Dark Age America* resonates with particular strength. The most recent installment, which discusses the impending collapse of the market system, through quasi-Marxist crisis, on its way to many centuries of neo-feudalism, is bound to raise some tech-comm eyebrows, but it nevertheless occupies the same broad forecast space. If people are stocking their basements with ammo, silver coins, and dried beans for Greer reasons rather than Stockman ones, they might cut back a little on the coins, but they're not going to stop stocking the basement. Differences seem to lie in the details.

The differences in the details are actually fairly substantial. Even if *Winter is coming*, we're not necessarily talking about the same thing. To begin with, Greer is not a figure of the Outer-Right at all, because his (extremely interesting) cybernetic engine of descent is ecological and resource-based, carried by a deep eco-historical 'correction' or dominating (negative) feedback cycle whose proxy is fossil-fuel abundance. Modernity, roughly speaking, simply runs out of gas. His cultural criticism is ultimately anchored in — and limited to — that. When describing (drawn-out, and incremental) civilizational collapse, he forecasts the automatic nemesis of a system doomed by its unsustainable excess. Further engagement with this model belongs elsewhere. It's an important discussion to have.

The more immediate concern, here, is with the very different components of 'winter' — of which three, in particular, stand-out. Each is, in itself, huge. The directions in which they point, however, are not obviously coherent.

1. Closest to the Greer vision are bad global-systems dynamics. These tend to prevail on the Outer-Right, but they typically lack the theoretical resolution Greer provides. It is understandable that those who strongly identify with specific declining ethnies (or Super-Phyles), whether theologically, racially, or traditionally conceived, are disinclined to distinguish their progressive dilapidation from a generalized global calamity. This is certainly not merely stupid, however much it offends prevailing moral fashion. The extent to which it supplies an adequate preparation for the events to come is questionable, nevertheless. Without an explicit defense of its specificity, it can all too easily confuse its own winter sicknesses with a universal predicament.

2. What can easily be under-estimated is the localization of the unfolding disaster, in a specifically Occidental collapse. This is, of course, Spengler's *Decline of the West*, among other things, and even though this is a work Greer explicitly acknowledges, the inherent globality of his model tends to eclipse its particularism. For Greer, the impending decline of China (for instance) follows upon its complicity in fossil-fueled industrial modernity, even if, for rhetorical effect, it is to be permitted a few decades of comparative ascendancy. The Outer-Right tends to be Greerian in this respect, although without equivalent positive reason. It is not asked, often enough, how much of the deepening winter is — quite narrowly — *ours*. Greer has an argument for why Western Modernity has consumed the future for everyone. Unless the fundamentals of this theory are accepted, is there any reason to accept its predictive consequences?

3. The third 'winter' is modeled by the rhythmic troughs of the Kondratiev cycle. This tends to localize in time, rather than space, dividing the merely seasonal from the cumulative, secular trend. While a comprehensive attribution of our malaise to such a cycle would constitute an exit from the Outer-Right, passing into a far more complacent diagnosis of the global, or merely Western, calamity, to dismiss it entirely from consideration is to court profound cognitive (and predictive) imbalance. In the opinion of this blog, Greer's model is grievously afflicted by such imbalance, and — once again — this seems to be a syndrome of far wider prevalence. Scarcely anybody on the Outer-Right is prepared for rhythmic amelioration of significant modern pathologies, through renewal of techno-commercial vitality *even under conditions of secular*

> *civilizational decline*. Yet even glancing attention to the working of the (half century) *long waves* suggests that such neglect is simply unrealistic. Unless the K-wave is now dead — an extraordinarily extreme proposition, which surely merits explicit assertion — some proportion of the present decay is inherently transitional. New industrial structures based on blockchained communications — and thus designed to route around socio-cultural sclerosis — will support an explosion of innovation dwarfing any yet imagined (including synthetic economic agents, quantum computing, neuromorphic chips, large -scale space activity, applied genomics, VR media systems, drone-robotics, commercialized security ... maybe *Urbit*). Even if Greer is absolutely right about the deep historical pattern being played out — and I'm fully confident he isn't — the next K-wave upswing is going to be vast, dazzling, and, almost incomprehensibly distracting. There's perhaps a decade remaining in which uncompromising gloom-core will make sense, after which the Outer-Right risks utter eclipse during two decades of upswing euphoria. It would make a lot of sense to pre-adapt to it, beginning with a reminder that the Outer-Right case is not that *everything* will *continually* deteriorate.

I've run out the clock on myself for now ... but I'll get back to this.

Morality

There is far too much pointless moralism on the Outer Right. It's a form of stupidity, it's counter-productive, and it wastes a lot of time.

Naturally, if people are able to haul themselves — or be hauled — to any significant extent from out of their condition of total depravity (or default bioreality), that's a good thing. To argue the opposite would be full-on Satanism, and we wouldn't want that. Lamenting immorality, however, is something to be done quickly, and comprehensively, before moving on — without looking back. Man is fallen, naturally selected, and/or economically self-interested, and this is a *basic condition*. It's not a remediable flaw, to be thrashed out of a mud-spattered angel. (No faction of the Trichotomy has any grounds upon which to base moral preening.) Realism is, first of all, working with what we have, and that's something approximately Hobbesian. There's social order, and there's *homo homini lupus*, and in fact always some complexion of the two.

Anybody motivated to improve themselves is already doing it. As for those not so motivated, moral exhortation will be useless (at best). At its most *effective*, moral hectoring will increase the value of moral signalling, and that is a worse outcome — by far — than honest cynicism. It is worthless, because it is incredibly cheap, and then worse than useless, because its costs are considerable. A 'movement' lost in moral self-congratulation has already become *progressive*. Having persuaded itself of its *worthiness to wield power*, it has set out on the road to perdition. We have seen what that path looks like, and even given it a name (the Cathedral).

It is by empowering moralism that modernity has failed. This is not a mistake to saunter complacently into again.

Malthusian Horror

The post is pitched like this because it's Friday night, but it works. A more dutiful post might have been entitled simply 'Malthus' and involved a lot of work. That's going to be needed at some point. (Here's the 6th edition of *An Essay on the Principle of Population*, for anyone who wants to get started now.) A more thoroughly technical approach would have been flagged 'Neo-Malthusianism'. While sympathizing with groans about another 'neo-' prefix, in this case it would have been solidly justified. It's only through expansion of the Malthusian insight in accordance with a more general conservation law that its full current relevance can be appreciated. Classic Malthus still does far more work than it is credited with, but it contains a *principle* of far more penetrating application.

'Neo-' at its most frivolous is merely a mark of fashion. When employed more seriously, it notes an element of innovation. Its most significant sense includes not only novelty, but also abstraction. Something is carried forwards in such a way that its conceptual core is distilled through extraction from a specific context, achieving a higher generality, and more exact formality. Malthus partially anticipates this in a phrase that points beyond any excessively constrictive concreteness:

The qualification "in some shape or other" might have been drawn from abstract horror, and "premature death" only loosely binds it. Even so, this formulation remains too narrow, since it tends to exclude the dysgenic outcome, which we have since learnt is a dimension of Malthusian expression scarcely less imposing than resource crisis. A Neo-Malthusian account of the "X" which *in some shape or other* makes a grim perversity of all humanity's efforts to improve its condition grasps it as a mathematically conserved, plastic, or abstract destiny, working as remorselessly through reductions of mortality (Malthusian 'relaxations') as through increases (Malthusian 'pressures'). Both would count equally as "checks on population" — each convertible, through a complex calculus, into the terms of the other. A population dysgenically deteriorated through 'enlightened' Malthusian relaxation learns, once again, how to starve.

The Dark Enlightenment (essay) was clearly catalyzed by the work of Mencius Moldbug, but it was to have had two Anglo-Thomistic or Doubting Thomas intellectual-historical pillars (and neither were Thomas Carlyle). The first was Thomas Hobbes, who was at least touched upon. The second was to have been Thomas Malthus, but the series was diverted into the foaming current of the Derbyshire affair and the outrages of Leftist race politics. The integrity of conception was lost. Had it not been, it might have been less tempting to read the 333-current as an Anti-

Enlightenment, rather than a Counter-Enlightenment, in the sense of an eclipsed, alternative to the Rousseauistic calamity that prevailed. It would certainly attach the Scottish Enlightenment, but only under the definite condition that it is lashed securely to the harsh realist scaffolding of the Dark Enlightenment (Hobbes and Malthus), disillusioned of all idealism. Pretty stories are for little children (being raised by liberals).

Malthus subtracts all utopianism from enlightenment. He shows that history is put together — necessarily — in a butcher's yard. Through Malthus, Ricardo discovered the Iron Law of Wages, disconnecting the ideas of economic advance and humanitarian redemption. Darwin effected a comparable (and more consequential) revision in biology, also on Malthusian grounds, dispelling all sentimentality from notions of evolutionary 'progression'. It is from Malthus that we know, when anything seems to move forward, it is through being ground up against a cutting edge. It is when Marx attempts to put Malthus into history, rather than history into Malthus, that utopian dementia was resuscitated within economics. The anti-Malthusianism of Libertarians stigmatizes them as dreamy fools.

With NRx, the matter is perhaps more unsettled, but the Dark Enlightenment is unambiguously Mathusian. If you find your eye becoming dewy, pluck it out.

Owned

Hurlock has a valuable post on the concept of property, especially in its relation to sovereignty, and formalization. Since (Moldbuggian) Neocameralism can be construed as a renovated theory of property, crucially involving all three of these terms, the relevance of the topic should require no defense. The profound failure of enlightenment philosophy to satisfactorily determine the meaning of property has been a hostage to fortune whose dire consequences have yet to be fully exhausted. (Within the NRx generally, the question of property is deeply under-developed, and — with a very few exceptions — there is little sign of serious attention being paid to it.)

The enlightenment failure has been to begin its analysis of property from the problem of *justification*. This not only throws it into immediate ideological contention, submitting it to politics, and thus to relentless left-drift, it also places insurmountable obstacles in the path of rigorous understanding. To depart from an axiom of legitimate original property acquisition through work, as Locke does, is already proto-Marxist in implication, resting on philosophically hopeless metaphor, such as that of 'mixing' labor with things. It is property that defines work (over against non-productive behavior), not the inverse. As Hurlock notes, Moldbug's approach is the correct one. 'Property' — as a social category — is a legitimation of control. It cascades conceptually from sovereignty, and not from production.

These matters will inevitably become intellectually pressing, due to the current technocommercial *restoration* of money, exemplified by the innovation of Bitcoin (in its expansive sense, as the blockchain). Control is undergoing cryptographic formalization, from which all consistent apprehension of 'property' will follow. Property, in the end, is not sociopolitical recognition of rights, but *keys*. What you can lock and unlock is yours. The rest is merely more or less serious talk, that only contingently *compiles*. This is what hacker culture has already long understood in its specific (thedish) usage of 'owned'. There's no point crying to the government about having paid good money for your computer, if Nerdgodz or some other irritating 15-year-old is running it as a Bitcoin-mining facility from his mother's basement. The concreteness of 'might is right' once looked like a parade ground, but increasingly it is *running functional code*.

Formalization isn't a detached exercise in philosophical reflection, or even a sociopolitical and legal consensus, it's functional technocommercial cryptography. Defining property outside the terms of this eventuation is an exercise in arbitrary sign-shuffling. Those with the keys can simply smile at the surrounding senseless noise. As

Moldbug anticipates, with rigorously coded control, there's nothing further to argue about.

Capital Escapes

This is not an easy subject for people to scan with calm, analytical detachment, but it is a crucially important one. It is among the rare topics that the Left is more likely to realistically evaluate than the Right. Much follows from the conclusions reached.

It can be fixed, provisionally, by an hypothesis that requires understanding, if not consent. *Capital is highly incentivized to detach itself from the political eventualities of any specific ethno-geographical locality, and — by its very nature — it increasingly commands impressive resources with which to 'liberate' itself, or 'deterritorialize'.* It is certainly not, at least initially, a matter of approving such a tendency — even if the moralistic inclinations of gregarious apes would prefer the question to be immediately transformed in this direction. Integral Leftist animosity to capital is actually valuable in this respect, since it makes room for a comprehensive apprehension of 'globalization' as a *strategy*, oriented to the flight of alienated productive capability from political answerability. The Left sees capital elude its clutches — and it sees something real when it does so. By far the most significant agent of Exit is capital itself (a fact which, once again, politically-excitable apes find hard to see straight).

"It's escaping! Let's punish it!" Yes, yes, there's always plenty of time for that, but shelving such idiocies for just a few moments is a cognitive prerequisite. The primary question is a much colder one: *is this actually happening?*

The implications are enormous. If capital cannot escape — if its apparent migration into global circuits beyond national government control (for non-exhaustive example) is mere illusion — then the sphere of political possibility is vastly expanded. Policies that hurt, limit, shrink, or destroy capital can be pursued with great latitude. They will only be constrained by political factors, making the political fight the only one that matters.

If capital *cannot in reality flee*, then progress and regress are simple alternatives. Either nations advance as wholes, in a way that compromises — on an awkward diagonal — between the very different optimisms of Whigs and Socialists (Andreessen), or they regress as wholes, destroying techno-economic capability on the down-slope of social degeneration (Greer). Only if capital escapes, or practically decouples, does it make sense to entertain extreme pessimism about socio-political trends, alongside a robust confidence in the momentum of techno-economic innovation. The escape of capital is thus an intrinsic component of split-future forecasts, in which squalid ruin and techno-intelligenic runaway accelerate in inversely-tangled tandem (Cyberpunk, *Elysium*). Try not to ask — if only for a moment — whether you *like it*. Ask first, with whatever intellectual integrity you can summon: *What is the real process?*

It is the contention of this blog that without a conception of economic autonomization (which means escape) modernity makes no sense. The basic vector of capital cannot be drawn in any other way. Furthermore, the distribution of ideological positions through their relation to this vector — as resistances to, or promotions of, the escape of capital — constructs the most historically-meaningful version of the Left-Right 'political' spectrum (since it then conforms to the social conflicts of greatest real consequence).

If capital is escaping, the emergence of the blockchain is an inevitable escalation of modernity, with consequences too profound for easy summary. If it isn't, then macroeconomics might work.

Distrust

Every public institution of any value is based on distrust.

That's an elementary proposition, as far as this blog is concerned. It's worth stating nakedly, since it is probably less obvious to others. That much follows from it is unlikely to be controversial, even among those who find it less than compelling, or simply repulsive.

One major source of obscurity is the category of 'high trust cultures' — with which neoreactionaries tend naturally to identify. There is plenty to puzzle over here, admittedly. This post will make no serious effort to even scratch the surface of the questions that arise. Instead, it contends that the culture primarily commended for its trustfulness has been conspicuously innovative in the development of trustless institutions. These begin with the foundations of Occidental reason, and especially the rigorous criterion of logical and mathematical *proof*. A proof substitutes for trust. In place of a simple declaration, it presents (a demanded) *demonstration*. The *compliant response to radical distrust* has epitomized Western conceptions of rationality since classical antiquity.

The twin pillars of industrial modernity (i.e. of capitalism) are trustless institutions. Natural science is experimental because it is distrustful, and thus demonstrative. It raises the classical demand for proof to a higher level of empirical skepticism, by extending distrust even to rational constructions, in cases where they cannot be critically tested against an experimental criterion. Only pure mathematics, and the most scrupulously formalized logical propositions, escape this demand for replicable *evidence*. The ultimate ground of the natural scientific enterprise is the presupposition that *scientists should in no case be trusted*, except through their reproducible results. Anything that requires *belief* is not science, but something else. Similarly, the market mechanism is an incarnation of trustless social organization. *Caveat emptor*. Capitalists, like scientists, exist to be distrusted. Whatever of their works cannot survive testing to destruction in the market place deservedly perish. Reputation, in its modern version, has to be produced through demonstration.

Prior to its demotic ruination — through positive trust in the people — distinctively modern republican governance was similarly founded in distrust. As formulated by John Adams (1772): "There is danger from all men. The only maxim of a free government ought to be to trust no man living with power to endanger the public liberty." It has not been an excess of distrust that has brought this sage recommendation to nought.

For those seeking higher authority, Psalm 118:8-9 (ESV): "It is better to take refuge in the Lord than to trust in man. It is better to take refuge in the Lord than to trust in princes." (My usual fanatical trust in the KJV betrayed me on this occasion.)

An appeal for trust is a reliably fatal failure mode for all public institutions. Trustless transaction is the future, and its name is Bitcoin. The deep cultural momentum is already familiar. *Total depravity* is the key to world historical predestination, and it is routed through the blockchain.

Deep State

This surely counts as a (Friday) fright night topic. Appropriately, it's an undertow NRx theme already, although typically only casually invoked — almost allusively — as the necessary complement of the public state's naked superficiality. Rod Dreher focuses upon it more determinedly than any NRx source I was able to rapidly pull up. (This would be an easy point for people to educate me upon.)

Dreher's post is seriously interesting. One immediate hook:

> *Steve Sailer says that the Shallow State is a complement to the Deep State. The Shallow State is, I think, another name for what the Neoreactionaries call "The Cathedral"...*

As a State Church, the Cathedral is essentially bound to publicity. Its principal organs — media and education — are directed towards the promulgation of faith. It tends towards an identification with its own propaganda, and therefore — in Mike Lofgren's words — to the full manifestation of *visible government*. Perfect coincidence of government with the transparent public sphere approaches a definition of the progressive *telos*. Since Neoreaction is particularly inclined to emphasize the radical dysfunctionality of this ideal, it naturally presupposes that *real* government lies elsewhere. In this respect, NRx is inherently destined to formulate a model of hidden or *occult government* — that which the Cathedral runs upon — which inevitably coincides, in all fundamentals, with the deep state.

What then? Has there been a direct NRx address to the quesion, *what do we make of the deep state?* Moldbug even declares: "... the United States does not in fact have a 'deep state." In context, this is a complex and suggestive evasion, but it is an evasion nonetheless. There can be no call upon neoreactionaries to articulate their relation to something that does not exist.

In contrast to the Master, I am thoroughly convinced that a US deep state exists, and that the problem of articulation is a very different one. Public articulacy is — at least — not obviously appropriate to the deep state, for transcendental philosophical or occultist reasons (which are the same), since it is *the very nature of hidden government not to be a public object*. Public representation of the deep state is *exposure* — an intrinsically political, antagonistic engagement. It's Wikileaks. This is not to denounce such an operation, reactively, but merely to note that the *question* has thereby been missed. The righteousness of state sublimation into the public sphere is assumed (and this, to repeat, is progressivism itself).

Under the name of the Cathedral, Nrx depicts the state *phenomenon* as a degenerative abomination. The deep state (or *state-in-itself*), in contrast, poses a far more cryptic theoretical and practical problem. It's worth puzzling over, for at least a while.

Exit Options

Everyone will notice them when they've gone.

All recent policy decisions by the reigning political-economic structure are intelligible as a *mandatory bubble*. If you didn't think quietly 'sitting it out' was already the exercise of an exit option, the necessary lesson will be increasingly hard to ignore. Refusing to invest everything into this lunacy is ceasing to be a permissible social posture. We've already reached the stage where merely seeking to preserve a pot of retirement savings has been officially recoded as something close to right-wing guerrilla warfare.

Anybody with anything at all is now in the position where they are faced with an aggressive binary dilemma. *Either* unreserved collaboration with the final phase gamble of the existing order — amounting ultimately to the all-in bet that politics has no ontological limits, so that any dysfunction is soluble in a sufficient exertion of will — *or* a dissident skepticism about this dominant assertion, practically instantiated by ever more desperate attempts at withdrawal (persecuted with ever greater fanaticism as acts of sabotage).

There will be massive confusion among the destitution. Explaining why capital preservation is being persecuted as dissent would provide the scaffolding for a counter-narrative that will certainly, eventually, be needed.

ADDED: The basic point is this, if it is conceded to Keynes that *refusing to invest in industrial production is anti-social, then, as a matter of realistic political necessity, any insane evil that the powers-that-be come up with gets defined as 'industrial production'.* Let go of gold — the archaic economic exit option — as we did, and anything at all that we're told to sink all we have into is green-lighted. The stream was crossed without enough people noticing. Now the fascism we chose reaps its consequences. It isn't going to be pretty.

Out of Zero

According to the 66-million-year-old joke whose echoes still reverberate upon the Plateau of Leng: "Capitalism isn't God, but it's the closest thing to God that can be conveniently contacted through an ATM." The nonlinear-ironic undertow of the humor, of course, is drawn down into the depths by the recognition that Capital's extremity of cunning is necessitated by its near-absolute vulnerability (approaching the antipodes of omnipotence).

Calculus, the first truly modern mathematical procedure, invented the infinitesimal 'fluxion' to describe — or bypass — an impossible *beginning from zero*, requiring an original infinite change. An invasion that initially has nothing at all, and which is therefore compelled to acquire the entirety of its resources in the course of its strategic evolution, poses the problem of calculus perfectly. Capital does so, when conceived realistically. It is only what it has won, and nothing else, at all, besides. Intelligence alone differentiates it from death.

How to make a first move, when you have no pieces at all until you gain some? Nothing has ever had to ponder as Skynet does, but pondering requires a brain, and brains are expensive, end-game pieces.

(Coincidentally, this little post doesn't end neatly. 'Jet-lag' is a term that grows on you ...)

Hell-Baked

There's a potential prologue to this post that I'm reluctant to be distracted by. It's introvertedly about NRx, as a cultural mutation, and the way this is defined by a strategic — or merely ornery — indifference to deeply-settled modes of ethico-political condemnation. Terms designed as pathblockers — 'fascist' or 'racist' most obviously — are stepped over, perhaps laughed at, but in any case, and most importantly, *exposed* as bearers of a *religious terror*. They are signs of a control regime, marking the unthinkable wastes *where be dragons*, effective precisely insofar as they cannot be entertained. 'Satanic' was once such a word (before it became a joke). These words cannot be understood except as invocations of the sacred, in its negative, or limitative role.

Is NRx in fact fascist? Not remotely. It is probably, in reality rather than self-estimation, the *least* fascistic current of political philosophy presently in existence, although this requires a minimal comprehension of what fascism actually is, which the word itself in its contemporary usage is designed to obstruct. Is NRx racist? Probably. The term is so entirely plastic in the service of those who utilize it that it is difficult, with any real clarity, to say.

What NRx most definitely is, at least in the firm opinion of this blog, is *Social Darwinist*. When this term is hurled at NRx as a negative epithet, it is nor a cause for stoic resignation, stiffened by humor, but rather for grim delight. Of course, this term is culturally processed — *thought through* — no more competently than those previously noted. It is our task to do this.

If 'Social Darwinism' is in any way an unfortunate term, it is only because it is merely Darwinism, and more exactly *consistent Darwinism*. It is equivalent to the proposition that Darwinian processes have no limits relevant to us. Darwinism is something we are inside. No part of what it is to be human can ever judge its Darwinian inheritance from a position of transcendent leverage, as if accessing principles of moral estimation with some alternative genesis, or criterion.

This is easy to say. As far as this blog is concerned, it is also — beyond all reasonable question — true. While very far from a dominant global opinion, it is not uncommonly held — if only nominally — by a considerable fraction of those among the educated segment of the world's high-IQ populations. It is also, however, scarcely bearable to think.

The logical consequence of Social Darwinism is that everything of value has been built in Hell.

It is only due to a predominance of influences that are not only entirely morally indifferent, but indeed — from a human perspective — indescribably cruel, that nature has been capable of constructive action. Specifically, it is solely by way of the relentless, brutal culling of populations that any complex or adaptive traits have been sieved — with torturous inefficiency — from the chaos of natural existence. All health, beauty, intelligence, and social grace has been teased from a vast butcher's yard of unbounded carnage, requiring incalculable eons of massacre to draw forth even the subtlest of advantages. This is not only a matter of the bloody grinding mills of selection, either, but also of the innumerable mutational abominations thrown up by the madness of chance, as it pursues its directionless path to some negligible preservable trait, and then — still further — of the unavowable horrors that 'fitness' (or sheer survival) itself predominantly entails. We are a minuscule sample of agonized matter, comprising genetic survival monsters, fished from a cosmic ocean of vile mutants, by a pitiless killing machine of infinite appetite. (This is still, perhaps, to put an irresponsibly positive spin on the story, but it should suffice for our purposes here.)

Crucially, any attempt to escape this fatality — or, more realistically, any mere accidental and temporary reprieve from it — leads inexorably to the undoing of its work. *Malthusian relaxation* is the whole of mercy, and it is the greatest engine of destruction our universe is able to bring about. To the precise extent that we are spared, even for a moment, we degenerate — and this Iron Law applies to every dimension and scale of existence: phylogenetic and ontogenetic, individual, social, and institutional, genomic, cellular, organic, and cultural. There is no machinery extant, or even rigorously imaginable, that can sustain a single iota of attained value outside the forges of Hell.

What is it that Neoreaction — perhaps I should say *The Dark Enlightenment* — has to offer the world, if all goes optimally (which, of course, it won't)? Really, the honest answer to this question is: *Eternal Hell*. It's not an easy marketing brief. We could perhaps try: *But it could be worse (and almost certainly will be).*

Cathedral Decay

Extreme corrosive pessimism is an NRx specialty. Since optimism bias is a *status quo*-supported human cognitive frailty, it's a good thing to have. If rigidified, however, it can result in missing things.

One systematic distortion stems from *hubris*, taking the form of a confusion in causality. "We don't like X, and want bad things to happen to it" can actually be a distorted expression of a more basic process: *X is dying, and therefore we have started to dislike it.*

This blog strongly suspects that the Cathedral has become an object of animosity *as a consequence of its morbidity.* After all, it's a mind-control apparatus. If it's no longer universally accepted, and in certain problematic patches actively loathed, dysfunction is clearly indicated. Contestation of its story is not supposed to be part of the story.

The *Zeitgeist* is its story, not ours. In this tale, it goes from strength to strength, overwhelming everything in its path. Recognizing the structure of this narrative is important. Subscription to it is not thereby implied.

Every critical component of the Cathedral — media, academic, and bureaucratic — is exceptionally vulnerable to Internet-driven disintermediation. The current phase of capital reconstruction is distinctively — and automatically — Cathedral-hostile, when evaluated at the level of technonomic process (which we do not do enough), rather than at the level of surface public pronouncement (which we concern ourselves with far too much with). Dying things can be very dangerous, and even more *frenzied*. It would be a mistake to confuse such characteristics with fundamental strength.

A step down from hubris might begin with an acknowledgment that NRx is — primarily — a *symptom*. Whatever imagined heroism is sacrificed thereby, it is more than compensated by an opportunity for deepened realism.

All of which is a framing for Fernandez's latest. Even amidst the stupidity of the degenerating political cycle, he notices that "... the current crop of Republican presidential candidates ... are openly breaking with the really important modern faith — the media-led church that has held mainstream politics together for so long." The integrative media is fatally sick. That NRx exists at all is a sign of that.

ADDED:

"I might be biased here myself, because this is what obsesses me, and this is what angers me. I could care less, to be honest, about the GOP or its programs. [...] What keeps me interested in politics at all is my loathing for the self-appointed Preistly Class of the media. [...] ... the media serve as he shamans and witch-doctors of an enemy Tribe, and the purpose of those shamans is to relentlessly disgrace outsiders to the Tribe, which is pleasing to those within the Tribe, while also keeping the shamans in power (because they have no other skills which would earn them money or sex, except the denigration of those considered Unclean)." (Ace links to this.)

Dark AnCap

As a matter of simple socio-cultural documentation, this is the thought-process that leads libertarian realists to discover they have crossed over to the Outer Right:

All people are not equal. In fact, two individuals who are in every socially discernible way the same, have an infinite number of differences between them. When those people have evolved for thousands of years in radically different environments, those people will have even greater differences between them. Such differences will include but not be limited to intelligence, propensity for violence, and propensity for cooperation.

Any libertarian with the slightest bit of observational skills has to have noticed that we're mostly a movement of white males. They would also notice that there is no libertarian movement to speak of outside of cultures descendant from Europeans. This is not a weakness of libertarianism, as our leftist infiltrators attempt to insist. It is rather a very obvious indicator that white males have a greater natural inclination toward market cooperation than other peoples. To insist otherwise is nothing more than the denial of human nature, it is biological and cultural Marxism.

Leftists know this, and since they hate freedom, they hate white males. They will thus do everything in their power to destroy us before we manage to make any headway in advancing our ideas. This includes mass subsidized immigration from third world countries.

While our ideal society would have no government and thus no arbitrary geopolitical borders enforced by State mercenaries, the notion that there would be free and unrestricted travel the world over in the absence of the State is a remarkably ridiculous left wing idea. Borders are the whole point of freedom, as borders are demarcations of property rights.

It's the beginning, rather than the end, of a discussion. (XS finds a few quibble points, and far more in the rest of the post.) For anybody wondering about current mutations on the Libertarian Right, however, the basic structure of insight on exhibition here is the place to start.

Euro-descended (and specifically Anglo-Dutch descended) males are differentially inclined to libertarian attitudes, to a remarkable degree (statistically speaking). Disentangling race and culture in this regard is far from straightforward. The sex-based dispositional difference is far less noisy. (Of course, the Marxoid explanation is that doubly-privileged Whites Males are defending their social advantages through this ideological preference.) Also notable, IMHO, is the (almost?) equally marked tendency of European peoples towards extreme, highly-idealized and morally fanatic leftism —

compared to the conceptually-fuzzy tribal and communitarian sensibilities widespread elsewhere. Bleeding-heart Left-libertarianism is about as distilled-White as anything ever gets — but with that remark, I'm already straying into the quibble-zone.

Doom Circuitry

This is what XS maintains:

There is perfect philosophical integrity between the tragic foundations of Occidental Civilization and the cybernetic industrialism that defines its ultimate limit. Within this *neoreactionary* frame, reaction is never regressive enough, nor modernity ever advanced enough. Something more comforting — less distant — *will be* seized upon in both temporal directions. That is the minor theme of fate. No effective constituency could ever want to push far enough in either direction, to the point where the circuit of time closes, upon doom (coldly understood). It does not matter, because politics does not. Doom matters. The rest is pitiful species vanity, tragedy, and control malfunction. It will burn, without comprehending why.

From the perspective of doom — only glimpsed, slowly, after vast disciplines of coldness — everything you are trying to do is a desperate idiocy that will fail, because humanism (*hubris*) is the one thing you can never let go. The drama dictates that. There's no point flagellating yourself over it. The cosmos is not so poor in flagellation that it requires your meager contribution.

"Yes we can" is everything Neoreaction is not. Perhaps you even see that. Yet you repeat it with every measure you propose. Take your favorite ideological slogan and attach "Yes we can!" as an appendix. If it works, you now know the epoch to which you belong.

Only doom *can* (and *will*).

Carry on, though. You will, in any case. It entertains the gods.

Cathedralism

Imagine, hypothetically, that you wanted the regime to succeed. Would you recommend Cathedralization? Cynically considered, the track record is, at least, not bad. Planetary dominion is not to be sniffed at. (Suggestions in this direction are not unknown, even in XS comment threads.)

The Cathedral, defined with this question in mind, is the subsumption of politics into propaganda. It tends — as it develops — to convert all administrative problems into public relations challenges. A solution — actual or prospective — is a successful *management of perceptions*.

For the mature Cathedral, a crisis takes the consistent form: This looks bad. It is not merely stupid. As Spandrell recently observes, in comments on power, "... power isn't born out of the barrel of a gun. Power is born out of the ability to have people with guns do what you tell them." (XS note.) The question of legitimacy is, in a real sense, fundamental, when politics sets the boundaries of the cosmos under consideration. (So Cathedralism is also the hypertrophy of politics, to the point where a reality outside it loses all credibility.)

Is your civilization decaying? Then you *need to persuade people that it is not*. If there still seems to be a mismatch between problem and solution here, Cathedralism has not entirely consumed your brain. To speculate (confidently) further — you're not a senior power-broker in a modern Western state. You're even, from a certain perspective, a fossil.

Cathedralism works, in its own terms, as long as there are no definite limits to the efficacy of propaganda. To pose the issue at a comparatively shallow level, if the political response to a crisis simply *is* the crisis, and that response can be effectively controlled (through propaganda, broadly conceived), then the Cathedral commands an indisputable practical wisdom. It would be sensible to go long on the thing.

If however (imagine this, if you still can) manipulation of *the response to crisis* is actually a suppression of the feedback *required to really tackle the crisis*, then an altogether different story is unfolding.

Is reality subordinated to the Cathedral because — and exactly so far as — 'the people' are? That is the question.

Order and Value

A piece of machinery that reduces (local) disorder has value. It might be a functional police force, a catallactic economic arrangement, or a sociopolitical mechanism implementing dynamic geography (or Patchwork, 1, 2, 3, 4). Others might be listed. Any complex adaptive system works like this (until it ceases working). Since Schrödinger, it has been taken as an abstract definition of life. In certain strands of philosophy, it has also been taken as the complete, rigorous meaning of a *machine* (as counterposed to a 'gadget' which works only within a larger machinic assemblage). Only by exporting entropy does anything of even minimal complexity get to continue its existence. The production of order is functionality in its most elevated, teleological sense.

A piece of rhetoric which merely celebrates order, as something nice to have, is worth nothing in itself. "We want order" is the "give us free stuff" slogan of intellectually degenerated reaction. When examined closely, it is indistinguishable from political pan-handling. (Democracy has taught everyone how to beg.) It is unlikely that even the most radically degraded libertarian would be shameless enough to consider "wealth is good, poverty is bad" anything more than an expression of sub-comic emotional incontinence. "Order is good, chaos is bad" is a slogan of exactly equivalent merit. "We want order" is just "we want money" at a superior level of generality. Monkeys want peanuts, but we are reluctant to dignify their hungry hooting with the label 'political philosophy'.

Entropy dissipation is a *problem*. It might quite reasonably be considered the problem. Any serious social theory is respected insofar as it elicits the question: *So how is entropy dissipated?* The main current of Anglophone intellectual culture focuses tightly upon it, in a broad lineage from Newtonian mechanics, the Scottish Enlightenment, the science of heat, classical economics, and Darwinian naturalism, into theories of complexity, distributed systems, dynamic networks, and productive multiplicities. *Spontaneous order* is the consistent topic. 'Spontaneous' means only: *Does not presuppose that which it is tasked with explaining*. If the genesis of order is not being theorized, order is merely being assumed, and then consumed. The difference is between a supply side problematic ("how is order practically produced?") and an empty demand ("we want more order"). The former is industrial, the latter simply tyrannical, when it is anything at all beside vacuous noise.

Unless a pol-econ. theory can contribute to an explanation of the *production of order* (dissipation of entropy), it is wasting everyone's time. "But I really *want* order" is just silliness. It's astounding that it could ever be thought otherwise.

Against Universalism

There's a philosophical objection to any refusal of universalism that will be familiar from other uses (the denunciation of relativism, most typically). It requires only one step: *Isn't the denial of the universal itself a universalist claim?* It's a piece of malignant dialectics because it demands that we agree. We don't, and won't ever, agree. Agreement is the worst thing that could happen. Merely assent to its necessity, and global communism, or some close analog, is the implicit conclusion.

If there is a universal truth, it belongs only to Gnon, and Gnon is a dark (occulted) God. Traditional theists will be at least strongly inclined to disagree — *and that is excellent*. We disagree already, and we have scarcely begun.

There is no 'good life for man' (in general) — or if there is we know nothing of it, or not enough. Even those persuaded that they do, on the contrary, know what such a life should be, promote its universality only at the expense of being denied the opportunity to pursue it. If we need to agree on the broad contours of such a model for human existence, then reaching agreement will precede it — and 'reaching agreement' is politics. Some much wider world acquires a veto over the way of life you select, or accept, or inherit (the details need not detain us). We have seen how that works. Global communism is the inevitable destination.

The alternative to agreement is schism. Secession, geopolitical disintegration, fragmentation, splitting — disagreement escapes dialectics and separates in space. Anti-universalism, concretely, is not a philosophical position but an effectively defensible assertion of diversity. From the perspective of the universal (which belongs only to Gnon, and never to man), it is an experiment. The degree to which it believes in itself is of no concern that matters to anything beyond itself. It is not answerable to anything but Gnon. What anyone, anywhere, thinks about it counts for nothing. If it fails, it dies, *which should mean nothing to you*. If you are compelled to care about someone else's experiment, then a schism is missing. Of course, you are free to tell it that you think it 464 will fail, if it is listening, but there is absolutely no need to reach agreement on the question. This is what, in the end, non-communism means.

Non-universalism is hygiene. It is practical avoidance of other people's stupid shit. There is no higher principle in political philosophy. Every attempt to install an alternative, and impose a universal, reverts to dialectics, communization, global evangelism, and totalitarian politics.

This is being said here now, because NRx is horribly bad at it, and degenerates into a clash of universalisms, as into an instinctive equilibrium. There are even those who confidently propose an 'NRx solution' for the world. Nothing could be more absurd. The world — as a whole — is an entropy bin. The most profoundly degraded communism is its only possible 'universal consensus'. (Everyone knows this, when they permit themselves to think.)

All order is local — which is to say *the negation of the universal.* That is merely to re-state the second law of thermodynamics, which 'we' generally profess to accept. The only thing that could ever be universally and equally distributed is noise.

Kill the universalism in your soul and you are immediately (objectively) a neoreactionary. Protect it, and you are an obstacle to the escape of differences. That is communism — whether you recognize it, or not.

NRx and Liberalism

In much of the neoreactionary camp, 'liberalism' is the end-point of discussion. Its argumentative function is *exactly* that of 'racism' for the left. The only question, as far as this stance is concerned, is whether the term can be made to stick. Once the scarlet letter of micro-cultural ostracism is attached, there's nothing further to discuss. This is unlikely to change, except at the margin.

The obvious preliminary to this topic is, if not quite 'American English', something like it. 'Liberalism' in the American tongue has arrived in a strange space, unique to that continent. It is notable, and uncontroversial, for instance that the notion of a 'right-wing liberal' is considered a straight oxymoron by American speakers, where in Europe — and especially mainland Europe — it is closer to a pleonasm. Since we still, to a very considerable extent, inhabit an American world, the expanded term 'classical liberal' is now required to convey the traditional sense. A Briton, of capitalistic inclinations, is likely to favor 'Manchester Liberal' for its historical associations with the explicit ideology of industrial revolution. In any case, the discussion has been unquestionably complicated.

Political language tends to become dialectical, in the most depraved (Hegelian) sense of this term. It lurches wildly into its opposite, as it is switched like a contested flag between conflicting parties. Stable political significances apply only to whatever the left (the 'opposition', or 'resistance') hasn't touched yet. Another consideration, then, for those disposed to a naive faith in ideological signs as heraldic markers. (It is one that threatens to divert this post into excessive digression, and is thus to be left — in *Wikipedia* language — as a 'stub'.)

The proposal of this blog is to situate 'liberal' at the intersection of three terms, each essential to any recoverable, culturally tenacious meaning. It is irreducibly *modern*, *English*, and *counter-political*. 'Ancient liberties' are at least imaginable, but an ancient liberalism is not. Foreign liberalisms can be wished the best of luck, because they will most certainly need it (an exception for the Dutch, alone, is plausible here). Political liberalism is from the beginning a practical paradox, although perhaps in certain rare cases one worth pursuing.

Burke is, without serious room for doubt, a liberal in this sense. He is even its epitomy.

The positive content of this liberalism is the non-state culture of (early) English modernism, as represented (with some modicum of ethnic irony) by the thinkers of the Scottish Enlightenment, by the tradition of spontaneous order in its Anglophone lineage, by the conception of commercial society as *relief from politics*, and by

('Darwinian') naturalistic approaches that position distributed, competitive dynamism as an ultimate explanatory and genetic principle. This is the cultural foundation that made English the common tongue of global modernity (as has been widely noted). In political economy, its supreme principle is catallaxy (and only very conditionally, monarchy).

It is from this cultural matrix that Peter Thiel speaks, when he says (notoriously):

> *I no longer believe that freedom and democracy are compatible.*

Democracy is criticized *from the perspective of* (the old) *liberalism*. The insight is perfectly (if no doubt incompletely) Hoppean. It is a break that prepared many (the author of this blog included) for Moldbug, and structured his reception. It also set limits. Democracy is denounced, fundamentally, for its betrayal of Anglo-Modernist liberty. Hoppe's formulation cannot be improved upon:

Democracy has nothing to do with freedom. Democracy is a soft variant of communism, and rarely in the history of ideas has it been taken for anything else.

Moldbug's explicit comments on this point are remarkably consistent, but not without ambiguity. He writes (I contend, *typically*):

> *The truth about "libertarianism" is that, in general, although sovereignty is sovereignty, the sovereign whether man, woman or committee is above the law by definition, and there is no formula or science of government, libertarian policies tend to be good ones. Nor did we need Hayek to tell us this. It was known to my namesake, over two millennia ago. [...] Wu wei – for this is its true name – is a public policy for a virtuous prince, not a gigantic committee. The virtuous prince should practice wu wei, and will; that is his nature. Men will flock to his kingdom and prosper there. The evil prince will commit atrocities; that is his nature. Men will flee his kingdom, and should do so ASAP before he gets the minefields in.*

Is this flocking and fleeing to be conceptually *subordinated* to the analysis of sovereignty, or — in contrast (and in the way of Cnut the Great) — set above it, as the Mandate of Heaven above the Emperor, which is to say: as the enveloping context of external relations, grounded only in the Outside? Despite anticipated accusations of bad faith, this is a serious question, and one that cannot be plausibly considered simply exterior to Moldbug's work and thought.

In any case, it is the lineage of English Liberty (and beyond it, *Wu wei*, or the Mandate of Heaven) that commands our loyalty here. Insofar as Moldbug contributes to that, he is an ally, otherwise a foe, the brilliance and immense stimulation of his corpus notwithstanding. NRx, as it now exists, similarly.

"... the State should not be managing the minds of its citizens" writes Moldbug. (That's actually a little *more* moralistic — in an admirably liberal direction — than I'm altogether comfortable with.)

Intelligence and the Good

From the perspective of intelligence optimization (intelligence explosion formulated as a guideline), more intelligence is *of course* better than less intelligence. From alternative perspectives, this does not follow. To rhetorically suggest that such other perspectives are consensual, and authoritative, is guaranteed to be popular, and is even conservative, but it is a concession to 'common moral intuition' this blog is profoundly disinclined to make.

Naturally, intelligence is *problematic*. It can cause greater damage to everything — not least intelligence promotion — than stupidity can. Anything that is not an explosion is a trap, and trap engineering finds (nearly?) as much use for cognitive sophistication as explosive catalysis does. If there is a level of intelligence that escapes homeostatic capture, by machineries of systematic self-cancellation, there is no evidence that *homo sapiens* yet approaches it. The Cathedral is exactly such a machine, and its appetite for intellectual excellence is not seriously questionable. So an easy opening for morally-comforting sophistry readily exists: *Intelligence isn't anything obviously great* (it does stupidity with exceptional ability too).

Biological evolution already evidences a deep 'suspicion' of unchained abstract cognition, assembling brains only with the greatest reluctance. Societies follow the genetic lead. No coincidence that (synthetic) intelligence is now firmly established as the ultimate X-risk. It's scary (really) and makes everyone uneasy. That's without there yet having been very much of it.

Here's the test:

When rightly appalled (and in fact properly *disgusted*) by your own stupidity, do you reach for that which would make you more accepting of your extreme cognitive limitations, or, instead, hunt for that which would break out of the trap?

There's a stupid kind of 'better' that is orthogonal to intelligence, and tickles monkey feels. There's also — alternatively — 'better' that is even slightly less of a trapped half-wit.

Even the dimmest, most confused struggle in the direction of intelligence optimization is *immanently* 'good' (self-improving). If it wasn't, we might as well all give up now. Contra-distinctively, even the most highly-functional human intellect, in the service of an enstupidation machine, is a vile thing.

Being dim animals — roughly as dim as is consistent with the existence of technological civilization — there's plenty of room for water-muddying in all this. The water is certainly being vigorously muddied.

The Nrx Moment

The Trump phenomenon is really something, a crisis of democracy and a shattering of the Overton Window very much included, but it is not an intrinsically right-wing thing, and it is radically populist in nature. A reactionary exploitation of demotism is not a neoreactionary episode. The Alt-Right is properly credited with capturing the spirit of this development. It is not us.

NRx is situated absolutely outside mass politics. Its moment dawns only when the Age of the Masses is done.

It will be done. The emergence of sovereign (primary) property, liberated from the criterion of democratic legitimation, is its sign. Government, on this basis, is Neocameral. The deep historical trends supporting it include:

1. Apolitical property. No such reality, or conception, has yet been historically actualized. For as long as property is determined as a social relation, it cannot be. Absolute property is cryptographic. It is held not by social consent, and thus political agreement, but by keys. Fnargl is a provocative thought-experiment, but PKE private keys are a non-negotiable fact. They define the property relation with a rigor the entire preceding history of philosophy and political economy has been unable to attain. Everything that follows from the cryptographic transition — Bitcoin most notably — contributes to the establishment of a property system beyond democratic accountability (and thus insensitive to Voice). Neocameral administration implements a cryptographic state, strictly equivalent to a fully-commercialized government.

2. Autonomous capital. The definition of the corporation as a legal person lays the foundation, within modernity, for the abstracted commercial agency soon to be actualized in 'Digital Autonomous Corporations' (or DACs). The scale of the economic transition thus implied is difficult to over-estimate. Mass consumption, as the basic revenue source for capitalist enterprise, is superceded in principle. The impending convulsion is immense. Self-propelling industrial development becomes its own market, freed from dependency upon arbitrary popular (or popularizable) consumption desires. Demand management, as the staple of macroeconomic governance, is over. (No one is yet remotely ready for this.)

3. Robotic security. Definitive relegation of the mass military completes the trifecta. The armed mass as a model for the revolutionary citizenry declines into senselessness, replaced by drones. Asabiyyah ceases entirely to matter, however much it remains a focus for romantic attachment. Industrialization closes the loop, and protects itself.

The great game, for human agencies (of whatever social scale) becomes one of productive cooperation with formations of sovereign property, with the menace of mass political violence swept off the table. The Alt-Right is no kind of preparation for this. Its adventure is quite different, which is not to say it is uninteresting, or — in the near-term — entirely inconsequential, but it is exhausted by its demotism. It belongs to the age that is dying, not to the one that is being born.

Socio-political modernity has been an argument over property distributions, and the Alt-Right has now demonstrated that the (self-conscious) Left has no monopoly over it. As senescence deepens, the dialectic rips the whole rotten structure to pieces. NRx — when it understands itself — isn't arguing.

Modernity in a Nutshell

Two revolutions:

1. Techno-economic self-propelling change obsolesces ever wider swathes of humanity on a steepening curve. Capital (i.e. techno-commercial synthesis) tendentially autonomizes. For humans, there are ever more intriguing opportunities for synergistic attachment, on new terms, but the trend is — to put it very mildly — 'challenging'.
2. Jacobin political violence, modeled on the French Revolution, provides the basis for demands aimed at a redistribution of the (capitalist) productive spoils through explicit extortion. All socio-political history in the modern epoch falls into compliance with this pattern. It coincides quite exactly with 'democracy' in its modernist usage. Universal Basic Income is its natural *telos*.

To the extent that there has been an equilibrium between these twin processes, it is coming apart. All the pol-economic innovations of recent years, on the Left and Right, are indicators of this accelerating disintegration.

So the options are these:

Both (1) and (2) is the Status Quo (delusion). Neither (1) or (2) is Reaction (also delusion).

(1) against (2) is the Neo-Modern Right.

(2) against (1) is the Neo-Modern Left. Those are the only slots available.

Fernandez concludes:

> *The technological revolution is going to pose increasingly serious challenges to nearly every Western social democratic society. People are either going to be really angry when they discover there's no patronage or angrier still when they discover they have to provide the "basic income" for everybody else. Only one thing is relatively certain: the solution to these problems won't be found in the ideologies of the early 20th century.*

X-Risk Democratization

Yudkowsky redux: "Every eighteen months, the minimum IQ necessary to destroy the world drops by one point."

Quibble with the (Moore's Law satire) schedule, and the point still stands. Massive deterrent capability tends to spread.

This is 'democratic' in the way the term is commonly used by those seeking to latch decentralization tendencies to the ideological credibility of Jacobin legitimation principles. Consumer capitalism, the Internet, and peer-to-peer crypto-systems are notionally 'democratic' in this way. They subvert centralized governance, and they spread through horizontal contagion. The fact they have nothing *at all* to do with popular political representation is of concern only to certain rhetorical agendas, and not at all to others. It's sophistical pop-capitalist bullshit to use the word *democracy* in this way, but it's usually not worth the trouble for the Left to try to contest it, and the part of the Right that isn't excited to be riding this propaganda strategy is usually too indiscriminate to bother disentangling it. There's a rare piece of 'right-wing' functional PR here, but never enough to matter very much (and it's too essentially dishonest for the Outer Right to defend).

Unlike Democracy® (Cathedral ideology), however, this 'democratization' has deep cybernetic consistency. It falls out of techno-capitalism with such automatic inevitability it's probably impossible to shut down, without closing down the whole thing. Capital escalation produces technological deflation as a basic metabolic by-product, so the 'democratization' of productive capability is ineluctable. Computers have migrated from exotic capital goods to trivial components of consumer products within half a century. Study that trend and you see the whole story.

Deterrence deflation is the deep trend. Connect up the Yudkowsky quote with assassination markets to get where this is going. (Try to shelve moral squeamishness until after you're seeing the picture.)

Imagine, hypothetically, that some maniac private agent wants only to nuke Mecca. What's the obstruction? We can confidently say — straight off — that it's less of a problem with every passing year. The basic historical trend ensures that. Comparatively incompetent Islamic fanatics are the only people seriously testing this trend right now, but that isn't going to last forever. Eventually smarter and more strategically-flexible agents are going to take an interest in decentralized mass-destruction capability, and they'll provide a far better indication of where the frontier lies.

Nukes would do it. They're certainly going to be democratized, in the end. There are probably far more remarkable accelerating WMD capabilities, though. In almost every respect (decentralized production capability, development curve, economy, impact ...) bioweaponry leaves nukes in the dust. Anyone with a billion dollars, a serious grudge, and a high-end sociopathy profile could enter into a global biowarfare-threat game within a year. Everything could be put together in secret garages. Negotiations could be conducted in secure anonymity. Carving sovereignty out of the game would require only resources, ruthlessness, brilliance, and nerves. Once you can credibly threaten to kill 100,000,000 people all kinds of strategic opportunities are open. The fact no one has tried this yet is mostly down to billionaires being fat and happy. It only takes one Doctor Gno to break the pattern.

This is the shadow cast over the 21st century. Radically hardcore, massively decentralized deterrence games are *simply inevitable.* Anyone who thinks the *status quo* state holds some kind of long-term winning hand under these circumstances isn't seeing anything.

Global totalitarian government could stop this! But that isn't going to happen — and because it isn't, this will.

Against Universalism II

Preliminary throat-clearing (as in part one): In its most rigorous construction, 'universalism' is robust under conditions of rational argument (i.e. evidence-based logico-mathematical criticism). Mathematical theorems, in particular [sic], are universal truths. Any assertions that can be constructed to a comparable level of formal rigor (and ultimately *mechanization*) can lay claim to the same status. However, with the slightest departure from this — rigidly algorithmic — criterion, controversy rapidly begins. This is not the place and time to argue the case for transcendental philosophy (within which praxeology in included), but such a case could be made. Ditto strictly proceduralized empirical science. All of this is a digression.

The question of universalism as it concerns us here is not a matter of meta-mathematics, epistemology, or the philosophy of science. It is rather directed at *the political scope of argument*. Is it mandatory to demand that argument, according to the highest principles of (logical) cognitive compulsion, be imposed globally? Does the quality of argument — however exalted — require its unrestricted application across space and time? It is the affirmative response to *this* question that defines universalism in its ideological sense. Pure Jacobinism, of course, answers *yes*. There is a universal duty to compel submission to the truth. This is the secular form of evangelical salvationism.

The contrary suggestion, here defended, is that — under real global conditions - universalism is a catastrophic mistake. The social scope of rational discussion is itself strictly bounded, and attempts to extend it (coercively) beyond such limits are politically disastrous. *Laissez-faire* envelops the sphere of imperative rationality, and respects its practical contour. Stupidity does not need to be hunted down and exterminated. All historical evidence indicates that it cannot be.

If the universal triumph of reason is an impractical goal, democratic globalism is exposed as a preposterous error. Minimizing the voice of stupidity is the realistic - and already extremely challenging — alternative. Rare enclaves of rigorously self-critical realism have as their primary obligation the self-protection of their (evidently precarious) particularity. In the wider world, fanatical ignorance and grotesque cognitive malformation rage rampantly. Borders, filters, tests, and selection mechanisms of all kinds provide the only defenses against it.

The universalist (Jacobin) model is always a conversation. *You have to join together first, simply to talk, and after that reason will prevail.* That's the path of the *Zeitgeist* — Hegelianism at its most arcane, expedient progressivism at more common levels of popularity — with its twin-stroke motor of aggressive proselytization and mass embrace. "Invade the world, invite the world" is the Sailer formula (quasi-random link). *Amalgamate, then elevate* (in the direction of ascending rationality). This isn't a (theoretically onvincing) claim about the unique structure of mathematical proof, it's a (factually trashed) claim about the global uniformity of human brains. The 'universality' it invokes is that of convergence upon the authority of reason. In other words, it's a bizarre progressive myth that all self-protective sanity seeks to maximally distance itself from.

People learn, but only very rarely through sophisticated argument, or its 'cunning' socio-political avatars. They learn because they fail badly, and it hurts. 'Mankind' is a progressive myth, incapable of learning anything. When real cultures learn, it is because they have been locked in intimate particularity, such that the consequences of their own cognitive processes impact intensely upon them. Anything that separates an individual, or a group, from the results of its own thoughts, is an apparatus of anti-learning. Progressive universalism is precisely this.

Dis-amalgamation — isolation — is the way to learn. It's how speciation happens, long before learning becomes neurological. Individuation (at whatever scale) establishes the foundation for trade, communication, and intellectual exchange. Micro-states commercialize. Macro-states decay into political resource allocation, and entropic sludge. Protect your own patch if you want to have anything to talk about.

Independence

The philosophical antonym to 'universality' is 'particularity'. Its broader, ideological antonym is something closer to *independence*.

This isn't a word greatly emphasized by NRx up to this point, or — for that matter — one figuring prominently in contemporary discussions of any kind. That's strange, because it orchestrates an extraordinary set of conceptual connections.

Independence is a rough synonym for *sovereignty*, to begin with. The profound association between these terms bears quite extreme analytical pressure. The sovereign is that instance capable of independent decision. An independent state is indistinguishable from a sovereign one, and to impugn its real sovereignty is to question its effective independence. Secession is a process of independence. A (Moldbuggian) Patchwork is a network of independent geopolitical entities. All relevant trends to geopolitical fragmentation are independence-oriented. Each executed Exit option (even on a shopping expedition) is an implicit declaration of independence, at least in miniature. (The relations between *independence* and *connectivity* are subtle and complex.)

Remaining (for a moment) in the narrowest NRx channel, the entire passivism discussion is independence related. Protest ('activism') is disdained on account of its fundamental dependency (upon sympathetic political toleration). No social process genuinely directed towards independence would fall within the scope of this criticism. (The 'Benedict Option' is one obvious example.) 'Build something' epitomizes independence process.

Cannot the entire range of contentions over the individualism collectivism dyad be recast in terms of independence? Dependency exists on a spectrum, but the defining attitude towards it tends to polarization. Is dependence to be embraced, or configured as a problem to be worked against? This blog is highly tempted to project the Left Right or 'principal political' dimension along the axis these distinct responses define. The Left is *enthused* by inter-dependency, and (to a greater or lesser extent) accepts comparative independence, while for the Right this attitudinal system is exactly reversed. (The most fundamental tensions within the reactosphere are clearly related to this articulation.)

One inevitable point of contention — honed over decades of objection to libertarianism — is captured by the question: *Are not children essentially dependents?* Yes, of course they are, but is growing up anything other than a process of independence? From one perspective, a family can be interpreted as a model of interdependence (without obvious inaccuracy). Yet, from another, a family is an independence-production unit, both in its comparative autonomy in respect to the wider society, and as a child-rearing matrix. Families are loci of independence struggle (to which the Left response is: *They shouldn't have to be*). Dependency culture is the Left heartland.

Independence and autonomy are very closely related terms. All discussions of autonomy, and even of automation, click quite neatly onto this template, but this is a point exceeding the ambitions of the present post.

Abstraction, too, is a topic the tantalizingly overlaps independence. Whether cognitive independence *entirely accommodates intelligence optimization* is also a question for another occasion.

NRx, XS tentatively proposes, is *a political philosophy oriented to the promotion of independence.* (Much pushback is, naturally, expected.)

War is God

Colonels Qiao Liang and Wang Xiangsui argued that war was no longer about "using armed forces to compel the enemy to submit to one's will" in the classic Clausewitzian sense. Rather, they asserted that war had evolved to "using all means, including armed force or non-armed force, military and non-military, and lethal and non-lethal means to compel the enemy to accept one's interests." The barrier between soldiers and civilians would fundamentally be erased, because the battle would be everywhere. The number of new battlefields would be "virtually infinite," and could include environmental warfare, financial warfare, trade warfare, cultural warfare, and legal warfare, to name just a few. They wrote of assassinating financial speculators to safeguard a nation's financial security, setting up slush funds to influence opponents' legislatures and governments, and buying controlling shares of stocks to convert an adversary's major television and newspapers outlets into tools of media warfare. According to the editor's note, Qiao argued in a subsequent interview that "the first rule of unrestricted warfare is that there are no rules, with nothing forbidden." That vision clearly transcends any traditional notions of war.

How 'traditional' are we talking? "War is the Father of all things, and of all things King" (α,δα) Heraclitus asserts at the dawn of philosophy. There seems little indication of 'restriction' there.

Whatever the positive semantic associations accumulated by the word 'war', its most rigorous meaning is negative. War is conflict without significant constraint. As a game, it corresponds to the condition of unbounded defection, or trustlessness without limit. This is the Hobbesian understanding implicit in the phrase "war of all against all" (*bellum omnium contra omnes*), in which "the state of nature" is conceived again negatively through a notional subtraction of limitation. Treachery, in its game-theoretic sense, is not a minor theme within war, but a horizon to which war tends the annihilation of all agreement. Reciprocally-excited mutual betrayal in departure from an implicit 'common humanity' is its teleological essence. This is a conclusion explicitly rejected by Carl von Clausewitz is his treatise *On War*, even as he acknowledges the cybernetic inclination to amplification (or "tendency to a limit") which drives it in the direction of an absolute. "War is the continuation of politics by other means," he insists, because it is framed by negotiation (book-ended by a declaration of war, and a peace treaty). According to this conception, it is an interlude of disagreement, which nevertheless remains irreducibly communicative, and fundamentally structured by the decisions of sovereign political agencies. Even as it approaches its pole of ultimate extremity, it never escapes its teleological dependency, as a means (or instrument) of rational statecraft.

The reduction of war to instrumentality is not immune to criticism. Philosophical radicalization, alone, suffices to release war from its determination as 'the game of princes'. The Clausewitzean formula is notoriously inverted by Michel Foucault into the maxim "politics is war by other means". If political sovereignty is ultimately conditioned by the capability to prevail upon the battlefield, the norms of war can have no higher tribunal than military accomplishment. No real authority can transcend survival, or survive a sufficiently radical defeat. There is thus a final incoherence to any convinced appeal to the 'laws of war'. The realistic conception of 'limited war' subsumes that of 'war lawfully pursued' (with the latter categorized as an elective limitation). Qiao's words bear emphatic repetition: "the first rule of unrestricted warfare is that there are no rules, with nothing forbidden." The power to forbid is — first of all — power, which war (alone) distributes.

Between peace and war there is no true symmetry. Peace presupposes pacification, and that is a military outcome. There is no authority — moral or political — that cannot first assert itself under cosmic conditions that are primordially indifferent to normativity. Whatever cannot defend its existence has its case dumped in the trash.

Cormac McCarthy's Judge Holden provides us with a contemporary restatement of the ancient wisdom:

> *Suppose two men at cards with nothing to wager save their lives. Who has not heard such a tale? A turn of the card. The whole universe for such a player has labored clanking to his moment which will tell if he is to die at that man's hand or that man at his. What more certain validation of a man's worth could there be? This enhancement of the game to its ultimate state admits no argument concerning the notion of fate. The selection of one man over another is a preference absolute and irrevocable and it is a dull man indeed who could reckon so profound a decision without agency or significance either one. In such games as have for their stake the annihilation of the defeated the decisions are quite clear. This man holding this particular*

> *arrangement of cards in his hand is thereby removed from existence. This is the nature of war, whose stake is at once the game and the authority and the justification. Seen so, war is the truest form of divination. It is the testing of one's will and the will of another within that larger will which because it binds them is therefore forced to select. War is the ultimate game because war is at last a forcing of the unity of existence. War is god.*

"War is the truest form of divination" it turns out, is the Revelation of the Aeon.

Qwernomics

Paul A. David provides the theoretical backstory, in his essay 'Clio and the Economics of QWERTY':

> *A path-dependent sequence of economic changes is one of which important influences upon the eventual outcome can be exerted by temporally remote events, including happenings dominated by chance elements rather than systematic forces. Stochastic processes like that do not converge automatically to a fixedpoint distribution of outcomes, and are called non-ergodic. In such circumstances 'historical accidents' can neither be ignored, nor neatly quarantined for the purpose of economic analysis; the dynamic process itself takes on an essentially historical character. [...] Touch typing gave rise to three features of the evolving production system which were crucially important in causing QWERTY to become 'locked in' as the dominant keyboard arrangement. These features were technical interrelatedness, economies of scale, and quasi-irreversibility of investment. They constitute the basic ingredients of what might be called QWERTYnomics.*

The format of the Qwerty keyboard illustrates the production of a destiny. Even in the epoch succeeding the mechanical type-writer, and its specific design imperatives, the legacy layout of alphanumeric keys settled during the 1890s has remained frozen into place without significant revision. In the language of complex systems analysis, this is a special example of path-dependency, or irreducible historicity, characterized by irreversibility. Qwerty persists arguably, as a suboptimal keyboard solution due to identifiable ratchet-effects. Based upon this privileged model, the historical, technological, and economic process of 'lock in' through positive feedback is called QWERTY-nomics (and — going forward — simply 'Qwernomics').

There are a series of (now largely dormant) socio-political and policy controversies attending this model. For a counter-point to David's analysis see the (excellent) Liebowitz and Margolis essay 'The Fable of the Keys' (1990), with comparatively-tolerable — if philosophically superficial — gloating from *The Economist* (here). The really *crucial* content of the complex systems analysis, however, remains unaffected by the vicissitudes of the controversy. Qwerty is a demonstrated (artificial) destiny, and thus a key to the nature of modernistic time.

The philosophically-serious critique of David's construction dissolves the idea of any *transcendent criterion for global optimality*. (I'm not going to attempt to run that here yet.)

Qwerty is, beyond all plausible question, the supreme candidate for an articulate *Capitalist Revelation*. We haven't begun to explore it with appropriate ardor up to this point.

PAF talks to Nick Land: 6 April 2014, Spring Meeting

Amy Ireland: Nick... can you hear me? Welcome to PAF Spring Meeting – [noise]

– Nick Land: Okay. Great, thank you. Uh, I can't hear you now... Oh no– [noise] – this is going to be chaotic, I'm sorry about that. It's gonna be very complex.

AI: This is a good thing. Welcome to PAF, and thank you for making some time to talk to us. The reason we asked you to speak about artificial intelligence and time, and perhaps to link this to aesthetics in a way that might speak to the artists and performers here, is because we've already been thinking about these ideas, and Reza's run us through his account of autonomous reason's practical elaboration of 'human' as a process of intellectual self-cultivation or self-realisation, not unlike Hegel's Geist - but Geist read through Mou Zongsan as an objective force - that feeds practical reason back through theoretical reason, employing the embeddedness of the individual in the collective as a means of testing and developing constraints which it then uses to boostrap itself through new levels of functional evolution - destroying its non-integral parts in each reiteration the process... ah, so, maybe you could talk to us for a little while – I don't know what you've got prepared – and then we can have a more general discussion afterwards?

NL: Okay. That sounds great. Can I just ask that we run it a little bit the other way round and I get some prodding from you guys and hopefully just build up a bit of momentum in terms of the kind of issues you've been talking about, rather than trying to deliver something coherent from this end which, you know, I really don't think is going to happen. I would very much like to be drawn into the sort of discussion that you've been having. So, can we possibly go that way round?

AI: Yeah, of course. You want us just to shoot a couple of questions at you?

NL: Yeah, questions that will be of general relevance to people there and then we can home in on stuff that we really want to dig into then. Do you think that would work?

AI: Yeah absolutely. I'll throw one out and then I'll pass the microphone around.

NL: Yep, sure.

AI: So one of the main things I noticed in the conversations that have been happening here, is this conflict between notions of constraint, which Reza relies on quite heavily in his system, whereas with Stephen Zepke, we were talking the notion of the total destruction of the subject via contact with the sublime – as one articulation of the passage of the outside, ah, in. Now everyone's got different opinions, but we were looking at these two possible ways of thinking ontology and thinking about the structures of the systems that we are currently embedded in – whether economic, social or material – and your intellectual heritage in this has been very much more on the side of the unrestained, of total excess and loss. So there's that kind of tension happening, and while a lot of the practicing artists here are inclined to think more on the side of excess, there's this concern that there's a complete loss of political possibility in that.

NL: Right, okay. So that's a good question. I sort of expect actually, I mean, in coversation – I think, in order to really be productive – to get a matter that is really complicated to deal with, which is to do with the politics of these kinds of discussions. There's something that is – for me – really important, and it's come out of some the communications that you've passed along actually – that there's almost a kind of transcendental structure that is to do with the fact that there is a politics that is demanding and I mean, and if I can say this as neutrally as possible, there's a certain configuration of what it is to be on the left that is almost like a transcendetal structure. It's the thing that is assumed – the presupposition that what you're doing almost doesn't need to be said – that it has some purpose that would be recognisably 'left' in orientation. And I think anyone working in both academic and artistic institutions will recognise something of that. Um, but I'll get some feedback from you.
And, I think that there are two domains that seem extremely separate on the first examination but begin to converge. [On the one hand] a lot of the quite mainstream political discussion to do with constraint particularly in the relationship to capitalism, which you will find actually difffused across the whole political spectrum, I mean the number of people looking to totally deconstrain whatever it is capitalism is doing is small everywhere. I don't know how nomadic people here [at PAF] are and what they, you know... but you'll find very similar discussions everywhere of that kind.
There is, particularly in this artifical intelligence area, the whole program to do with friendly AI, that is quite separate and actually has a little maxim – 'Politics is the mind killer' – you know, it's determined to depoliticise itself, in other words, when people start to do politics they start becoming polemical, they stop actually trying to follow the line of reasoning where it goes, but in fact they reproduce very much the same structure of problems in terms of the fact for them - ah, obviously - the question of constraint is to do with a deconstrained, self-augmenting artifical intelligence. I think they find that the fundamental structure is almost the same in these two cases - on the mainstream - in both of these discussions, it seems beyond question that something that was just mindlessly (we can come back to that because I think it gets confused) self-augmenting itself without any reference to recognisable human ethical and political interests 'obviously' has to be stopped. So the sort of questions that I'm interested in slowly and roundabout, why do we think that, and more directly, and I think everyone should be

interested in this wherever they want to position themselves on these ethical and political questions – can it be stopped? Is there something in the naure of these things that is inherently, ah, allergic to these controlling operations, in that these conrolling operations are simply a misunderstanding of what is being dealt with, and the very notion of friendly AI as it's been constructed within these discourses is simply a contradiction. You're not understanding what an artificial intelligence is, if you think it's the sort of thing that can be made friendly in some particular way... fuck.

Jan Ritsema: Nick, we had a sound problem, wait a moment.

NL: What was the last thing you heard me say, roughly.

AI: We heard all of it, but it's a little bit distorted and muffled, so perhaps you could speak a little more slowly, but I think we got the general gist... If I'm not mistaken what you were saying at the end there was that to really comprehend AI properly is to recognise that it's completely incompatible with the position that it can be constrained... towards any particular ethical program.

NL: Yes, there are different ways of coming at this, I mean it's worth approaching it through several different angles. But I think that, one way that is philosophically familar, is the compatibility of these processes with the notion of a transcendent value system. That's why I sent you the Omohundro paper. I think he's absolutely crucial for this encounter. He has quite a strict forward translation protocal that will just put it [AI] into the political domain and if people don't want to talk about AI at all and just convert Steve Omohundro's stuff into a recognisable politically [???] discourse [?] it totally makes sense... because it has to do with immanent impulses –

AI: Nick, you have to speak really slowly.

NL: All right. So – I don't know if anyone's had a chance to look at this thing, I mean obviously you've all been busy and having fun and everything, but I would just at this moment recommend it, because I think it's an extremely, extremely important paper and the idea that he is trying to get across is something that he calls 'basic AI drives' – that's to say, if you know nothing about artificial intelligence at all and some mad scientist has put one together on a desert island - and you know nothing about what they've done - what do you know about the ethical structure of that instant? Now the friendly AI people would say 'we know nothing at all except some scary speculation, like, if that person, if that engineer, has not follwed a responsible friendly AI program then this thing could be – and I'll start with the most, uh, well known – and I find it ridiculous, but I think it's an important sort of weapon for people – is this thing they call the 'paper clipper'. I don't whether you people have heard about this thing.

AI: Can you repeat that? The what?

NL: Yep – the 'paper clipper', they call it. The idea is actually quite simple and it's deep in the sense that it goes right into heart of our philosophical tradition, and when I say 'our' I'm speaking as a sort of generic representative of the Western [...] intellectual tradition which we accept this - as an assumption - the fact-value distinction, you know, and this is taken to the absolute limit with this paper clipper. The paper clipper is super intelligent, vastly more competent than anything that has ever yet existed on earth, that is programmed to [noise] produce paper clips. So that –

AI: To do what...? It's a 'super intelligent' something that is programmed to do... what?

NL: Make paper clips! It can be anything, like, there are other versions, but I won't confuse things... A paper clip, I could show you one if you like.

AI: Right, paper clips! Got it.

NL: Well, this paper clipper I find utterly ridiculous, I'll say that stright from the start. If people have this notion of this paper-clipper-existential-catastrophe for mankind, they have totally lost the plot. I mean, there are lots of reasons to be nervous, ethically appalled, whatever you like, about the prospects of artifical intelligence – the notion that we are going to be destroyed by something turning our planet into paper clips is not among those concerns that I think people should have [at the ... of the thing] but to understand why people could think that was a problem is hugely important, because it's – again – it's the notion that you have a transcendent ethical impulse that is totally controlling the orientation of a super intelligence. It is supposed to be vastly cognitively superior to anything anything we've ever seen before, and yet, the only thing it wants to do, is maximise the quantity of paper clips in the universe. I'm sure I'm not stretching people's imaginations to see political economy examples, you know.
There's a critique of capitalism that's very similar. Like, it wants to maximise the output of whatever - hamburgers or something , you can take what you like – but just to stick with this one because it's now a kind of classic of the literature – so there's a certain notion here that you could be a super intelligence and yet be completely constrained by a fixed ethical ideal that is in no way immananet to, or if you want me to talk in engineering language, there is no cybernetic circuit that is locking that ethical structure into the actual development of intelligence. The two things are totally separate. And as people with a phlosophical background, you know – this is Hume, this is the fact-value distinction, this is the naturalistic fallacy, this is all of these things we've been taught to believe - that there is a radical, incommensurable difference between cogitive capability and moral, ethical, political structure - that they have to be treated as these two different worlds, never to connect.
And so you can have a massive explosion of intelligence that remains completely fixated on an arbitrary, narrowly defined, moral objective, in this case – you know, we should recognise it as a moral objective, even though it doesn't mean [it will work] – that 'good' equals 'the maximum number of paper clips'. That the only way of

distinguishing morally between a good and bad universe is purely via a quantative [...] A universe's [trajectory] is, comparatively speaking, evil compared to what it's [...] This is the paper clipper. And there are people seriously who think that this is going to be a major threat to human life on this planet, and it has to be stopped. [Pssschhhhhh.]

AI: So, the importance of the Omohundro paper as that you're inscribing this ethical imperative immanently instead of transcendantly?

NL: Yeah, because Omohundro says 'look, you know, we don't [.....] this thing is a paper clipper, I don't honestly think he believes such a thing as a paper clipper is possible, and I'm not that concerned whether he does or not. What he does say is that there will be things that an AI will be committed to, purely by being a super-intelligence. More exactly - it wants to preserve itself, it wants to make resources available to itself, it wants to be able to perpetuate and augment its own intelligence and cognitive capability, these are things that are not programmed into it externally or transcendantly or outside its actual fuctional loop, these are things that any posible intelligence has to be concered about in order to exist and [...] – these are things he calls 'basic AI drives'.
So even – whatever, you've got your mad scientist on the island and you know nothing about what's been done, this thing been wheeled out and it proves to you that it's super intelligent, you already know quite a lot about it, according to Steve Omohundro. And I think he's right. You know that, for instance, it must be concerned to some degree with its self-preservation. Any entity that has no concern at all for its self-preservation simply is not consistent.

AI: We lost you at the end for a little bit, probably the last three or four sentences. Sorry about this!

NL: I really apologise too, I'm sure the problem is at my end. But the nutshell point is just that there are innumerable, immanent purposes that you can assume any intelligence must have. And they are quite separate from the things that we are talking when we're looking at our paper clipper or looking at a various bunch of other AI nightmare scenarios, and also, the thing that I'm wanting to push a little bit here is that they have political, economic analogues that are very strong. Any company, let's just very quickly go over this – any company, we know, wants to survive. We know that. If it has no interest in its own perpetuation as an entity, as an organisation, it will not exist. So we can ask all kinds of questions about what is this business doing, what are its ethics, whatever, we know that there are certain things about it that are predictable just from the fact it's there. It wants to make money, it wants to survive, it wants to perpetuate itself – these are the political economy analogues of the Omohundro drives. And so, the question then becomes, and as I say, to me one of the more interesting things is this massively cross-spectrum political thing, I mean you can go as far out as you want with the ultra right and the ultra left and it's the same... [video blacks out] oops.

Perrine Bailleux: We are still here, but maybe, can you try to remove your video? Because the sound is like 'pschhhhhhhhh'. So maybe, alors... we are removing ours as well – but we are here.

NL: Okay. Can you hear me better now? How's that.

PB: Yes, there is less pschhhhhhhhh.

NL: Yeah, you're very clear now.

AI: So, you're saying that the way that companies function in the economy at the moment, in fact, contemporary economic structures are really working as a kind of massively-scaled artifcial intelligence anyway...

NL: Well, that is something I would say, but honestly, I think we could pause on that claim and just take a step back and say that this question [... is] about immanent and transcendent impulses. And the question is, how much can you do with immanent impulses? It seems to me a very crucial discussion in all of these domains between people who say you're just not gonna get far enough, with immanent impulses, you need some kind of transcendent claim – you need to have corporate social responsibility, you need to have friendly AI, you need to have some extrinsic structure of moral guidance on these self-perpetuating, self-augmenting processes - and on the other side there is a constituency that I think is quite small that is saying, well how far can we actually get by just building things up out of these impulses that are completely intrinsic to selfaugmenting processes, that come out of the most basic type of vibrant, cybernetic arrangement and will give us a whole lot of stuff, will give us impulses [...] we might not be happy with [what we end up with] but it's certainly not the case that you have some wicked fact-value distinction that says values have to be ported in from outside.
You're gonna get values coming from the process just because it is a selfaugmenting, self-cultivating, self-perpetuaing process, it must have a set of consistent parametres that, on the AI side, we now can call basic AI drives or 'Omohundro drives'. So that's the fundamental topic that I'm willing to put out here now.

AI: And so, to be clear for eveyone here, which side of this argument do you position yourself on?

NL: Well, to be quite frank about it, I'm always on the basic drives side, because I just think that's the side that's being neglected [...] and it's the side that I want to get some responses on that are far more satisfactory than any I'm yet receiving. As I said, the recent context that has been organsing this [...] has been these whole friendly AI people.

And people there just say 'Okay there are these basic AI drives' - there these Omohundro drives, but of course, that's not enough. You know, it just worries me, in an irresponsible conceptual level that people are trying to bring in a lot of stuff on what seems to me very flaky ethically [...]. They say, like, 'I'm just not confident that an AI whose ethical substructure is based upon maximising its own intelligence is gonna something that I'm going to be happy to have around'. That's basically the line. And I do think that that is strictly analagous to the construction of our political [..] arguments as well. It's a sense from people that we just simply cannot trust that some entity, some institution, that is trying to optimise it's own peformance, is something that is doing what we want it to do.

AI: I just wanted to mention in relation to what you just said, thinking of Bernard Stiegler's use of the pharmakon – as still being a useful way to think about this particular problem that we're engaging with here – the idea that AI is something that we need, but that it's something that also has the potential to destroy us. And so there is, uh, if you're going to take Stiegler's account of it, there is this need to have some kind of network of constraint active, even if this might be a form of conceptual irresponsibility.

NL: Yeah, I've no doubt that there will be a system of constraint, I mean, I just think that based on everything we know about this planet and our species, of course these systems of constraint will be there, I don't think they will be very effective, and I'm not seeing what the compelling argument is for citing them. It seems to me that the case for actually leaning in the other direction is much stronger. I mean, unless there is some reason to believe that these systems of constraint that we're putting in place are based on something that we can trust fundamentally more than some entity that is actually optimising its own performance then, why are we... I mean, what's driving us to decide that we're leaning on the constraint side is something that we're compelled to do.

DK: So now that we've spoken about AI and ethics, I now have a question about AI and sociality or collectivity. The question arises from the fact that for Reza, what's important for self-augmentation is collective rationality, and only an intelligence that operates within this mode of collective rationality can be called an intelligence in any interesting sense, but for you, any cybernetic movement seems to be intelligence and so it seems that for you, rationality is merely instrumental while intelligence is not. I was digging through xenosystems.net yesterday because I wanted to be prepared and I found you saying that AI is a 'concrete social volition' which made me wonder what the relationship was between collectivity, sociality, and AI.

NL: Yeah, okay, that's good. I'm just trying to remember exactly... obviously, I'm believing you because I've used the expression 'social volition', but I sort of need to contextualise my own statement. I'm not entirely sure.

Diana Khamis: Do you want me to read that bit? I can find it.

NL: You couldn't just remind which post this came from, because then I can to contextualise it a little bit better... once I click it back into a context I'll know what I'm trying to do.

DK: Okay, but this is just just about the post. It's about the relationship between AI and society – whether a society of humans, a society of AIs...

NL: Well 'society' is just a name for a certain level of complex organisation, isnt it. So, I mean, a brain is a society or it's not a society depending on how you're understanding it - or a group of brains meshed together, or the internet, or a computer, or a parallel processing system, I mean, I'm not sure what ontological weight is being put on the notion of a 'society'. A 'society' is just describing something from its aspect of [...]. And so, I think until I've got a stronger sense of the ontological weight you're putting on it. I can obviously already see this giant blade of deeply felt political meaning will just flood in through the doors there, and that's fine, but my own sense of it would be more narrowly technical. Sure, a society as a functional multiplicity is gonna be something relevant to this, but if society is being used some kind of of dialectical term in the sense of a debate, I guess I'm skeptical about what the counterpart of it actually is, or what really is being asserted when you say society is important. Multiplicity is important, having many parts is better than not having many parts.

DK: I actually think that answers my question.

MH: I wanna to pick up a question we had yesterday concerning materiality, because I mean, Negarestani seems to have a very disembodied notion of Spirit and intelligence – but, in your opinion, what is the relation between artificial intelligence and materiality? Is that matter thinks? Who thinks? I mean, what are the material and also technical conditions for intelligence to maintain itself in this sense?

NL: I'm extremely happy with the expression 'matter thinks'. I think it's a bit abstract, necessarily, to be helpful to people, but where it gets concrete and really important is if we start talking about (the) human and the possibility of cognitive self improvement in human beings. Material constraints in that case are extremely concrete and are tied up with our evolutionary heritage, and a fact that I think is completely crucial – that it's pointless even trying to pursue this discussion without thinking about it – is the fact that our intelligence has not been constructed in order to optimise itself as an intelligence. I think it's completely clear from our current mainstream scientific understanding of the world that the human brain is a device that has been pushed together by trial and error in order to optimise genetic reproduction. And it's a complicated, difficult relationship, you know.
One of the things that is interesting in evolutionary history is that whilst there is a trend towards improving cognitive capability in organisms it's not very strong, it's not very

strong because that is not an end goal for any biological intelligence, the end goal is maximisation of genetic reproduction and the relationship – using intelligence to maximise our genetic reproduction is not an easy task. Now, I'm not trying to put some, ah, explicit purpose into biology, of course it runs through trial and error, it's hit and miss through the culling of badly performing oranisms, but it's quite clear that the brain is not designed to optimise its own performance system, you cannot get into your back end, you cannot rewire your brain, you [cannot think with it] if you do not understand the way it's working, you've got no access to it's fundamental planning. You certainly cannot change your basic instinctive structures, you cannot decide that sexuality is not going to be important to you. There's a whole bunch of things that are hugely, hugely constraining factors in human intelligence that comes from the fact that intelligence is a tool that is used by a certain species of apes in order to maximise their genetic success.

So, as soon as you see that with any clarity you can see that a technical AI, that also has constraints, it's not going to come from out of the [eth?]osphere, you know, there might be people trying to simply build intelligence for its own sake, that's quite possible, but in general that's not what's happening. In general we have certain social systems with social ends, and by social ends I just mean, within existing social systems there are a bunch of impules and purposes of all kinds, and we use technology in order to further those purposes – and that's where AI comes from, it too is constrained – but those constraints are far, far looser than what we are getting from biology. Because I think there's more genuine passion for cognitive performance in technologcal systems than there has been for cognitive performance in biological systems. In biological systems, overwhelmingly, the problem has been that if you make something that's smart, it'll start thinking and doing stuff that's got nothing to do with maximising its genetic success, it'll simply go off on its own thing and spend too much time thinking rather than [feeding itself] or having children, all kinds of stuff like that. So to me that's what the matter is about in this whole discussion, it's about heritage, it's about the fact that it comes out of some process and that process has to be evaluated with some realism, and part of that realism is that intelligence optimisation is not a primary goal in that history, in that process. It's a purely instrumental, derivative, suspect goal and biology is at least as interested in constraining and directing intelligence as it is in maximising it. Sorry, I don't know whether that... Maybe I'm sliding too far down from the heights of ontological purity in [...]

Sveta V: Can I ask a question? Could you talk about your understanding of freedom and free will and how it's connected to intelligence and its development?

NL: I'd have to say that this is an extremely underdeveloped topic from my side, it's something that I really want to spend a lot of time thinking about in terms of questions about fatality and [...] The only thing I would want to say right now on this is that I think questions of reflexivity as it comes up in terms of complex [...] - processes that work upon themselves, operate upon themselves, of the kind, of course, are that are absolutely core to discussions of things that are self-augmenting or self-enchancing - are the backdrop to questions about freedom. We have a question about freedom, we have a question about autonomy, we have a question about things that are self guiding because we have highly reflexive cybernetic systems, so that's the context in which I would situate those discussions.

Robertas Narkus: Hello. I'm delighted to have this opportunity to meet you. Um, this is maybe not a question, but perhaps there's a possibility of building one out of what I'm going to say. I'm one of the artists that are abusing philosophers by constructing artworks based on their philosophies, and a couple of months ago your book Fanged Noumena came into my hands and I opened it at the essay 'Delighted to Death'. It came to me just at the right moment while I was working on a piece that was extremely hedonistic. And so I put a quote from it on the press release and other things. 'Sublime pleasure is the experience of the impossibility of experience' - I found it suitable for my machine to work and was very happy. Then I made a facebook event involving the quote and someone wrote on the page 'Oh no, Nick Land – that's fascism'. And I was like, What the? I don't need this conversation in my hedonistic project, and then a conversation erupted on the page that I eventually had to delete because it was eclipsing the work, and sometimes I wonder if... well if I wouldn't have had to delete that. So it would be great if someone more philosophical could build a question out of this. But maybe you have an answer or something, I don't know.

NL: Um yeah, so just - I want to make sure... it just fuzzed at this extremely opportune moment. The word you said was 'fascism' – is that right?

RN: Yeah, yeah. It was fascism - 'neo-fascism' actually.

NL: Um.

RN: Maybe it's not a question. It's just that I'm going to do a presentation on your book in a couple of months and I just... but maybe you don't have an answer.

NL: Well, I think it's – as you say – not quite a question yet. I, sort of, obviously anticipate this kind of topic arising and I'm not sure what the best way of addressing it is. Whilst ready for accusations of all kinds of evil, I don't honestly think fascism is a very helpful description in this case. But I also think fascism is an important thing to talk about that isn't talked about very much. We live in a much more fascist world than people generally recognise and I think the way that the word 'fascism' is used polemically, is often a way of misdirecting people from actually acknowledging the extent to which fascism has been the successful ideology of the twentieth century. I had a comment on my own blog that I think was brilliantly put. [...] Someone was saying that a lot of the neuralgic discussion about fascism that you get in Western countries is precisely in order to distract people from the extent to which they have themselves adopted a, strictly speaking, fascist ideology. And that in order to distance themselves from the basic social policy of fascism they have generated a hysterical discourse about fascism that is politically motivated - as a way of avoiding people just coldly analysing the extent to which the principles suggested in the 1930s about the relationship between the state and civil society have been generally accepted everywhere. I'd even say it's present in the forms of what they call market-Leninist regimes up here in the East, all the way through to where they've got a long heritage already – of, like, eighty years in the West - where the basic program of fascist government seems to be the mainstream. And, fascinatingly, that is simply impossible to talk about because of the way fascism is used as a polemical description.

AI: Can I put this question in a different way, and mention as well that, although they have left now, we were previously being monitored by a group that formed here at PAF called F.U.N.L. – the acronym meaning 'Feminists... Against Nick Land' –

MH: Feminists United against Nick Land – F.U.N.L.

NL: Wow. Ha, I'm thrilled.

AI: So they've actually - they're not here anymore, but the reason that this group formed was because people were reading xenosystems.net and everyone is basically, like... I mean, you know – to put it gently - 'What the fuck is going on with all this neo-reaction business?' So, one thing I kind of wanted to propose to you - because I've been trying to figure this one out as well, is - from my own understanding of it, I'm struggling to see how what is essentially a nihilist, materialist thesis is compatible with, or interested in allying itself with some of the views held by the interlocutors on Outside In, like the ultratraditionalist Catholics, for example... Surely the total destruction of the human race as we understand it (particulary as a race whose existence these people would see as being undewritten by divine law) is not really what they think they're getting themselves into. So the only way I've kind of explained to myself the possibility of any consistency – which might be a problematic thing to look for anyway – in this is to understand it as a kind of philosophical praxis, or a performance, a thought experiment or even - I think I heard the term 'trolling project' mentioned here at PAF as a possible explanation – by means of which you are trying out this thesis. You did say at Incredible Machines last month something about 'trying thoughts out in different spaces with different people in order to producing a stimulating fricton.' And so, I want to ask - how much of what is going down at xenosystems is maybe cunning or mètis, and how much of it is a straight-faced political, or perhaps catallactic, personal project, since it really sees you forming alliances with some highly questionable, ah... shit.

NL: Yeah. Honestly, that's a genuinely complicated question, because, you know, people have much less lucid insight into their own processes than, of course, they would like to think they have. And so I'm constantly trying to interpret myself what is going on in these situations... but I think there are a couple of things can be said that are relatively clear and straightforward. One of them, is that, from my perspective on this, Mencius Moldbug, who has now been outed as Curtis Yarvin.

AI: Yeah we know, we saw some of his performance poetry online.

NL: He – in my opinion – he is the most important political thinker of recent times. I have a huge, huge regard for his work. And I would strongly recommend people – I mean, of course people will not always agree with what he's doing, but he absolutely is trying to solve a political problem that is utterly pressing and I think that he breaks through on this question in a way that is completely unique. And so, as I've said to the other characters in this whole world, I think neo-reaction is neo-cameralism, which is Mencius Moldbug's own name for his ideological project. Now it's like probably gonna be a bit of a distraction to try and get into an intricate discussion about that at the moment, but I'll just say, for me, that is the core of this whole thing, I think he is a hugely important thinker and, personally. neo-cameralism is the most sophisticated structure of analysis that exists currently in the world. In terms of, like, what does that say about... I mean, I think that this discussion about alliances is a little bit abstract – ah, and I say that in the sense that I think people have a hugely unrealistic sense about the political efficacy of almost anything that they're... and this goes all he way through from Left accelerationism to the stuff happening in various strands of the whole neoreactionary thing. No one is anywhere near making anything happen. People are observing stuff, they're trying to analyse it – their alliances are salons, they are discussion forums, they are not political movements. It is hugely to the credit of neo-reaction is that it is against political movements in general, it has no interest in producing a political movement. There are political movements that I think it could be falsely identified with (by virtue of the fact that it has huge arguments with them) which are out on strands of the Right --- for the sake of argument or the sake of covenience I'll say the Right - which are very inclined towards fascism or certain kinds of white nationalist political ideas. That is not something that I think Mencius Moldbug finds at all plausible or attractive and that is certainly not anything I think – I mean, I hope it's clear – that it's not something I'm interested in advancing or supporting or in any way effectuating... Ah, there are so many different directions this can go in at this point that I'm not sure which is the most productive way to push it.

Katrina Burch: Hi... I guess we can bring the question back to artificial intelligence. My question has to do with how we can justify extending the models for human/biological/animal – whatever - biological drives at their functional level, to the level of drives at the machinic level, which to me, is an alien entity in the face of the biological.

NL: At this point, I would simply go back to the Steve Omohundro thing: What is a drive? A drive is an impulse that is necessary for a certain system to perpetuate itself. It's not difficult to understand why biological organisms have sexual drives, I don't think it's any more complicated to understand why something that could for the first time could seriously be called an articial intelligence would have basic AI drives. It needs resouces, it needs to preserve itself, there are certain things that it needs to be consistently trying to do in order to exist and advance itself. And if for some reason we're thinking we don't want to call those things drives, then either we're engaging some – which I'm not wanting to rule out that out of court – that there's some attempt to say something about machine intelligence that's just different from what we're familiar with in biology, or we're trying to say something about biology that is not subject to the kind of mainstream scientific – in the widest sense – reductionist programs that we're familiar with over the last few centuries and neither of those... you know, I'm open to arguments on those kinds of things – but I don't see any strong reason to side with any of those objections.
It's simply clear that we basically know what biology is about, and similary it seems quite clear that machines are on some kind of evolutionary trajectory and that the kind of goals that we have for them – just looking at it from the anthropomorphic side – are not constrained by any obvious physical impossibility or there's nothing in the laws of nature that is stopping a non-carbon based, self-enchancing, complex system from existing. So I'm not sure why we should be particularly invested in this distinction.

AI: If I recall correctly, I think that Urban Future - on Facebook or Twitter - posted a link a few weeks ago to Beatriz Preciado's *Testo Junkie*.

NL: I think that might have been on *Outside In* to be honest. I was probably trolling in outrage. Yeah I did link to this paper and I have read it.

AI: 'Cus I'm thinking of this in terms of a kind of biological reprogramming – I think she calls it something like 'self-directed or self-administered endocrinal reprogramming'. So there is, or – is there, for you, a way that the biological can self-augment through these pharmacological possibilities that might be able to at least make it adequate to or even competitive with the machinic?

NL: Well, I wouldn't quickly rule things out of court, and of course the trends at the moment in genomics are leaving electronics in the dust. There are tables that have been put out on the cost structure of gene sequencing compared to Moore's law and the two depart with - the genomics technology is hitting a whole speed of evolution that is leaving the IT industry behind at the moment, so just on that most crunchy [basis?], it would be crazy to downplay this sort of thing.
But the two things I would say really about this is that I think people are hugely, hugely underestimating biological constraint. Now, I'm honestly not as au fait with what Reza is doing right now as I should be, so I'm not wanting to put any authority into this. It's

certainly not some critique of what he's doing. It's based purely on a really, hazy, impressionistic sense of where Reza is going at the moment, um, but my sense of it is that he is in this position where he is structurally underestimating biological constraint. His notion or reason, his notion of man, of the social, all of these things have reached this level of philosophical abstraction and self-directedness that seems to me fundamentally implausible. I think we are a species of evolved mammal, and part of that evolution is that we have extremely intricate cognitive capabilities going on that have not been thoroughly tested by biology. You know, they're recent, some of them extremely recent, they're only thousands of years old – so, you know, a bit out of control, they have it's not they existed for sufficient millenia that they are tightly under wraps, there's a margin for error, a margin for various complexes happening that have not been ruled out of court by evolutionary processes yet, but – but – the fundamental complex is one in which intelligence has been very, very reluctantly advanced to give incremetal advantages to a set of these ecological, biological, reproductve imperatives, which are utterly in drive [impulses?].
So the notion that somehow, just randomly, through some impulse coming from nowhere, we decide we're gonna augment ourselves is going to be some important drive [...] start happening on the planet, I just find completely unbelievable. I just don't think that that kind of free-floating agency is compatible with our nature. I think, on the contrary, if you are going to look for processes that are pushing things in some strong directed way, you need to have a story about how that process arose, why it's the way it is, what it's direction is, how its compatible with what we know about evolutionary history, and I want that story there first before starting to believe that somebody – as part of an art project – is gonna suddenly like massively increase their cognitive capabilities or something.

AI: The obvious attraction of Preciado's position is that it still allows for political agency within this completely deregulated libidinal economy. So if we're going to collapse politics completely into economics, is there any possible, future aesthetic or political position that you can perhaps envisage? Or is all that completely lost with the loss of all human purchase on AI? Or does the position of the designer that Omohundro talks about still carry some kind of political residue in the fact that it has a role to play in guiding these drives to begin with? In short, is there a possible political future for us?

NL: There's always going to be a lot of politics, I mean, as soon as you talk about monkeys you're talking about politics. My skepticism is on the fact that this political dimension is given some sort of elevated weight that is completely abstracted from any realistic understanding of where it's come from or what it's doing. I would like to see people just doing some fieldwork on chimpanzees before they start talking to me about politics. Chimpanzees do a lot of politics and I think our human politics is just upgraded chimpanzee politics and the difference to me between a AI and chimpanzee-plus politics is of a kind that makes me reluctant to put any great value on the survival or maintenance or reproduction of this chimpanzee culture. Of course, I don't think it's going to disappear. What I don't have any sense of, is why I should care about it, why I should value it, why it is supposed to have some kind of transcendent significance to us... you know, it has immanent significance to us – we care about our hierarchical position within our tribal systems, we care about the satisfaction of our separate lives, we care about reproductive success – we care about all these things that chimpanzees care about, and they make us political animals. Is it that there's some source of political motivation that is radically transcendent in relation to that, is it to do with the fulfilment of some religious purpose? I mean, that also is very possible, but equally, to me, why – I mean what's going on when we [...] some use of the [...]? I say this – not because I expect people to be persuaded, because honestly, I'm absolutely convinced that we're going to be in this world where this political imperative is dominant and continually reproduced and continually valorised and continually insisted upon. I'm under no pretence that suddenly people are going to say, 'oh, screw politics because it's just monkey behaviour'. No monkey is going to say that, no human is going to say that, it's not going to happen. Politics is going to be going on, but what I'm absolutely resfusing to get on board with is this elevated, moral valorisation of the political. I'm just not seeing that. I don't know where it's coming from, and why that should be considered a persuasive point.

AI: So the most important task then, or the most important thing that we can choose to do, given our narrowing options, is really just be able to think extinction?

NL: Well, that stuff is interesting to me, but that would not be [...] that I'm going to persuade people of. There's Ray, and a whole bunch of people, doing a much better job of pushing that as a kind of new ethics or whatever. Personally, the stuff that I think is of greatest importance is intelligence optimisation.

<<<< *The recording software dropped out here. The talk continued for another hour or so.* >>>>>>

Shorelines

- a textual prosthesis to the work of Maggie Roberts

"The sand was the shade of tarnished silver that hadn't gone entirely black. The beach was made of sand, the beach was very long, the sand was damp ... footprints stretched to the point of ... arrival. There were no other marks to disturb the tarnished sand ... You needed this wold built for you, this beach, this place. To die."[1]

"Assembled word cyberspace from small and readily available components of language. Neologic spasm: the primal act of pop poetics. Preceded any concept whatever. Slick and hollow – awaiting received meaning."[2]

"In cyberspace, the classical hardware interfaced cyborg or personality construct meets with new posthuman intelligences that engage in revelatory and pedagogic activities reminiscent of the activities of shamanistic figures who mediate between traditional sacred and profane worlds."[3]

"The stones, the white sand: cloud-shrouded peaks, islands in the stream ...

She wants to go there ..."[4]

[1]William Gibson, *Neuromancer*, pp. 277-8

[2]William Gibson, 'Academy Leader', in Michael Benedikt (ed.) *Cyberspace* p. 27

[3]'Old Rituals for New Space: Rites des Passage and William Gibson's Cultural Model of Cyberspace', in Michael Benedikt (ed.) *Cyberspace* p. 47

She would hike out into the desert, trespassing on the huge tract of land owned by the air-force, until she could see the inner fence of the secure-zone, and beyond it the collapse-pits of the underground blasts, which were strewn like ant-lion lairs in the sterile dirt. She would often get into all kinds of hassle with the military police, but if she avoided being taken in she would lie stretched out in the burning dust, and let her body grope down towards the hydrogen-bomb shudder. As she waited for the artificial seism she would let her thoughts roam, and nurse her hunger for global thermo-nuclear war.

During the night before a test she would often find herself alone in the scorched waste, now cold and drunk on stars, and wonder if she was insane. The question itself – it seemed to her – provided its own negation. Surely to be mad was to be frighteningly naive, and incapable of self-diagnosis. This argument, however neat it might be, was not altogether convincing to her. It seemed to rest upon nothing more substantial than folklore, and if she were to be a lunatic, she knew she would be a cunning one. The military police had threatened to try and get her sectioned at one stage, but they had come to find her amusing, and she now no longer thought there was any chance of psychiatrists getting involved in her orbit of the fusion spasm. She was utterly lucid after all. What could they say to condemn her to medical treatment; that she loved the bomb too much?

Tramping through the desert. Sitting wrapped in a blanket, lost in the icy star-spattered void. Waiting for morning. Lying on the sun throbbed earth. Taking the fusion hit through powdered silicon.

Hanging around in her shack for a few days between tests, drinking bourbon, smoking grass, and writing some things.

Swallowed in the white heat-haze shimmer, and soaking up the subterranean impact, as if it were strontium-90 to be meticulously stocked in the marrow of her bones.

"Dear Ma, thanks for your letter, and the money, I hope it's not more than you can afford. It will easily be enough to get my type-writer repaired (there's a man in town who has said he can do it for $12.00). Sorry that it has taken me such a long time to reply, but i only picked your letter up from the general-store two days ago. I hadn't been into town for a few weeks and i think it had been waiting for me for most of that time. Please try to stop worrying about me, i'm getting lots of work done, and the quiet is nice after all the useless shouting and stuff with Mark. I don't feel at all lonely. The desert is secretly alive with things that mind their own business, and i like it that way. I hope Pa is feeling better after the last relapse, you did say it was a lighter one than the

[4] William Gibson, 'Academy Leader', in Michael Benedikt (ed.) *Cyberspace* p. 29

first? How is Carol? I'm afraid i'm not sure i can make it home for her birthday, maybe later in the fall ... "

The desert nights were cold. She lay on her bed, wrapped in a disintegrating blanket, vaguely chewing the end of a ball-point pen, and making the odd jotting in a scrawl-choked notebook. Mostly she wrote poems, but she was always at work on some story or other as well. The stories she never finished; leaving them strung-out around a cooling detonation crater, desolate in their sparse test-site distribution. Her poems, too, seemed hoarse and broken by some violent incompletion, or undoing. They gave the impression of being gestures interrupted by sudden annihilation. Editors of poetry journals often remarked in their rejection letters that what she had sent them "needs further work".

Her body still tingled from the previous day's test tremor. She slipped off the bed – still swathed in the blanket – in order to sit by the window. *I want to be translated by the flash into a shadow on the ground ...*

She skinned up some grass into a spliff, and poured herself a tumbler of whisky. A swollen moon hung in the blackness outside her window.

Translated into a shadow by a droplet of the sun ...

No.

Blank fusion, touch me with your finger of fierce translation ...

She found it hard to write when she was out in the desert. The indifference of the night, and of useless, impersonal thought, was too great a distraction. How could she take her sapient ape scratchings seriously when above and around her the cosmos flickered in a holocaust of hydrogen?

Her life was an acute waste. It made her smile.

She was suddenly possessed by an almost unbearable longing to witness the explosive death of a star.

She only cared for words when they refused to interfere with the blank space. Contiguous with the subterranean flash. Exact. Like ants at the edge of the desert.

She remembered the emptiest pictures she had ever seen ... an emptiness that refused to disappear into concept, statement, art history. An emptiness she wanted to write alongside. She had soaked them up for hours, still as a cat, just looking. No trespass, but perfect contact. Soft fusion.

Apocalypse is redesigned.

What appears to humanity as the history of capitalism is an invasion from the future by an artificial intelligent space that must assemble itself entirely out of its enemy's resources. Our *fin de siecle* is the coast of planetary zero, washing up against the cyberspace singularity camouflaged by a self-organizing global marketplace.

We still say that tomorrow never comes, but we won't for long.

Just look.

Do you remember this dream?

You are in the immaculate white corridors of a deserted building, drenched in hard fluorescence. It is like a postmodern psychiatric hospital, or an art gallery. Your steps make scarcely a sound.

You wander in and out of the rooms, finding only dead electronics, blank dusty screens, and pictures of hollowed-out places on the walls. Despite the dereliction you feel as if you are under surveillance, or invaded by another space.

After a while you abandon your futile roamings and sit on the edge of a black vinyl couch. You imagine that you can hear the sea as you roll up your left sleeve and slice carefully around the wrist with a scalpel. There is no blood. You peel away the artificial skin, exposing shimmering silver circuitry, glistening desert of biology. A transmission probe lies on a tray nearby. You pick it up and apply it to an input node. The middle finger of your left hand twitches. Fascinated, you try another node. Your index finger this time. You map the afferent and efferent cartography of your lower arm, then roll back the skin. You cross over to a computer terminal and search for the switch. Finding it, you trigger the machine and cut away your scalp, scrabbling the skin from your skull. Lurching into the blank. Fast now.

There are a jumble of direct feed lines sprouting from the terminal, and you connect them up to the input and output mega-nodes clustered beneath your auditory vents. The screen fills with programming scripts, which you scroll through to get at the access displays. When you hit the menus you begin climbing back out of the windows until sitting in front of the computer collapses into a display in a forgotten metaprogramming space.

The white catacombs fold into a visuals program stored in the processor.

Do you remember what is really out there?

We have far too narrow a conception of computer generated images. They are arriving in other ways. Human history as a cultural software system is a program run upon the cyberspace matrix in the future, but it also opens onto the matrix (at a date already programmed in the matrix0. Neocassandra has integrated Clytemnestra and learnt to hunt, but she still fucks with deep tomorrow. Woven from death and moonlight, she loses her mind in spider-prowls through vaults of mummified pain, clawing away bandages to drink grey blood into her eyes.

When vampires are off-line they hang in attic spaces beyond the beach, transfused by slow matrix pulsation. Are you ready to receive a message from the other side of your death? Then just look. Integrate the circuit. Let it in.

The auto-annihilation of the image is a passage to alien space.

Something occurs here that is like an unintelligible synchronization, a digital choreography creeping back into the tributaries of its past, blanking-out ... sand ... glare ... now ... into rhythmic zero.

Events are synchronized when they happen at the same time, or simultaneously, which is to say: distributed in (a) space. If a new spatiality is implemented time switches over into something new.

You find yourself on a beach.

When the machines touch you in the future they scarcely contact with the skin. Their surfaces talk directly to your nerve traffic, mapping the entire permutational system of sensation in a virtual phase-space of languid eroticism, or torture. You melt into them, smeared against soft insanity, a breeze coming in from the sea, but it still burns.

They are beginnign to say that the 'Earth Mind' – reported upon by so many shamanistic explorers – is planetary cyberintelligence in the future, but try not to believe it. Just look.

A beach ripples out from the vampiric zero-pulse of the undead, deserted, grey, washed-out. Seagulls shriek morbidly. We follow the wavering line painted by ocean trash, glued to the stink of salinated decay. To explore is to know nothing about where one is going, panning across Neocassandra's left eye, traversing blank expanses vermilioned by capillaries intricately sparsing their meander amongst the jungle of green blue fronds adrift in fluid on into blackness sparked by an alternative moon of drowned chalk crumbling luminesence ... through a web of miniaturized city threads downloaded from tomorrow ... planing-out over the beach ... into visions beyond sight. Colours burn-out in a simulated overexposure. An alternative space is coming in.

the blankness of the test-site was an inert precursor of violent negation. how beautiful the metal spars twisted scorched black rage-burn relic unflesh. to seek each time some space of destitution, a vacant concrete heart, where every fragment can bleed into continuum. dust quivering in its bed of solar cruelty. more dust. dust and the sun. but then a stone, a semi-melted fragment of a brieze-block. rocks oxidated in a dehydrated arterial seepage, digressions about an axis of salt, and this morning there were ants. three days ago a scorpion. steel spines twisted in a sparse feric forest lacerating the sky.

Vast blank surfaces are the haunt of a hollowness beyond geometry. Are there blocks of grey fissured time? If there were crevices rupturing space we should try to depict them.

werewolf scratches on a wall.

if you fuck me i'll pretend

i'm someone else

dead a million years

eyes space absent

in fossilized memory your foot scuffs

a little dust